The Chef Manager

Second Edition

Michael Baskette, CEC, CCE, AAC

PEARSON
Prentice
Hall

Upper Saddle River, NJ 07458

Library of Congress Cataloging-in-Publication Data

Baskette, Michael.
  The chef manager / Michael Baskette,.—2nd ed.
    p. cm.
  Includes bibliographical references and index.
  ISBN 0-13-118913-1
  1. Food service management. 2. Cooks. I. Title.
  TX911.3.M27B367 2006
  647.95068—dc22

               2006006649

Editor-in-Chief: Vernon R. Anthony
Senior Editor: Eileen McClay
Editorial Assistant: Marion Gottlieb
Executive Marketing Manager: Ryan DeGrote
Senior Marketing Coordinator: Elizabeth Farrell
Marketing Assistant: Les Roberts
Director of Manufacturing and Production: Bruce Johnson
Managing Editor: Mary Carnis
Production Liaison: Jane Bonnell
Production Editor: Mike Remillard, Pine Tree Composition
Manufacturing Manager: Ilene Sanford
Manufacturing Buyer: Cathleen Petersen
Senior Design Coordinator: Miguel Ortiz
Cover Designer: Marianne Frasco
Cover Image: Linda Bleck, Images.com/SIS
Composition: Pine Tree Composition
Printer/Binder: R. R. Donnelley & Sons Company

Image credits appear on pages 320–321, which constitute a continuation of the copyright page.

Pearson Education LTD.
Pearson Education Singapore, Pte. Ltd.
Pearson Education Canada, Ltd.
Pearson Education—Japan

Pearson Education Australia PTY, Limited
Pearson Education North Asia Ltd.
Pearson Educación de Mexico, S.A. de C.V.
Pearson Education Malaysia, Pte. Ltd.

10 9 8 7 6 5 4 3 2 1
ISBN 0-13-118913-1

Contents

Preface

The hospitality and food service industries demand a great deal more of chefs and managers than ever before in their over 5,000 year old history. Competitive markets, shortage of skilled workers and diverse workplaces have forced chefs and other hospitality managers to balance culinary artistry and personal service with business management and human relations skills in order to survive.

The role of the chef has evolved from the fancy/exotic cook who practiced during the rise of ancient Rome, through various stages of medieval and classical cuisine development in Europe, Asia and the Americas, to that of the modern cook, quality specialist, leader and kitchen manager. In addition to culinary and hospitality mastery, modern hospitality, foodservice and chef managers must also learn to lead, direct, coach, plan and protect quality in order to remain competitive in the industry.

The Chef Manager, Second Edition continues the tradition of exploring the management side of professional food service, from a practitioner's point of view, as did the first edition, but goes even deeper into the evolution of cooking, management theory and practices, and the quality management movement that has affected all industries since its start in the late 1950s in America and Japan.

Twenty-four expanded chapters cover the stories surrounding the evolution of cooking and management to teach young and practiced culinarians the art of managing people, policies and procedures. Subjects include a discussion of Frederick Taylor's scientific management theory, Elton Mayo's discoveries at Western Electric's Hawthorne Plant, Walter Shewhart's quality control cycle, W. Edwards Deming and Kaoru Ishikawa on re-engineering Japan's management structure, Joseph Juran and Philip Crosby's unique approaches to quality management, the Fishbone Diagram, the Pareto principle and more.

The Chef Manager, Second Edition is a special collection of insightful lessons and analogies that bring management theory to life for professional culinarians. This is just the beginning of what a lifetime of learning and practice can achieve for chef managers everywhere; this time the product is people, the flavors are motivation and leadership, and the menu is held together by quality planning, management and control features throughout.

ACKNOWLEDGEMENTS

The Chef Manager, Second Edition would not have been possible without the support of my friends, family and colleagues. My personal thanks go out to my wife, Donna Baskette, for her support throughout the process, and to the professionals at Prentice Hall who helped me every technical step of the way. Of all the people at Prentice Hall I owe a special thanks to Vernon Anthony who continues to encourage me every day.

My professional and personal gratitude is also owed to the many chefs who have shared bits of their career stories to inspire others who plan to follow in their footsteps. These include: Dan D'Angelo, CEC, AAC; Barbara Hulick, CEC; Nancy Longo; Tom Macrina, CEC, AAC; Cary Neff; James Paul, MS, CCE, FMP; Reimund Pitz, CEC, CCE, AAC; and John Zehnder, CEC, AAC. These consummate professionals are inspirational leaders who took the hard road to success. Now everyone can learn from their adventures.

I continue to owe thanks to the people at the Culinary Archives & Museum at Johnson & Wales University in Providence, Rhode Island, particularly Stephen Spencer, who helped me secure photos of Auguste Escoffier, Antoine Carême, and Caesar Ritz to accent a few stories. The university's commitment to preserving culinary history is unparalleled in modern times.

A special thanks to the following reviewers: Katrina Warner, Tarrant County College; Doug Fisher, Spokane Community College; William Paternoster, Center for Culinary Arts; Anthony J. Strianese, Schenectady County Community College; and Delma Denice Woods, Tarrant County College–Viking Culinary.

Also, to Roger Adams, Special Collections, Hale University at Kansas State University for his help in securing title pages and folio covers for a couple of the culinary world's greatest literary masterpieces: *De Re Coquinaria, Le Viander de Guillaume dit Taillevent* and Carême's *Le Cuisinier Parisien*. Only through history can we learn, and only through historical reference librarians can we remember.

Finally I'd like to thank the inspirational Dr. Joseph Juran, chairman emeritus of the Juran Institute, and Dr. Armand Feigenbaum, founder of General Systems Company, for their continued support of quality management, now crossing over into the food service industry, by allowing me the use of their personal photos in the telling of their own individual stories. It is through the inspiration of others that we can all be inspired to do more and make a quality difference.

THE STRUCTURE
OF FOOD SERVICE
IN HISTORICAL PERSPECTIVE

Chapter 1
The Changing Role of Chef
Chapter 2
New Values in Culinary Leadership
Chapter 3
The Structure of Kitchen Organization

The traditions of the professional chef are well preserved by centuries of evolution and practice. From their tall toque blanche (white hats) to their hound's-tooth patterned pants and leather-topped wooden clogs, modern chefs wear the same uniform worn by cooks in medieval France and practice a craft that parallels human existence.

From the earliest roadside inns to modern bistros, cafés, and restaurants, the traditions of professional hospitality and food service have grown. Those traditions are remembered and challenged on a daily basis. Successful chefs and restaurant owners take lessons from those traditions, yet open their eyes to new ideas and are dedicated to change.

CHAPTER 1

The Changing Role of Chef

OBJECTIVES

When you complete this chapter, you should be able to:

- Describe some of the influences that shaped the early developments of the hospitality and food service industries.
- Discuss the contribution of the epicure Marcus Gavius Apicius to ancient Roman dining and early European cuisine.
- Describe the contributions Giullaume Tirel (Taillevent) made to the modernization of cooking techniques in the fifteenth century.
- Explain some of the early influences of Italian chefs on French kitchens thanks to the marriage of Catherine de Medici to the Prince Regent of France in the fifteenth century.
- Describe one of the earliest attempts to transition regional French foods into a unified French cuisine.
- Describe why La Varenne became known as one of the early great innovators of French cuisine.
- Describe the young life of the chef who overcame many obstacles to become the King of Chefs and the Chef of Kings.
- Describe the evolution of the restaurant in the eighteenth and nineteenth centuries.
- Describe the professional cooking career of Auguste Escoffier and the contributions he made to modern food service.
- Describe some of the accomplishments of America's first great chef Charles Ranhofer.
- Describe the evolution of chef from fancy cook to business manager and list some of the new competitive skills required of modern chefs.

EARLY DEVELOPMENTS

If hospitality can be defined as the sharing of one's home and dinner table with friends, family, and acquaintances, then its development can be linked to mankind's earliest days. Humans learned early to depend on others for security and to hunt and share food as groups. It was when they banded together that they could protect themselves and their families from larger and stronger animals, and eventually to learn to hunt and kill them for food. If humans had not learned to depend on each other, they might not have survived.

The social evolution of mankind was essential to the survival of the race. It eventually spirited the development of civilizations, as people became even more dependent on living in groups for security and food. Soon the groups grew to become towns and then cities, with each one strategically based where food could be easily grown or hunted.

Besides security or safety, the harvesting or growing of food has always been a priority for people and civilizations. Cities flourished where food could be easily found or grown, and withered or disappeared altogether when food became scarce. Examples of this can be found in India around 3500 B.C., where cities sprang up along the Indus River to use its water for both travel and irrigation, and again in China along the Yellow River, where cities began to evolve during the same time. Other examples are the cities of ancient Egypt, such as Heliopolis (near present day Cairo), and dozens of other Egyptian cities building their foundations along the banks of the fertile Nile River and thriving there for many centuries.

As civilizations grew, the world trade between them also grew and became good business. Foods that could be easily grown or harvested in one area of the world could be traded for foods grown and/or harvested in other areas. Long before gold and silver were traded, salted fish, spices, grains and domesticated animals were grown, raised, harvested and traded for the accumulation of great wealth.

Ancient trade routes soon began to flourish throughout the ancient world, causing great migrations of people and goods from one portion of the known world to the next. The King's Highway was one such route, stretching from Heliopolis at the northern part of the Nile across deserts and mountains to Damascus, the ancient trading city in Syria over 400 miles away. Eventually multiple trade routes connected Egypt, India and China to other parts of the ancient world. The Mediterranean Sea ferried merchants from port to port carrying food, spices and oils from Greece to Southern France and northern Africa.

The business of hospitality, where housing, food and friendship could be purchased from a stranger, took shape early in the form of inns for the travelers who occasioned along those ancient trade routes, leaving their homes, family and friends far behind. Merchants, religious pilgrims and eventually citizens summoned to their home towns for census taking (an early Roman tradition to count citizens around the expanding empire for the purpose of taxation) would travel hundreds of miles in distant and foreign lands, occasionally looking for the comforts of good cheer, freshly prepared food and a soft bed for the night.

Inns were such a large part of society by the late thirteenth century A.D. that they became the focal point of one of the world's greatest works of early literature, *The Canterbury Tales*, by Geoffrey Chaucer (c. 1343–1400 A.D.) of London, England. In his chronicles, Chaucer describes the different people he (the narrator) met along a religious pilgrimage from London to the Shrine of St. Thomas à Becket, located inside the Roman Catholic cathedral in Canterbury, England; each of the colorful travelers told their stories over a pint of beer or leg of mutton in a local inn. Chaucer's *Canterbury Tales* captured for the first time in literature the anticipation of a good meal and a clean bed for travelers a long way from home.

The extent and quality of hospitality services continued to evolve hand in hand with the development of civilizations. Religion, social engineering, art, politics, and technology have all influenced and been influenced by the world of hospitality and culinary arts. As human matrices developed, through need and pleasure, the business of supplying food, shelter, and a friendly hand nourished world cultures.

Even today the hospitality industry, and particularly food service, touches on all aspects of human life with just as much diversity and complexity as the cultures it serves. Its need is primal and, therefore, survives all time. Its value is measured on a personal bias that has as many factors as there are dreams and desires of people throughout the world. Providing shelter, food and beds is not a difficult business, but delivering them in the true spirit of hospitality with good value and comfort while meeting the demands of a discriminating and diverse customer base makes it an intricate and highly competitive business.

Chaucer's Knight from
Canterbury Tales

As does every industry, the business of hospitality services must strive to keep up with diverse values, changing trends, tighter budgets, and fierce competition in order to succeed in the evolving modern world. Hospitality services are complex and competitive businesses to own, manage or supervise, where success needs to be a planned and well managed task. Every facet of its services is measured by the evolving standards of the human race and changes with the idiosyncrasies of each customer. Therefore, managers and chefs need constantly to develop their service strategies, menus and business practices accordingly. Hospitality service is a major contender in the business world, touching countless lives, from those it serves to those who work under its umbrella.

The spectrum of hospitality operations and services in the twenty-first century spans economic, political, and social boundaries. Workers come from a vast variety of backgrounds in ethnicity, culture, race and religions. The fastest growing groups of workers in American hospitality and food service operations are Asians, Latinos and African Americans. Women also continue to gain better positions and better pay in all aspects of hospitality, even at the executive manager and executive chef levels. While white males still dominate the leadership positions in hospitality, that matrix is changing.

Customers, likewise, come from various economic and social backgrounds. Customers on a budget and customers with open wallets can often frequent the same operation. Single parents, families, mature customers, disabled customers, professional workers, sports celebrities, politicians and even famous actors frequent hotels, clubs and dining facilities all over America. While there are some private clubs which remain very exclusive and hotel dining rooms with menu prices higher than the typical traveler could afford, most hospitality and food service operations attract and service everyone they can. This can be described as an open market, where the diversity of customers seek out a diversity of services and prices to accommodate their basic, luxurious and their frivolous needs.

To better manage the diverse population of workers and the ever-increasing business complexities of hospitality services, particularly food service, the roles of managers and chefs have had to change over the years. In traditional European settings, the chef was respected first as an artist and then as a master of culinary skills. In today's high tech, international hospitality industry, the chef's role encompasses both art and craft, with new emphasis on business, personnel, human relations, and strategic planning. The chef has become a manager in the twenty-first century.

THE ARTIST CHEF

Over centuries of development the art of cooking improved in direct proportion to advancements in trade, technology and culture. The ancient trade routes expanded across seas and oceans; the science of metallurgy gave cooking the knives, pots, and pans vital to its success; the science of viniculture, its wines; and distillation, its brandies and liqueurs. As the civilizations of the world expanded, explored, and conquered, the world's larder of exotic and unusual foods also expanded.

Thanks to the power, wealth and ambition of Egyptian, Indian, European, Middle-Eastern, Russian and Asian royal families and trade merchants, regionally indigenous foods found their way to the kitchens of the world, where chefs could experiment and transform them into dining treasures.

Monarchs were the first to be lavished with the new culinary treasures because they could afford the luxury of choosing what to eat and paying for only the best and most exotic ingredients. Banquets could be fitted with hundreds of different dishes of ten, twelve, or twenty portions each, and everyone invited could have a taste from each plate. By the middle of the fourteenth century dining had become an adventure, and the cooks' abilities were judged by the vastness of their culinary repertoire.

Apicius

Sometime between 44 B.C. and 117 A.D., during the rise of the great Roman Empire, there lived at least three men by the name of Apicius. One lived during the early rise of the Republic, a second during the reign of Tiberius (c. 42 B.C.–37 A.D.) and a third in the late fourth or early fifth century who collected ancient Roman cooking recipes and prescriptions and compiled them in a single book entitled *De Re Coquinaria* (*On Roman Cooking*). It is believed that the third Apicius, Caelii Apicius, the author of the first book on Roman cookery, not only borrowed the earlier Apicius' recipes for the book, but also his name as a marketing ploy, and was not a true relative at all.

Marcus Gavius Apicius, the second Apicius, is the one who has garnered particular interest from culinary scholars. He served un-

De Re Coquinaria title page (1541 printing)

der Augustus and Tiberius Caesar as a culinary expert, and it is his recipes which survive today, thanks to the entrepreneurism of Caelii.

Known for his sauces and extravagant dishes, Marcus Apicius served exotic dishes such as flamingo, nightingale tongues, camel heels, roasted ostrich and stuffed sterile sow's womb. These dishes were intended to startle the middle class and excite the appetites of royalty.

The Roman philosopher and archivist Pliny (c. 24–79 A.D.), in his book of *Natural Histories* (19:137), credited Apicius with the practice of force feeding pigs with dried figs and then drowning them with honey wine. The particular mixture of honey wine, figs and fresh pork roasted over an open fire must have seemed ingenious in the cuisine of the day. A similar process was used on geese to enlarge their livers to produce a rich, fatty culinary delight, indicating that the origins of *foie gras* were founded in ancient Roman culture.

The main difference between modern cuisine and the ancient Romans is the style. Apicius based his famous sauces on the balance between crushed green herbs and ground spices. Lovage, oregano, and thyme, for example, are matched by pepper, cumin, and coriander. To these seasonings he added a second level of flavors, the sweetness of honey or the sourness of a spoonful of vinegar. In slightly more elaborate recipes he used a third element such as raisins, dates, plums, almonds, walnuts and chestnuts. Practically all of Apicius' recipes incorporate a wine and pre-made stock appropriate for the particular meat, seafood, or vegetable.

De Re Coquinaria also contains many festive dishes reserved for great holidays, some with rich, elaborate fillings. Often a variety of herbs, exotic spices, fruits, and nuts are mixed with seasoned ground meats and bread crumbs, and cooked inside the poultry, suckling lamb, or kid. The whole dish, decorated with plumes of feathers, antlers or other part of the animal, bird or fish that is then being served, is carved at the table so the guest gets a portion of stuffing and meat all on the same plate.

De Re Coquinaria is actually a collection of ten smaller books:

1. Epimeles, *The Chef*
2. Sarcoptes, *Meats*
3. Cepuros, *From the Garden*
4. Pandecter, *Various Dishes*
5. Ospreos, *Peas, Beans, Lentils, Chickpeas, etc.*
6. Aeropetes, *Game Fowl*
7. Polyteles, *Domestic Fowl*
8. Tetrapus, *Quadrupeds*
9. Thalassa, *Seafood*
10. Halieus, *Fish*

Here is an example of one of Apicius' recipes for Guinea Hen:

Almond Sauce for Guinea Hen or Chicken
3 lb guinea hen or chicken
1 tsp ginger
1 tsp ground pepper

Roman Kitchen circa 24 A.D.

Sauce:

1/4 tsp ground pepper
1/2 tsp cumin
1/2 tsp coriander
pinch of fennel
pinch of rosemary (or rue)
1/4 cup dates, finely chopped
1/4 cup almonds or filberts, grated
1 tsp wine vinegar
1 cup chicken stock
1 tsp olive oil or butter
ground pepper

Sprinkle ginger and pepper over the dressed guinea hen or chicken. Roast in a hot brick oven for 1 hour or till done.

For the sauce, grind pepper, cumin, coriander, fennel, and rosemary (or rue) in a mortar. Add to finely chopped dates, and grated almonds or filberts. Blend with vinegar, stock, and olive oil or butter. Bring the sauce to a boil and pour over the roast bird. Sprinkle with a little pepper, and serve.

It is rumored that Marcus Apicius, although very wealthy himself, spent all his fortune on the exploration of exotic foods. When his fortunes finally waned, he committed suicide so not to have to face life with only common food and drink for nourishment.

Guillaume Tirel (Taillevent)

Philippe VI
of France
(1293–1350)

One of the first key figures to play a part in the evolution of what is known today as modern European cuisine was a cook in the court of King Philippe VI of France, in the middle of the fourteenth century. Chef Guillaume Tirel (c. 1310–1395), who was also known by the name Taillevent, took advantage of the court's power and money to furnish his kitchens with the most advanced culinary cookware and exotic foods available.

Taillevent standardized hundreds of traditional recipes and created hundreds of new ones using the cooking technologies that he helped to perfect. Borrowing recipes and methodologies from the Roman cook Apicius, Taillevent searched for new applications and took the lead in reorganizing culinary knowledge, utilizing the developing technologies and subsequent skills of his day. Whole roasted peacock stuffed with white truffles and served au plumage (decorated with the colorful feathers of the host bird) or cockscombs simmered in cream and honey with cinnamon and cloves were two dishes Taillevent likely served to the royal family.

Taillevent collected many of his original and regenerated recipes in a book simply referred to as *Le Viandier*. The full title is much longer. Translated into English the full title states:

> Hereafter follows the Viandier describing the preparation of all manner of foods, as cooked by Taillevent, the cook of our noble king, and also the dressing and preparation of boiled meat, roasts, sea and freshwater fish, sauces, spices, and other suitable and necessary things as described hereafter.

Viandier literally refers to the position of butcher in the kitchens of Taillevent, which was also responsible for all the meat preparations and sauces. This was by far the most important cooking station in a noble's kitchen since meat, seafood, and poultry made up almost ninety percent of the entire meal.

Very little emphasis was placed on such "peasant" foods as vegetables and rice. The emphasis was on the many types of meats and poultry that were available to the king's kitchen, with no care given to the expense or difficulty of preparation. For the noble class, this represented a complete turnaround from the dependency on vegetables for sustaining life to the flaunting of them as testimony to material wealth.

Here is an excerpt from Taillevent's *Le Viander:*

Here Follow the Meat Roasts

31. Roast pork.

Eaten with verjuice. Some make a sauce (to wit, add garlic, onions, wine and verjuice to the roast drippings in the pan). In a pie; eaten with verjuice.

32. Veal.

Parboiled, larded, and roasted; eaten with Cameline [Sauce]. In a pie, add some Spice Powder, pork fat and saffron; eaten with verjuice.

33. To make calf mesentery that one calls *charpie*.

Take your meat when it is completely cooked, cut it up very small, and fry it in lard. Crush ginger and saffron. Beat some raw eggs, and thread them onto your meat in the lard. Crush spices and add some Spice Powder. However, some do not wish any Spice Powder in it, and eat it with Green Verjuice [Sauce].

34. Roast mutton.

Eat it with fine salt, Cameline [Sauce] or verjuice.

35. Kids, lambs.

Refresh them in boiling water, pull them out soon, brown them a bit on the spit, lard them, and roast them. Eat them with Cameline [Sauce].

36. Stuffed piglet or pig.

Scald it, wash it well, and put it on the spit. The stuffing is made of pork pluck, cooked pork meat, some egg yolks, harvest cheese, cooked peeled chestnuts and good Spice Powder. Put everything in the piglet's belly, stitch up the slit, and put it to roast. Baste it with a spoon, while turning the roast, with vinegar and good boiling drippings. Eat it hot with Yellow Pepper [Sauce]. Some lazy persons eat it with Cameline [Sauce].

Le Viandier front insert

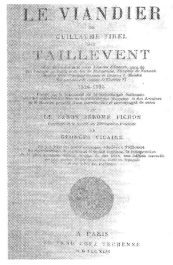

Le Viandier title page
(1892 printing)

Taillevent also wrote descriptions of table art, perhaps the original grand decorative pieces used at great banquets and buffets. Here is another translated excerpt from *Le Viandier* describing these unique decoration pieces:

Painted Subtleties

202. [The Swan Knight.]

If you wish to make the Swan Knight in his right, have 12 pieces of light wood, with the 4 uprights stronger than the others. Assemble everything and nail it very strongly. Have some lead sheets 3 feet in length and as much in width (you will need at least 2 or 3 sheets of lead). Make it in the shape of a little chest about a foot deep that can hold two or 3 buckets of water. Make a little skiff of glued parchment in which will be put the image of the Swan Knight.

You need the likeness of a little swan made of glued parchment covered with fine hair or white down. You need a little chain resembling gold hung from the swan's neck and attached to the skiff within the lead box. For the box attach 4 wheels to 4 [inverted] chevrons attached here and there. You need some linen dyed like waves of water. Nail it to the top of the box so that one does not see the men who will be underneath.

203. A tower.

If you wish to make a tower covered with linen dyed as if it were masonry, have 4 windows at the 4 corners of the tower. Have a likeness of Saracens and Moors seeming to fire at a wild man who would assail them. To make the wild man have a handsome man, tall and upright, clothed in a linen robe, hose and shoes all joined together, with the robe covered with [strands of] painted hemp. In the tower you need the figure of a young valet disguised as a wild boy. He should have some leather balls full of wadding or carded wool, dyed to resemble stones, for throwing at the wild man.

204. To make the image of Saint George and his virgin.

Make a large terrace of pastry or light wood (like that from which one makes pavises). Make the likeness of a saddled and bridled horse, with the image of Saint George on the horse, a dragon under the feet of the horse, and the virgin holding the dragon tied by her girdle around its neck.

Le Viandier became the bible of French cooking for the next three hundred years. It was often used in conjunction with *De Re Coquinaria* as the only source for fine cuisine. Both books were so popular they were among the first books printed by the modern printing press, which was introduced in 1470.

Catherine de Medici

Catherine de Medici's arrival in France in 1533 to marry Henry II, heir to the French throne, had as much an impact on French cuisine as it did on French politics. The de Medicis were a very wealthy and powerful Italian family. Catherine's promise to wed the young prince was intended to bind political agendas between the influential Italian family and the French aristocracy.

Catherine de Medici (c. 1530)

Catherine de Medici (born 13 April, 1519; died 5 January, 1589) was the daughter of Lorenzo de Medici (II), Duke of Urbino (Italy) and Madeleine de la Tour d' Auvergne who, by her mother Catherine of Bourbon, was related to the royal house of France. Catherine had barely reached the age of thirteen when Francis I, King of France, Catherine's uncle, arranged a marriage between Catherine and his second son, Henry. Catherine was thirteen years old when the wedding took place.

To appease the young Catherine, those things she grew up with and became accustomed to in the Italian courts were brought to France for her continued enjoyment. Her particular interests lay in dance, music and fine dining.

Among her entourage were trained Italian cooks skilled in the fine cuisine of Florence and the grand style in which it was served. Among other things, Italian chefs were skilled in the cooking and serving of all types of mushrooms, truffles, garlic and infrequently used vegetables such as broccoli, eggplant and artichokes. Even popular filled pasta creations such as lasagna, ravioli and manicotti were soon being served to French nobility.

Catherine also brought with her the expectation that ladies would be in regular attendance at sumptuous feasts, and would dress in fashionable (and revealing) attire when doing so. Dinner, in France, was to become theater and not just a reason to gorge one's self with food and drink.

Catherine also refused to abandon the Italian custom of eating with a two-pronged metal instrument instead of with her hands or a knife, as was the older French custom. Once the royal court was convinced of the importance of using the early rendition of what is now the fork at the king's table in addition to the knife, the people too were convinced.

In 1559, Catherine's husband King Henry II died in a tournament accident and her eldest son Francis II came to the throne. Francis II, however, was very weak and ruled for a mere 17 months. Upon his death in 1560, Catherine's second son, Charles IX, inherited the throne at the age of ten. This allowed Catherine to become Queen Regent of France and garner great control over the dealings of the French court, and she served as such until Charles IX's death. She also served as Queen Regent for her third son, Henry III.

Henry II of France
(1519–1559)

Protestant followers had already begun to infiltrate the strong Catholic communities in fifteenth century France, causing quite a lot of upheaval and a civil war. Catherine was soon faced with making a decision either to join with or fight the new religious movement. Catherine wanted to remain neutral, and thought both religions could co-exist.

In 1564, she decided to try and put the battles to rest by traveling throughout France to show the monarchy's support for both religions and to encourage both to exist in peace. She traveled with her son, the new Dauphin of France, who was later to become Charles IX, and an entourage that toured France from coast to coast for two full years. Naturally, Catherine brought along the court's young chef, Guillaume Verger, with her.

While Catherine and her son were parlaying religious and political maneuvers, Verger was busy preparing meals for the royal family and for the dozens of people who accompanied them from foods he found along the way. Choosing from foods, herbs and wines that were readily available, Verger discovered great diversity in cuisine wherever he went. Transforming peasant meals into royal delicacies was not an easy task, but one which Verger undertook with great zeal.

On returning to Paris two years later, Verger had collected quite a repertoire of French regional cuisine. He continued to introduce the most popular of these dishes to the royal table in Paris, and perfected those using modern appliances of his day. For the first time, French regional cuisine had been united, prepared and served in a single kitchen.

By the middle of the seventeenth century, French cuisine had undergone tremendous refinements. Yet the apprentice chef had little to go on besides the bits of information handed down by his or her teachers. Contemporary cookbooks were merely collections of various recipes with little theme and no organization. These texts were difficult to reference and often only listed ingredients without measure. Therefore, whenever two chefs prepared the same dish, the results were often quite different.

François-Pierre de la Varenne

François-Pierre de la Varenne, chef under the Marquis d'Uxelles, Louis Chalon du Blé, was an adventitious student of culinary arts. He was committed to the foundations of cooking and became a great innovator of seventeenth century cuisine.

La Varenne's analytical nature led him to the great accomplishments of his life. His fervent studies and exhaustive work led him to realize that French cuisine lacked organization and consistency. To have a unified cuisine would require standardized recipes and procedures written in a format that cooks could easily understand. La Varenne committed a large part of his professional life to developing the first set of logically drawn books on French cooking.

La Varenne's first book, *Le Cuisinier Française* (c. 1651), was the first reference for some popular modern culinary creations such as roux, caramel, cooked meringue, mayonnaise and the leading sauce, béchamel. Béchamel was made slightly differently than its modern version, which utilizes a roux as a thickener. It was made by simmering milk and veal stock together with seasonings then strained and finished with cream. The sauce was named to flatter a courtier, Louis de Béchamel, Marquis de Nointel (1603–1703), a financeer of Brittany, who is sometimes mistakenly credited with having invented it.

The foundation of French cuisine, the *Le Cuisinier Française* became so popular that there were over thirty editions printed in the first seventy-five years of its publication.

Together, La Varenne wrote three books which became the leading sources for professional cooks and chefs wishing to practice the most modern French cuisine of the times:

Le Cuisinier Française (The French Chef), 1651.
Le Patissier Française (The French Pastry Chef), 1653.
Le Confiturier Française (The French Candy Maker), 1664.

THE CLASSIC CHEFS

What we refer to as classical French cooking today was considered modern cooking in restaurants, hotels and private houses in the nineteenth century. Cooking techniques had already been well defined through centuries of trial and error; food ingredients from all parts of the known world were readily available (for those who had money and power); and the vocation of cooking was already founded on hard work, dedication and study as a life-long quest to learn and perfect skills and knowledge. All that was needed to catapult French cooking into the global limelight was for those cooks and chefs, themselves in a position of influence because of places in which they work, to harness all of what was known about cooking, take advantage of the money allowed them for provisions to find and create the world's greatest foods, and chronicle both their learning and their recipes in such a way that other professional cooks and chefs could easily interpret the information and strategies and apply similar techniques in their own establishments.

Cuisine around much of the civilized world had evolved to a high level of sophistication with very definable characteristics by the time Antoine Carême started working for the kitchens of eighteenth century France. Italian cuisine was perhaps the best known; Spanish cuisine was building a good reputation; German cuisine was still very fragmented, yet its roots in charcuterie (sausages, hams, pâtés, etc.), cheeses and wines were already established; Asian cuisine was flourishing and evolving among the mainland and the various islands of the western Pacific; and Russian cuisine was gaining recognition in foods and style of service. The world's greatest chefs studied and learned each of the world's greatest cuisines as a means to improve their own country's cuisine and all of culinary art.

What Carême, Beauvilliers, Escoffier and Ranhofer accomplished for French cuisine by perfecting and chronicling it through their professional lives, prestigious careers and written works, soon became the foundation for high cuisine in other parts of the world as well. Particularly in those places these same trained chefs traveled and worked, the influences of the French kitchen lay the standard upon which foods would be measured from Europe to Russia to the Americas and through other parts of the civilized world.

Antoine Carême

Antoine Carême has been called the King of Chefs and the Chef of Kings. He was born the son of a stonemason on the Rue du Bac in Paris, France in 1784.

The youngest of seventeen children, Antoine was sent into the world when he was only eight years old to fend for himself. Perhaps it was this early life trauma that hardened Carême's spirit and drive. He was determined to succeed, despite the drama of hunger and poverty, no matter what the consequences. Though one of many who faced growing up in the chaotic

Antoine Carême
(c. 1810)

world of the Napoleonic empire and subsequent French Revolution, Carême fully realized that his success was entirely left up to him and him alone.

Young Carême was taken in as a kitchen helper at a low class restaurant near one of the main gates leading toward the center of Paris. He worked to exhaustion for long, hot hours with little compensation just to have a place to live, work and eat. At night, Carême taught himself to read and write by candlelight in the small corner of the room where he slept, for he knew it was his only way out of the grueling work he found himself doing. When his work was over, his studies began.

Carême remained at the cooking house for a six year apprenticeship and then moved on to apprentice with Bailly, the Paris pâtissier who was known for all kinds of pastries and cream tarts. Carême enjoyed working with pastries and candies, luxuries he was not privileged to enjoy himself. Although every formula was scientific and exact, he was allowed a certain amount of creativity in the final construction and decoration of Bailly's confections. He carried this notion of creative restraint for the rest of his life.

Carême left the pâtisserie to study architecture, for he loved the great arches, cathedrals, and palaces that dotted the countryside and cities of France. Caught up in the spirit of reconstruction that followed the revolution, Carême developed a great talent for design and construction. Symmetry was the most important aspect of Carême's designs in architecture and, likewise, in his later designs of sugar and buffet presentations.

Carême returned to the kitchen, but carried his flirtation with architecture in his work satchel. Carême has been credited with saying, "Of the five fine arts, the fifth is architecture, whose main branch is confectionery." His love for architecture and design was transformed into some of the most spectacular buffet presentations to be found in the world anywhere. Carême promoted the idea of the pièce montée, a decorated centerpiece for buffet platters, not necessarily edible, intended to lend a particular theme or purpose to the given party.

His first place of employment after leaving the study of architecture was with a then-famous statesman, the Duc de Talleyrand, who always insisted on organizing grand parties and dinners. Carême excelled with his first chance to be in charge of a kitchen brigade, including his specialty, which was still pastry.

In the early 1800s, France was gripped in global war, and French kitchens soon suffered with a loss of help, as young men were called away to the army. Money to buy fancy pastries and even the ingredients for the pastries themselves became scarce. Carême and his fellow cooks had to work harder and smarter in order to prevail.

One popular shortcut that Carême helped to develop was the creation and use of leading sauces to which other flavoring and garnishing ingredients could be added for a particular purpose. Prior to this, all sauces were made from scratch for each dish served, using only stock as a shared ingredient. Soon the use of sauces like espagñole, velouté, and béchamel, which had already gained popularity in French kitchens, to create smaller sauces for individual preparations became standard practice.

Duc de Talleyrand (c. 1812)

In 1815, Carême left Talleyrand to travel across the English channel to work for the Prince Regent, who later became King George IV of England. Unfortunately, Carême did not care for the weather in England and after only two years decided to leave it for good. Returning to the continent, he served the Russian Czar Alexander I in St. Petersburg, Russia, but hated the harsh cold weather there as much as the damp, foggy British air and the even more harsh politics, which had plagued the Russian monarch since his rise to the throne.

Soon Carême longed to return to Paris, and did so to be employed by the house of Baron James de Rothschild as head chef. James de Rothschild was a wealthy banking magnate in Paris, expanding his family business there in 1811 from his home of Frankfurt-am-Main, Germany, as financial advisor to rich and influential Parisians. Food, entertaining and hospitality were of great importance to Rothschild, and Carême was given free reign to produce the best foods money and power could provide.

Carême is often referred to as the father of grand cuisine, for he set the standard upon which food would be judged for more than a hundred years. Carême was a perfectionist, an architect, an artist, a writer and above all a passionate chef. He designed elaborate menus and picturesque displays utilizing the best foods available in his time to please the palates of the noble and the rich. By doing so, he chronicled thousands of recipes and standardized hundreds of cooking and pastry techniques toward the creation of the best foods money and power could afford.

Carême's concept of leading sauces was rather simple, yet revolutionary for the day. His plan was to perfect and then use three or four great sauces which

St. Petersburg, Russia
circa early 19th century

could still be made with proper care and ingredients in large quantities, stabilized by the use of the roux, which could be held for extended amounts of time during service. These leading sauces could then be used as the base for hundreds of variations depending on the meat, game, poultry or fish that they were going to accompany. Simply by adding a flavoring, such as herbs, and spices, a condiment like mustard or horseradish, any number of wines and garnishes, thousands of small sauces could be made very efficiently.

Carême promoted the use of four leading sauces. They were: espagñole, a velvety brown sauce borrowed from the kitchens of Spain; velouté, which literally translates as "velvet" and was made from veal, fish or poultry stocks; béchamel, the milk-based sauce which had been in use since Taillevent, now stabilized by the roux; and allemande, a type of thin velouté further thickened by the addition of eggs and cream often referred to as a type of liaison, or natural thickener. Other natural liaisons Carême would use were simple bread crumbs and cooked rice, which also thickened soups and sauces in which they were used.

Carême's legacy remains with us through his four books:

Le Patissier Pittoresque (Beautiful Pastries), 1815.

Le Maitre d'hotel Française ou Parallele de la Cuisine Ancienne et Moderne (A Study of Ancient and Modern Dining in French Hotels), 1822.

Le Patissier Royal Parisien (Royal Paris Pastry Maker), 1825.

Le Cuisinier Parisien ou l'Art de la Cuisine au XIX (The Paris Chef, or The Art of Cooking in the 19th Century), 1833.

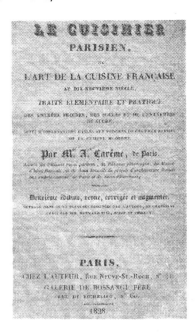

Le Cuisinier Parisien
(1828)

Carême earned the title of Chef of Kings and King of Chefs, for he worked for the rich and powerful people of his day. Some of his meals were even served to Napoleon Bonaparte while he worked for James de Rothschild in Paris. Carême will always be remembered for his great menus, opulent table settings and instructions for organizing kitchens which planted the seeds in the young mind of Escoffier over forty years later, who re-engineered the entire kitchen brigade. Carême died at the age of 48. It is said he burnt out under the fire of the kitchens and the passion of his heart.

Boulanger and the First Restaurants

In 1765, one year after Carême was born, a soup vendor named Monsieur A. Boulanger open a small shop where he could sell his soups, broths and other light meals to travelers and passers-by. The sign over his door read "Restoratives" which literally means "to restore," suggesting the need for light meals in between the formal meals to keep people going throughout their busy days.

Boulanger's menu quickly grew, and his business seemed to flourish overnight. It became the first successful operation where a patron could order from a menu offering a variety of dishes from which each person could choose, separately or in parts, to complete a whole meal. Whatever the customer was hungry for, light or full meals were presented to them with moderate style and service for a fair and reasonable price. By some accounts there were over 500 restaurants in Paris by the turn of the nineteenth century, merely thirty-five years later, attesting to their popularity.

Antoine Beauvilliers, a popular culinary writer and gastronomic authority of his day, opened his own restaurant—La Grande Taverne de Londres—in 1782. It was there that the more famous gastronomic writer, Jean-Anthelme Brillat-Savarin (1755–1826) bragged on the successes of Beauvilliers by writing "He was the first to combine an elegant dining-room, smart waiters, and a choice cellar with superior cooking."

In his chronicles of gastronomy (*The Philosopher in the Kitchen*, c. 1825), Savarin goes on to describe what he considered a novel scene from one of his dining experiences at Beauvillier's La Grande Taverne restaurant around 1808:

The far end of the room is occupied by a host of solitary diners, who order loudly, wait impatiently, eat rapidly, pay, and depart.

At another table is a family from the country, content with a frugal meal, yet relishing one or two unfamiliar dishes, and obviously enjoying the novelty of their surroundings.

Nearby sit a husband and wife, Parisians, from the evidence of the hat and shawl hanging above their heads; it is clearly a long time since they had anything to say to each other; they are going to the theatre, and it is a safe bet that one of them will fall asleep during the performance.

Farther on are two lovers, judging by the attention of one, the coquetry of the other, and the gourmandism of both. Pleasure shines in their eyes; and, from the choice that governs the composition of their meal, the present serves both to illuminate the past and foreshadow the future.

In the centre of the room is a table surrounded by regular patrons, who as a rule obtain special terms, and dine at a fixed price. They know the names of all the waiters, who let them into the secret of what is freshest and newest; they are like the stock-in-trade of a shop, like a centre of attraction, or to be more precise, like the decoys used in Brittany to attract wild duck.

There are a number of those individuals whom everyone knows by sight, and no one by name. These people are as much at ease as if they were at home, and quite often try to strike up a conversation with their neighbors. They belong to a type only met with in Paris, which has neither property, capital, nor employment, but spends freely for all that.

Finally, there are one or two foreigners, usually Englishmen; these last stuff themselves with double portions, order all the most expensive dishes, drink the headiest wines, and do not always leave without assistance.

The accuracy of our description may be verified any day of the week; and if it succeeds in rousing curiosity, perhaps it may also serve as a moral warning. (p. 269–270)

It was during the same time that many fine restaurants began to open up along the picturesque Palais-Royal near the Louvre in Paris. Among them was the famous Véry, which became a favorite stop of the novelist Honoré de Balzac and the gourmet Grimond de la Reynière. Reynière was so impressed with the fare and service that he proclaimed Véry the finest restaurant in all of France.

Brillat-Savarin, another frequent patron of Véry's, was also impressed with the food and service. It was quite a unique experience for him and his associates to find high quality food in the comfortable setting of the casual restaurant. Meals like them had heretofore only been available at the homes of wealthy gentlemen and the finest hotels. The impressive menu at Véry, reminisced Brillat-Savarin, contained these offerings:

12 soups

24 hors-d' oeuvre

15 or 20 beef entrées

20 mutton entrées

30 chicken or game entrées

16 or 20 veal dishes

12 pastry dishes

24 fish dishes

15 roasts

50 side dishes

50 dessert dishes

"In addition, the fortunate gastronome can wash his meal down with at least thirty kinds of wine, from Burgundy to Cape wine and Tokay, and with twenty to thirty kinds of liqueur, not to mention coffee and mixed drinks, such as punch, negus, syllabub, and the like" (*The Philosopher in the Kitchen*, pp. 274–275).
Less than fifty years later culinary history was again being made by Adolphe Dugléré, who was the chef of the nineteenth century restaurant Café Anglaise on the Boulevard des Italiens in Paris. Dugléré designed his restaurant menus according to the highest level of cuisine that was possible for the day and insisted on the highest quality in presentation and service. Two of his most popular dishes became classic favorites: Sole Dugléré (recipe 825 in Escoffier's *Le Guide Culinaire*) and Potage Germiny (recipe 724 in Escoffier's *Le Guide Culinaire*).

One of the most popular dinners served at Café Anglaise under the direction of Chef Dugléré was christened the Three Emperors Dinner on June 7, 1867, for it was intended for the Russian Czar Alexander II, his son—who would later become Czar Alexander III—and King William I of Prussia—who later became the first emperor of Germany.

The famous meal included a number of classic and local favorites (the numerical references given here are from Escoffier's *Le Guide Culinaire*, written in 1902):

- Soufflés à la Reine (with creamed chicken)
- Fillets of sole
- Escalloped turbot
- Poullet (Chicken) à la Portugaise (E. no. 1506)
- Homard (Lobster) à la Parisienne (E. no. 960)
- Caneton (Ducklings) à la Rouennaise (E. no. 1764)
- Ortolans (a small game bird) on toast

The restaurant evolved from selling soups and broths (Boulanger) to the fine tables of Café Anglaise in just over one hundred years (1765–1867). To accomplish the serving of grande meals in the restaurant format necessitated quite a few innovations. Among them the standardization of cooking stations and the menu items they were responsible for were paramount to the success of the fast paced preparation and service. It would not be long before the concept of à la carte service of haute cuisine would be championed by another French chef, Auguste Escoffier, who would become the most influential chef of the twentieth century.

Auguste Escoffier

Georges Auguste Escoffier (1846–1935), known today as the Father of Haute (High) Cuisine, was born in Villeneuve-Loubet, Alpes Maritimes, France, the son of a blacksmith. Like Carême, Auguste had a rough start in life.

Auguste Escoffier (c. 1922)

In 1859, Escoffier was just thirteen years old, and already had shown a preference for art in school and food from his maternal grandmother. Not even his father could predict he would put the two together to form one of the world's greatest cuisines.

Yet thirteen was the age that young boys chose or were directed to learn a particular vocation. Apprenticeship training was and still remains one of the preferred forms of training throughout Europe, and Escoffier began his cooking apprenticeship in his uncle's restaurant in Nice, France: Le Restaurant Française. Escoffier received no favors from his uncle, and struggled through the strict rigor and discipline he found there, which was typical of many French kitchens of his day.

In 1865, the owner of Le Petit Moulin Rouge in Paris had been visiting Nice and observed Escoffier working around the restaurant. He was so impressed with the young cook's energy and clean appearance that he offered him a job on his own kitchen brigade. Escoffier accepted, and worked for the famed

Parisian restaurant until 1878 (except for his military service). He climbed the ladder from cook to chef de cuisine and head chef through his perseverance and dedication to quality foods.

By 1870, when war broke out between France and Prussia, Escoffier was called into military service and had to take a leave of absence from the restaurant where he had been perfecting his skills. But his culinary career would not end; rather it would be improved because of the strict discipline and formal line of authority Escoffier experienced in the French army.

Escoffier's reputation landed him the appointment of chef de cuisine of the Rhine Army Headquarters in Metz, France (now in the southern portion of Germany) under Marshal Bazaine, who was given authority by Napoleon III to lead the entire French army during this war. Unfortunately for Escoffier, Metz came under siege by the combined German and Prussian armies in 1871 and fell to their dominance. Escoffier and some 140,000 other French soldiers became prisoners of war. However, the war was soon over, and Escoffier was free to return to Paris and continue developing his professional career.

Escoffier not only prepared meals for the officers, but supervised the preparation of food for the army soldiers. He was determined to serve the soldiers the best foods he could and became a driving force in the development of canned ragouts, soups and other hearty meals which he implemented for French army rations.

Prussia troops march past Arc de Triomphe in Paris, France (circa 1871)

After the war, Escoffier returned to Le Petit Moulin Rouge as head chef and remained there until 1878.

Escoffier held a variety of positions in and around Paris until he and his new wife Delphine (together they had two sons and one daughter) decided to move to the Mediterranean coast. There Escoffier assumed the position of Directeur de Cuisine of the Grand Hotel in Monte Carlo.

It was in Monte Carlo that Escoffier met a young hotelier from Switzerland named César Ritz (1850–1918). They decided to form what would become the most dynamic management team in the history of the hospitality industry. It was fortuitous that the two young professionals would find energy and ambition in each other, and shared the desire to transform both attributes into providing the best hospitality and finest foods and service money could provide; Ritz catered to guests through furnishings, decor, and guest services; Escoffier catered to their palates.

Escoffier and Ritz were recruited to the Savoy Hotel in London as Head of Restaurant Services and General Manager, respectively. They eagerly accepted the challenges. What they found was great demand for luxurious hospitality and dining services, but for a busy, more fast-paced clientele then what they were used to. The days of three, four and five hour dinners where patrons all shared from a variety of dishes was slowly disappearing. Escoffier and Ritz were forced to streamline all of the duties and responsibilities of dining room, hotel rooms, and kitchen staff into highly efficient operations utilizing standardized procedures to ensure a high level of consistency and control.

Escoffier borrowed the concept of serving meals à la carte from the new style of luxurious restaurants which were forming all throughout France to accommodate this quicker pace for dining. Dugléré and others had shown that haute cuisine could be served in the new style of fast service without suffering in presentation or quality, and Escoffier was determined to make the same transition possible for the very complex and tradition shackled hotel kitchens under his charge.

To accomplish this transformation, Escoffier had to re-engineer the entire organizational framework of the kitchen. First, he identified all the tasks and responsibilities within the kitchen, combined like items into groups of

César Ritz (c. 1885)

responsibilities, and then redesigned the kitchen work stations to accommodate the new groups of responsibilities. When the parts of the order came together at the center of the line, the food was plated and served, all under the scrutiny of the executive chef.

Escoffier wrote many books—*Le Livre des Menus (The Book of Menus), Le Ritz (The Ritz), Le Carnet d'Epicure (The Epicurean's Notebook),* and *Ma Cuisine (My Cuisine)*—but his legacy is carried primarily by his greatest book *Le Guide Culinaire (The Culinarian's Guide),* 1902.

Le Guide Culinaire gave names for hundreds of recipes and procedures, identifying for the first time exact ingredient lists and garniture for appetizers, hors d'oeuvres, eggs, fish and seafood, sauces, aspic jellies, court-bouillons and marinades, soups and soup garnishes, rélevés and entrées of meat, poultry, and game, roasts and salads, vegetables and starches, snacks and desserts. It became the most comprehensive and exacting description of the preparation and service of food ever compiled.

Escoffier studied Carême's works and believed as strongly as Carême did that good cooking begins with good solid foundations. The first several pages of *Le Guide Culinaire* emphasize this belief, outlining the correct ways to prepare stocks, glazes, and essences. It next introduces the different types of roux and their uses, then names the five "leading" sauces. Three of Carême's original four (espagñole, velouté, and béchamel) plus a tomato and a hollandaise sauce are listed. From these five sauces, Escoffier goes on to name over a hundred small sauces and lays the groundwork for thousands more.

Le Guide Culinaire remains today the most used reference for chefs around the world. Escoffier's reputation is indelibly marked in the profession of which he was so proud. Escoffier retired in 1919 at the age of seventy-three and was the first chef ever to receive retirement pay for his life's work.

Charles Ranhofer

America, like France, also played an important role in the rise of culinary art. Wealthy American diners enjoyed fabulous fare from the world renowned Delmonico's as early as 1827 in New York City's Madison Square. Charles Ranhofer (1836–1899), a predecessor of Escoffier, helped put Delmonico's on the map of fine world cuisine while he was executive chef from 1862 to 1894. He is noted as having cooked for presidents Abraham Lincoln, Ulysses Grant and Andrew Johnson, for the Grand Duke Alexis of Russia, the author Charles Dickens, and for countless admirals, generals, and heads of state.

Charles Ranhofer
(c. 1894)

Charles Ranhofer was born in St. Denis, France, the son of a restaurateur and grandson of a noted cook, so that his destiny as a cook seems to have been set at his birth.

When he was twelve years old, Ranhofer was sent to Paris to learn the art of pastry-making, and quickly excelled at the craft. After completing his three year apprenticeship he became the head baker at a Parisian restaurant; he was only fifteen years old.

A year later Ranhofer began cooking for the house of Prince Henin of Alsace, where he first learned how to prepare feasts and banquets on a grand scale. Through perseverance and an excellent work ethic, Ranhofer was made chef de cuisine by the time he was twenty years old.

Ranhofer came to America for the first time in 1856, but for only a few short years. He was engaged as a chef by the Russian Consul in Washington D.C. While in America he also had the chance to visit and work in some of the kitchens in New Orleans, and learned to love the flavors of the Creole and Acadian foods he found there.

In 1860, Ranhofer returned to France to take the position of chef at the Tuileries Palace, where he was responsible for arranging balls for the Court of Napoleon III.

He returned to New York City after only one winter at the palace to manage the kitchen of the Maison Dorée, but in 1862 was hired by Delmonico's, located at the time on Fourteenth Street and Fifth Avenue in Manhattan.

Delmonico's in its original location, Fourteenth Street and Fifth Avenue, New York, New York

Delmonico's is given credit for being the first true restaurant in America. Although America had hundreds of taverns and inns that served food before Delmonico's opened its doors, none were at the same level of sophistication. If not the very first, Delmonicos was considered the finest restaurant in America for many years afterward.

It was a Swiss-born sea captain and merchant, Giovanni Del Monico, who observed the need for a full service restaurant, patterned after the successful ones in Paris and other European cities, to replace the common fare available at the many taverns and inns which already dotted American streets. He observed that successful New York bankers and businessmen had no real place to go for a high quality meal either to impress or entertain. In 1827 he convinced his brother Pietro, an accomplished pastry chef, to open Delmonico's in the heart of New York City.

Except for a period between 1876 and 1879, when Ranhofer returned to France to open his own restaurant—the Hotel American near Paris—Ranhofer remained with Delmonico's the rest of his life. A gifted manager as well as a chef, Ranhofer excelled at designing world class dinners for large groups, often with just a few hours' notice, all the while attending to the demands of regular patrons who lined up for Ranhofer's exquisite foods and elaborate desserts.

Delmonico's hosted some of the highest occasions that occurred in nineteenth century New York, and Ranhofer personally planned them all, including banquets for President Andrew Johnson, President U. S. Grant, Charles Dickens, and many foreign dignitaries. (President Lincoln would visit town quietly

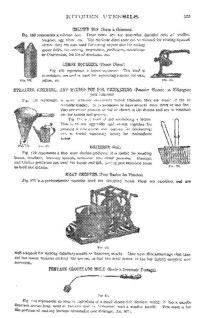

19th Century cooking utensils taken from The Epicurean, page 233

during the war for unpublicized meetings and stayed at rooms above the restaurant gratis at Lorenzo Del Monico's insistence.)

Ranhofer is given credit for inventing baked Alaska in honor of Secretary of State Seward's purchase of Alaska in 1867, and eggs Benedict after a famous financier and Wall Street broker LeGrand Benedict. He was also the first to popularize lobster Newberg in America, adapting a recipe brought to New York by a friend of Charles Del Monico.

Ranhofer was a member of several charitable and professional groups, including the Cercle Francais de l'Harmonie, the Société Culinaire Philanthropique, the French Benevolent Society, the French Orphan Asylum, the Chefs' Gastronomic Club of Chicago, and the Epicurean Club of Boston. He married and had three sons and two daughters. He died in 1899 of Bright's disease (a kidney ailment), and was buried at Woodlawn Cemetery in New York.

Ranhofer's legacy is remembered in his book *The Epicurean* (Dover Publication: New York, 1894). This is a huge treatise: 1,183 pages, 800 illustrations, over 3,000 recipes. By and large, the recipes are in the classic French tradition. However, a few popular American recipes also found a place in the text.

Among famous classic dishes are American favorites like: apricots à la Jefferson, striped bass à la Manhattan, corned beef hash. American style, Boston brown bread, Indian breakfast cakes, Jambalaia [sic] of chicken, chicken à la Maryland, Philadelphia style clams, corn on the cob, succotash, roasted canvas-back duck with hominy, New York hard-boiled eggs, California sherbet,

The Epicurean title page
published 1894

Standard dinner table set-up at Delmonico's taken from The Epicurean (1894)

American style lobster, Saratoga potatoes, peach pudding à la Cleveland, California quail à la Monterey, American style smoked salmon, and gumbo with soft-shell crabs.

The Epicurean also contains seasonal menus for up to 400 diners and a selection of historic Delmonico banquet menus dating between 1862 and 1894. The complete treatise also contains hundreds of illustrations and the discussion of utensils, platters, cooking pots, pans, carvings, and ornate presentations used in Ranhofer's kitchens.

THE MODERN CHEF

By the end of the eighteenth century in Europe, the role of the chef had evolved to one of fancy cook and artisan from its very meager beginnings. Figure 1–1 depicts historical milestones in this rich history. The new artisan chefs were expected to put their experience and learning to the test every day and create new and exciting menu offerings for an ever demanding clientele. In the aftermath of the French Revolution, the world was ready for a higher level of cuisine than it had ever demanded. This was accomplished in large part by the hard work and dedication to culinary art by the master chef Antoine Carême.

One hundred years later the transformation of the chef from fancy cook to culinary manager began to take shape in Europe and the United States thanks

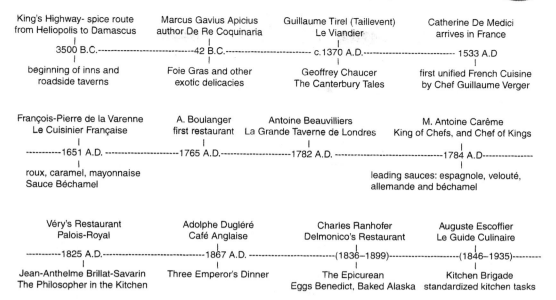

FIGURE 1–1   Hospitality and Culinary Timetable

to the efforts of Auguste Escoffier and Charles Ranhofer, who dedicated their lives to the study and improvement of culinary art. They both saw clearly the changes taking place in the social and political environments around them, and re-engineered their kitchens and menus to adjust to the evolving demands of customers.

Both *The Epicurean* (Ranhofer, 1894) and *Le Guide Culinaire* (Escoffier, 1902) became required reading materials for cooks throughout Europe and the United States wanting to emulate the success of the two authors. Eventually Asia, the Middle East and other parts of the world would also benefit from the writings of the two chefs, as trained chefs from Europe soon began to monopolize prestigious culinary positions around the world. Both chefs set the standard upon which other restaurant and hotel dining room food service would be founded and compared to for over a hundred years.

It was not only the recipes and the revised cooking and plating procedures that the two great chefs contributed to culinary art. They also helped to create a new form of culinary education and professional development for all cooks and chefs. Food alone was not enough; both Escoffier and Ranhofer understood and insisted on continual study and improvements in their craft and professional attitudes for themselves and their staffs.

Proper dress and hygiene became a priority for Escoffier in his French kitchens and Ranhofer in New York's Delmonico's. Where Ritz once said of Escoffier, "The master [Escoffier] has complete reign in his kitchen. It is his duty to prepare the finest foods and mine the grandest of tables for the

Lady's luncheon Delmonico's (c. 1902)

pleasure of our guests," Lorenzo Delmonico also said of Ranhofer, "He was perfect in dress and manner, and his attitude was such as to make me feel that he was doing me a great favor by coming into my employment. He gave me plainly to understand that he would be 'chief' indeed."

For both chefs, writing their treatises on cooking was not only a means of recording what they had learned and done, but to teach other culinarians about modern cooking as it was evolving around them. There were hundreds of recipes presented in logical order, but there were also great discussions of culinary theory and practice, proper culinary techniques, the need for standardized recipes, plating instructions and discipline within each kitchen work station.

During this evolution one chef, the executive chef, would be given ultimate responsibility and authority over the kitchens, the menus and the cooks preparing the meals.

It was natural for Americans to embrace the promise of fine cuisine for its emerging population of successful merchants, military leaders, judges and politicians at the turn of the twentieth century.

America had gained recognition as a global leader, thanks in large part to its success as an industrial nation, and was ripe for the exploitation of fine cuisine and grand hospitality. It was not long before fine hotels and exquisite restaurants expanded in American cities and dotted the American countryside from coast to coast.

Many European chefs immigrated to the United States to fill the ever growing number of positions of executive chefs in the emerging American industry, bringing with them their classical training and menus. America had neither a formal apprenticeship program for aspiring cooks or chefs nor culinary schools from which trained cooks could emerge, and depended on trained European and Asian chefs to run their hotel and restaurant kitchens.

The stock market crash in 1929, followed by the Great Depression—which was to become the worst depression in United States history—had a devastating effect on all American businesses, including the American hospitality industry. The rich and powerful people who had frequented the theaters, arts, and finer restaurants no longer existed. Rooms went empty, plays canceled, and restaurants and hotels closed their doors forever.

The U.S. depression had financial ramifications throughout the world. It was not until Europe prepared for war against Germany that the economy started to turn around. In 1941, America entered the war after the attack on Pearl Harbor by the Japanese (December 7, 1941), and soon its financially weakened industries were refurbished with federal funds and contracts and building supplies for the American armed services. As devastating as World War II was in terms of human life, it did end the Great Depression for Americans and helped start a whole new class of people—the middle class.

After World War II, as Europe and Asia were rebuilding and the rest of the world regrouping, Americans were enjoying a strong economy fueled by a huge increase in manufacturing. U.S. soldiers, sailors and pilots returned home to take up jobs in the expanded industries, which quickly turned from making military weaponry to cars, textiles and home appliances, in many cases side by side with their wives and the other women who were forced to enter the job market during the war to keep the war machine supplied with arms and equipment.

The quick gains American industries made during the reconstruction era following the war came from a huge export business. Record breaking domestic sales continued to supply jobs and money to American households. Men and women working hand in hand in order to pay bills, support a family and save for retirement became the standard rather than the exception. Good jobs and pay soon fueled the U.S. economy and enabled it to climb back to being one of the most prosperous in the world.

A lot of hard working families would maintain a good level of income and security. While many would never become rich they were significantly better off financially than the poor class, thus creating a new style of American life, one that was somewhere between that of the poor and the rich—a middle financial class of people.

This phenomenon fueled the creation of a variety of dining facilities, restaurants, clubs and even hotels for people who wanted the same services but not at the high prices of the classic properties. Both owners and chefs had to make changes in order to meet the needs of an expanding consumer market.

Food service continued to flourish in the '50s with the advent of diners, cafés and fast food service operations. Though these operations had existed before the 1950s (White Castle hamburgers first made the scene in 1922, and McDonald brothers opened their first hamburger restaurant in 1937), they began to gain popularity after the war as a fast and convenient way of servicing the needs of a quicker paced lifestyle and growing families.

Since these smaller establishments were less costly to open and operate, many individual chefs, business people and financiers opened their own restaurants to feed the ever growing middle class population. Chefs and other private owners found out there was more to running restaurants than cooking food, and quickly became business managers, hosts/hostesses, financiers, marketers, promotion experts, and human relation specialists for dealing with customers and staffing issues.

Chefs were also needed by the expanding fast food industry in their research and development departments, where their expertise in the construction of foods and flavors was invaluable to food manufacturers and expanding chain restaurant concepts. These research chefs were required to work side by side with food scientists, and learn much more food science themselves in order to create signature dishes for their prospective clients.

With competition rising, businesses becoming more complicated and personnel management a new priority, the chef's job became even more diverse than it had ever been before. Not only do chefs need to know how to cook and make money, but they have to learn how to motivate, train and properly communicate to a wide variety of people. Women, African Americans, Asians, Mexicans and other Latino groups found jobs that were once reserved only for white

McDonald's first restaurant opened 1948 by Dick and Maurice McDonald in San Bernadino, CA.

males; doors which had once been closed to minorities were all of the sudden swung wide open to fill tens of thousands of needed positions. Chefs trained in Europe, Asia and the United States had to learn how to deal with the problems and benefits of a diverse work force.

The modern chef has to be both a culinary technician and a business manager to stay in competition with the thousands of other restaurants and hotels from which customers have to choose. They must study the sociological changes that affect their customers and the food trends that influence dining around the world in order to stay competitive with the old and new restaurants and hotels opening by the thousands nation-wide.

While culinary art is founded on mastering the skills of cooking and baking, the business of running professional kitchens has a completely different set of required skills. Here is a short list of some of the new skills now required for the modern chef to stay effective with staff and to be competitive in the modern market:

- Communication skills
- Math skills
- The ability to plan and forecast
- Organizational skills
- Human relations skills
- Personnel development skills
- Management skills
- Quality control skills
- Computer skills

The chef's role has evolved many times over the past two thousand years since Apicius recorded his monumental work on Roman cookery. From the fancy cook to the classic chef to the supervising manager, the roles and responsibilities of the chef have risen to greater and more complex levels.

CHAPTER 2

New Values in Culinary Leadership

When you complete this chapter, you should be able to:

- Define the role of the modern professional chef.
- Describe the advantages of formal and informal culinary education to professional success.
- Describe some of the attributes of a quality oriented chef.
- Describe the academic subjects chefs need to study in order to be effective in modern kitchens.
- Describe ways a chef and other food service/hospitality managers can give back to the communities that support their businesses.
- Describe some of the career opportunities for chefs and the specific personal and professional traits needed to be successful in those types of operations.

LEADING KITCHENS TO SUCCESS

A rich culinary heritage has laid the groundwork for the position of chef today, and that position continues to evolve into the twenty-first century. Students of the culinary arts can take lessons from the past to help shape their plans and strategies for the future, yet they must remain current with trends and technologies. Culinarians should strive to study continuously in order to keep up with the changes and the progression of culinary arts and culinary management which is happening all around them. The legacy of the great chefs of Europe and America is not merely in the recipes and books that they left behind, but in the lives they led studying and perfecting their craft—the one lesson all culinarians can learn from.

The dedication and foresight of chefs from around the world continue to refine the art and science of the modern kitchen. As food trends and cooking technologies change, chefs too must change their repertoires of recipes, techniques and presentation styles constantly to meet the demands of their customers. The most successful chefs of the day take advantage of the changes in business and thrive on the challenges a discriminating customer may present.

The professional chef of today is a teacher, a leader, an organizer, and above all, a person willing to learn and try new things. Chefs must also be business and personnel managers in order to stay competitive in an increasingly complex industry. Motivation, training, organization, and planning are essential skills that must be mastered by the modern professional chef for them to able to lead their staffs to quality performance and production.

Leadership begins with a thorough understanding of the basics of the trade. Leaders demonstrate their knowledge and pass on their experience to the people who work with and for them. Chefs cannot be leaders without the respect of their employees, and respect is earned over the pots and pans and butcher blocks that taught them their craft.

Chefs must learn their craft from every aspect. History is just as important as current trends; technique is as important as foresight.

CULINARY EDUCATION

Culinary education is one of the fastest growing segments of the education industry in the twenty-first century, and has been for over twenty years. When the American Culinary Federation began its programmatic accrediting commission in 1984, there were only a few dozen schools promoting formal culinary education; according to *Shaw's Guide for Cooking Schools—2005*, there are now over 1,200 culinary art related programs offered on a continuing basis, with over 700 of them designed specifically for the training of professional cooks.

The growth of culinary schools and individual programs over the past twenty years is testimony to the rising interest in food for dining pleasure and for careers.

It has become big business for state operated and proprietary schools alike to offer culinary arts and hospitality management programs to help supply workers for the expanding industry and fill their classrooms. Hospitality and food service careers have never been more popular, perhaps in part because of the success of TV programs like those on the Food Network, but also for the celebrity status of a lot of local chefs who market themselves and their establishments with pride and finesse, often under the tutelage of a trained PR professional. A lot of people want to become chefs, for the spotlight it promises them if and when they become successful; for the freedom of running their own kitchens and wielding great authority in the operation; and for the glamour of cooking for the rich the famous and political leaders. These are great temptations. But to get there takes a lot of preparation, study and experience.

The need for new employees continues to outpace the availability of trained personnel in all areas of the hospitality industry. A school or college which can consistently educate entry level employees with the skills and knowledge to prepare them for management positions with a few years of industry training after graduation can keep their classrooms filled. Whether education is offered at a community college, a private college, or a state university, when delivered properly, a solid education can position motivated individuals for successful careers in the demanding hospitality industry.

A formal culinary education exposes students to many styles and techniques of cooking through their various instructors. In some schools, students are exposed to a dozen or more chefs in as few as fifteen to eighteen months. Students can learn the specialties and idiosyncrasies of each chef as though they've worked for them in the industry. Comparable industry experience could take many years to obtain.

The concentration and direct supervision given to students in a culinary classroom cannot be easily duplicated in the workplace. Although chefs tout themselves as natural teachers, teaching on the job, where the chef has the authority to hire and fire, is quite different from teaching in the classroom, where the student is the customer. To teach in a structured educational program requires a great deal more patience and special training in motivation techniques, learning behavior, and teaching methodologies than a typical chef needs to run a professional food service operation.

Students in formal culinary/hospitality educational programs need to take advantage of the time they have with professionals who are teaching them. The more information that can be given, the more practice can be tried and the more real-work experiences that can be shared under the direction of an experienced professional, the greater the successes the young graduates can achieve.

However, education does not only come in the classroom; it comes in libraries, in bookstores, and in working kitchens. Not all beginning cooks have the opportunity to enroll in a full culinary education program and must pick up courses and study one class at a time on their own. And for those who do earn a culinary degree, continual learning is made possible through a variety of seminars, workshops, on-line and correspondence courses offered by hundreds of organizations around the country.

The American Culinary Federation, National Restaurant Association, State Restaurant Associations and other trade associations offer a multitude of learning opportunities through conferences, trade shows (where food vendors display their products and give samples to enquiring cooks and chefs), localized meetings, publications and on-line platforms for sharing information about trends around the world. Likewise, some food companies host trade shows in strategic locations around the country to solicit business, but also to educate the professional cook and chef. This education comes in the form of seminars, culinary competitions and of course the trade show itself, where companies display their broker's products.

There are many other nationally recognized education companies offering a variety of seminars and workshops for professional supervisors and managers. Dale Carnegie and Dunn and Bradstreet are just two such companies which offer various learning platforms for professionals around the country. Many of their subjects include: First Time Supervisors, Organizational Leadership, Managing Multiple Tasks, Business Communication and other business and management related topics designed for a general audience. Although not culinarily or hospitality focused, these same general management, supervision and leadership workshops and seminars have applications in all industries. Experience in professional kitchens helps to transform those generic business and management theories into culinary leadership and practice.

Learning does not always have to come out of a book or a person's mouth; learning can take place by watching, observing and doing. Cooks and chefs can learn a lot, for example, just by going out to eat in various competing restaurants, hotels or clubs in their community. Observing what competitors are doing with service, ambience and food, scrutinizing the quality of service and food and comparing these to their own operations can result in learning for themselves and their staffs when they bring that knowledge back to their own kitchens.

The story of Antoine Carême, who taught himself to read and write by candlelight after working long hot hours in the kitchen, should be an inspiration both to young and to experienced culinarians. Learning, whether in a college program or on the job, must become a lifelong adventure.

PROGRESSIVE SKILLS

Becoming a professional chef requires progressive training and experience in addition to formal and informal education. Whether starting out working in a ware wash (dish or pot wash) or prep job and working up the career ladder to chef, working through a structured apprenticeship program, or graduating from a culinary school or college, all successful culinarians are those who have worked a variety of jobs in various types of operations under the direction of many chefs. Not only does having a variety of jobs and positions help build a solid repertoire of recipes, techniques and procedures, it exposes the young culinarian to different management styles and business strategies that are prevalent in the diverse food service industry. A young culinarian who can establish a good foundation in knowledge, skills and experience is setting the stage for a successful career.

There is such a large diversity in types of operations that a young culinarian may want to experience many before deciding to specialize in one field. The basics of service and food are the same, but the needs and wants of the customers change completely and the pressures and expectations of management and owners become increasingly demanding as menu price and style of service goes up.

The best way to learn if you will like working in free standing private restaurants is to work in one; if you feel you want to be a country club chef, then take a cooking job in one near where you live or study. By working the schedules, meeting and working alongside the other cooks and chefs, talking to the wait staff and seeing how the members of the club intermingle with the staff, you will learn in a short period if that is the atmosphere and style of work that you want to engage in. If you have set your goals on becoming a hotel chef one day, then you should get a prep cook's job in one of the better hotels in your neighborhood; in that way, you will see first hand how hotel kitchens work balancing room service, catering and dining room food services.

Private restaurants offer completely different experiences than themed or chain restaurants which follow a corporate model.

Hotel operations are different from both restaurants and resorts—they're a unique type that varies among downtown centers, airport hotels and discount hotels. They all offer the same services, but at quite different levels and in completely different environments.

Private city clubs and prestigious country clubs offer different experiences than restaurants or hotels, for they cater to very specific groups of people who are members and part owners of the clubs in which the cooks and chefs work. As clubs, private city clubs and country clubs have similar parameters within which they work, yet different business pressures, complexities and customer expectations.

Catering companies offer yet another set of experiences, as well as institutional food services, hospital food services, cruise ship food services and myriad other types of food service establishments.

Each venue offers the culinarian experiential classrooms from which they can learn innumerable lessons and ultimately decide which career path they want to follow.

ATTRIBUTES OF A PROFESSIONAL CHEF

The skills and knowledge required to be a successful chef today can be easily documented, studied and learned. Yet basic skills and knowledge are simply not enough to catapult the average culinarian to the rank of professional chef. What also is needed is a professional attitude, demeanor and command of these advanced skills:

- Leadership
- Decision making
- Work ethic
- Self-motivation
- Continuous education
- Organization
- Planning
- Quality control

Today's chefs must be leaders who can give sound direction and guidance, for the fast pace and complexity of running a professional food service operation demands quick decisions that create positive results. The best way to prepare ones' self for making those fast, accurate decisions is through hard work, constant study and many years of practice.

To fulfill the role of a professional manager as well as an accomplished cook, chefs must look the part, speak the part, and most important act the part of a professional manager with finesse, consistency and pride. Great leaders often become role models for others to emulate. It is their energy and drive that makes other people work harder and accomplish greater goals. Successful chef mangers must be ready to act and make quick hard decisions, yet must also be willing to admit their mistakes and those of others for the sake of learning. A leader who does not act like a leader can never truly be one.

Most successful chefs have worked their way up the career ladder from washing dishes to running big production lines. They learned early in their careers that all jobs in a professional kitchen are dependent on each other for their operation's success, and that the only way to get things done is by doing whatever it takes to create positive results. The best motivation to pass on to workers is a good work ethic that the chef possesses personally.

Even among chefs who began their careers by attending culinary schools or working apprenticeship programs, the most successful are those who understand and can communicate to others the critical relationship of and necessity for every job in the professional kitchen. Successful chefs are active chefs, helping their kitchen staff achieve their goals of quality food service by cutting, cooking and even washing dishes or pots and pans right alongside staff as needed.

The chef as a manager and leader must continue to work hard at training and education in order to stay ahead of the competition. It is a task that never ends.

There are always articles to read in business magazines like *Restaurants & Institutions, Restaurant Hospitality, Nation's Restaurant News, Chef Magazine* and *The National Culinary Review* to keep them abreast of industry news and trends. New books are constantly being written by authors with new perspectives on cuisine, professional cooking, baking or management, and perhaps even new ideas to stimulate thinking and challenge mediocrity. Chefs must stay ahead of the competition by keeping themselves and their staffs informed.

Mise en place is a common phrase in the culinary industry. What it means literally is everything in its place. What it means figuratively is organization. It dictates: Know what you have, how much there is, where you have it, and how to use it correctly, always. That is organization!

One way chefs organize production is by making lists; it helps to write things down. What is needed first? How long does it take to prepare each item, and who on the staff is most likely to prepare it? Organization includes knowing how long it should take to do a certain thing, the skills required to do it and the specifications on which it should be based. In this way the organized chef can judge professional progress.

Chefs must also learn how to organize their time throughout the day, for there are many things to be accomplished and only twenty-four hours in a day. The more successful chefs become at organizing their time, the least number of hours they need to work to accomplish results. Organized chefs combine tasks that require similar prep or cooking techniques to create efficiencies in production like devising a mise en place of ingredients with multiple uses, and thinking ahead before making another trip to the walk-ins or storeroom. They ask: What else do I need? What will I need later? They know that there's always something that has to be done later and that there's no better time than now to get started. Successful mangers and leaders don't wait for the next day if there is time that day to start a new project.

Chefs organize their work stations so that everything needed during production hours is within reach. It should not take more than two or three steps to accomplish a single cooking task. Reaching for items on the prep table or in the reach-in should be automatic by knowing exactly, instinctively, where everything is before getting started.

Planning is just as important to a chef's career as it is to the daily routine of the job. Chefs need short- and long-term goals and a time frame in which to judge their progress. Knowing the distinction is a priority to getting there.

The five Ps (proper planning prevents poor production) of business apply to food service as well as to any other business. The importance of the planning function cannot be over emphasized.

The planning function is analytical in nature and requires clear thought and a calculating mind. Analyzing numbers, ratios, and percentages in the light of historical and economical factors is the cooking method for a well seasoned plan.

Planning means thinking ahead; it saves time, energy, and stress when done correctly and consistently. What to do next? What to do tomorrow? Next week? Next five years? Time is the only relative factor in each of these questions; the need to ask these questions is timeless.

The control of quality in professional food service is another of the modern chef's many responsibilities. It's not enough to have standard recipe cards, pictures of plated foods, or even skilled staffs performing all the work; without the diligent supervision and constant inspections that professional chefs apply in their kitchens every day, consistency in food quality can be hard to guarantee.

The control of quality can be achieved by careful planning, training, supervision and follow-through. Yet it is not simply the application of policies or processes to food production that creates quality foods, but the inspiration of the chef in charge which drives quality production. A chef who strives for quality production always has a better chance of achieving it on a consistent basis than another chef who simply cooks and serves food.

Quality can be measured through comparison with set standards, but it can only be achieved when it becomes a deliberate outcome and not an accidental result. Successful chefs strive for quality in everything they do and pass their inner energy and passion for quality to their staffs, preparing and serving the foods they help create. A chef who is too busy, or disorganized, or impassive about quality may never achieve it in their professional life.

The Academic Chef

A chef's training must have a solid academic component in order to be successful in today's industry. Professional chefs need to be skilled in a variety of subjects, including supervision and human relations, marketing, finance, sanitation, nutrition, mathematics, business and communication.

Kitchens and dining rooms are no longer run on just good food and prompt, friendly service. They are complex work environments where a multiple set of skills play an integral part in keeping the team together.

Supervision and human relations teach managers how to deal with the human side of the working equation: motivation skills, leadership skills, time management, and conflict resolution skills and strategies.

Marketing skills keep chefs and their restaurants competitive in a fast-growing industry by teaching them how to create a competitive product in the first place; position the product in a community that demands or wants it; and promote the product and services that accompany it in a professional and appealing way. Marketing is one of the many business skills successful chefs need to have in their portfolios to stay on the cutting edge of business.

Finance skills include calculation of food and labor costs, recipe costing, inventory control, budgeting, and forecasting. These calculations are in the chef's domain of responsibilities. No matter how good the food and service are, without proper and accurate costing, the success of the business will be in jeopardy.

Sanitation is the study of food safety and, consequently, the science of food bacteria and food-borne illness. This is a serious subject because ignorance can spell disaster. Proper food handling practices, from receiving to service, can guarantee that the foods chefs serve are wholesome and safe to eat.

Whereas many forms of food poisoning are promulgated through human error and personal hygiene, food safety can be protected through proper training of the staff. Sanitation training must be given equally to managers as well as dishwashers, prep cooks, line cooks, and wait staff. Sanitation is everyone's responsibility.

Nutrition became increasingly important in the latter part of the twentieth century, and promises to become emphasized even more in the twenty-first. As more evidence surfaces regarding the benefits of healthful eating to preserving a quality standard of life, customers become more aware and demanding of their restaurant chefs and owners to supply healthier meals.

Nutritional cooking does not have to be bland or unoriginal. Normal everyday cooking can become more healthful when cooks have a better understanding of the roles of fat and salt in cooking, and make sensible substitutions in their recipes and cooking procedures. When the science of nutrition is accentuated by knowledge of taste and flavor, nutritional cooking can rival the splendor of classical and international cuisine.

Math skills become critical in the operational and business functions of a professional kitchen. Converting recipes to meet consumer demand, conducting yield tests (determining the actual price of usable cuts of meat, poultry, seafood and vegetables), costing recipes and pricing menus are everyday kitchen activities that require a working knowledge of math, particularly how to work with fractions, percentages, multiplication, and division. Guesswork in these areas can be disastrous to the efficient running of the kitchen and to the revenues and profits made at the register.

The need for a cook and chef to learn business skills is increasing as management roles descend down the organizational ladder. Whereas the owners used to be the only ones interested in the business of the operation, chefs became more involved in the business aspects of food service as the complexities of running a professional kitchen continued to increase. Now some of those responsibilities and concerns are working their way down the career ladder to other culinary positions such as sous chef, cold food chef and even some high level line cook (chef) positions where responsibilities include preparedness, quality checks, inventory control, product control, waste control and other standard operating procedures. There are many standard operating procedures (SOPs) in place for every successful operation to help control and monitor costs throughout the production and service periods.

Communication skills are critical to the chef manager's success, for only in communicating properly and efficiently to one's staff and supervisors can work get accomplished with quality precision. Communication comes in many forms; verbal, written and bodily expressions are all forms of communication, and not necessarily in descending order of importance. The structure and delivery of communiqués in any form determine whether messages are properly sent, received and interpreted so that intended results can occur. When done well, communications can lead, motivate and discipline when necessary to achieve great results. If done poorly or casually, communicating can cause confusion, fear and complacency.

The Chef Motivator

Another departure from traditional kitchen management is the evolution of chef from dictator to motivator. While many modern professional kitchens continue to follow some aspects of Escoffier's brigade system, they have lessened their use of the hierarchical style of management fashioned from Escoffier's military experiences.

Past practice allowed chefs to rule their kitchens with a strong, disciplinarian hand and strict hierarchical management. Workers were seen as tools to getting the job done, and there were plenty to go around. Lax employment policies allowed for a steady stream of employees in and out of the kitchens and contributed to a high rate of employee turnover. The employee, seen as a commodity, was considered expendable. Only the chef was considered essential to the success of the operation.

The modern industry acknowledges the importance of all workers in the operation of successful businesses. Good leadership is essential, yet the hard work and dedication of employees are what make restaurants run well and keep them competitive in an expanding market.

There's a direct correlation between the level of complexity within an organization and the level of expertise needed of its employees. Complex operations which deliver high quality foods and services need highly skilled and dedicated staffs to make them work. With thousands of new restaurants, hotels and clubs opening in the United States alone every year, let alone the rest of the civilized world, the supply of trained employees can not keep up with the demand.

The role and demeanor of the chef had to change in order to keep the highly skilled and motivated staffs that are now required of the hospitality industry from leaving their employment. Instead of following strict and highly disciplined organizational structures, chefs must become coaches and mentors to hold and shape diverse groups of skilled employees into productive and efficient teams.

The support and inspiration that chef leaders give their staffs keep employee turnover low, keep morale high and create success for the people and the business.

The Social Chef

The hospitality industry could not exist without the support of its communities and neighborhoods. Restaurant dining rooms, hotel rooms and banquet halls would be less full if not for anniversaries, weddings, birthdays and business meetings. People depend on these establishments for the services they supply. In turn, businesses depend on the loyalty of customers to fill their seats and pay the bills. This is a symbiotic relationship that benefits only if both sides are successful.

Many chefs and hospitality managers are giving back to the communities that support their businesses and protect their livelihoods and to less fortunate people around the globe. Social-minded managers know the importance of building relationships that go beyond guest checks and room charges. By catering to the emotional and social needs of people they build ties that create loyalty and goodwill far more lasting than paid advertisements, specials, and coupons could ever produce.

There are many ways chefs and hospitality managers give back to communities and the world around them. Here are some common ways to show support for other people outside of the business of selling foods and hospitality:

- Sponsor a local Little League baseball, soccer, girls hockey or other neighborhood sports team.
- Sponsor a Cub Scout, Boy Scout, or Girl Scout pack in your area.
- Participate in charity drives for the hungry and homeless.
- Encourage your workers to participate in walkathons or other charity fundraisers.
- Encourage workers to participate in blood drives for the Red Cross.
- Participate in community cleanup programs by paying workers who donate their time to clean sidewalks, alleys and roadsides.
- Set up recycling bins in the parking lots for customers to bring their aluminum cans, glass bottles and newspapers to your establishment.

▪ Participate in child hunger programs and other programs that support the less fortunate.

There are many ways of giving back to the community that supports your business and the world in which you live. A healthy community and a worldwide social conscience helps to promote strong, vibrant relationships between businesses and their patrons, especially in the food service and hospitality industries, where the service and comfort of people are primary goals.

THE DIVERSE INDUSTRY

Today's industry is as diverse as the people who populate the earth. The needs of the customer are many. It takes many forms and levels of food and hospitality services to meet the demands of such an expansive industry.

The modern chef finds work in hundreds of jobs. It is one of the most diverse arenas for work in any professional field. Some of the possibilities include the following.

Catering: On-premise or off-premise catering offers exciting opportunities for young culinarians today. In many areas of the country, there still exist excellent opportunities for growth in this market segment. For catering, chefs need special abilities in organization and planning, since parties are often performed in conjunction with several other parties and often at different locations. Catering done off site is the most difficult because it is performed away from familiar surroundings where things like hot water and electricity are taken for granted and anything can happen. Off-premise catering chefs can take nothing for granted. They make several trips to the catering site prior to the party to arrange services like delivery, setup of tables and trash removal. People skills also become extremely important to catering chefs and managers because of the more than usual contact with the guests of the party. Chefs and cooks are not closed off behind a kitchen wall, but many times are out serving the buffet or carving at the table.

Restaurants: Restaurants are as varied in theme and purpose as the people who go out to eat and their reasons for dining away from the home. They offer the greatest flexibility in jobs and job responsibilities to the largest part of the culinary workforce. Family style, theme, ethnic, and specialty restaurants are only a few of the many types of restaurants that are successful in today's market. In small, usually family-owned restaurants, the chef must play many roles, from cook and baker to purchasing agent, stock handler and promotions expert. In large restaurants, those duties might be delegated to others while the cooking and baking responsibilities remain with the chef.

Clubs: Private clubs, country clubs, and city clubs combine both catering and restaurant styles of service for their members. Depending on the type or location of the club, the percentage of business could be heavier either in restaurant or catering sales, and often shift depending on the season or other special events. Members are considered part owners by virtue of the membership fees they pay to support the club. Chefs need a higher sense of confidence in their own culinary skills and people skills in order to keep peace with so many bosses. Clubs have high and low seasons, which allows the chef a break from the heavy pace of a busy environment. The artistic chef truly has a place in private clubs since customers expect more than usual at their dinner tables and on the buffet. Ice sculpting and pastry arts are also good skills for a club chef to possess.

Corporate Chefs: Food service manufacturers offer great opportunities for chefs with an experimental eye. H. J. Heinz, Sara Lee, Nestlé and UBF Food Solutions are major players in the modern kitchen, and their teams are as likely to be chefs as scientists (practice and theory). Research and development (R&D) keep these companies and many more on the competitive edge. The job of the chef is to develop new products and improve existing ones, making them not only taste and look good but be convenient for mass production. These chefs must keep in touch with market trends and regional diversity.

Dietary: Food service within hospitals, nursing homes, and retirement communities (soon to become the fastest growing segment as populations age and life spans increase) is called dietary management. Chefs who choose this career must have special training in nutrition, sanitation, and kitchen management to make sure the dietary needs of patients are met exactly as required by the dietitian or doctor. Food not only has to be healthful, but exciting both in taste and appearance; therefore, chefs must be creative and modern in their techniques and menus. In many locations, hospital food service is now competing with the independent restaurant for walk-in customers. This is an area of food service which will continue to evolve as the population ages.

Education: With the rise in formal culinary education programs around the world, there has been a need for chefs to become teachers and college administrators to design the curriculums and teach the classes. In order for the schools to continue to teach appropriate skills for culinarians entering the modern industry, practicing chefs are brought into classrooms to share their expertise and knowledge. For a lot of chefs the practice of teaching is an attempt to inspire as well as educate young culinarians. Teaching allows a chef to give fully of themselves, their backgrounds, their education, their experiences and their drive for professionalism that can instruct and inspire hundreds of people entering or progressing in the culinary and hospitality industries. Teaching is hard work, itself requiring a lot of study and practice to succeed, yet teaching is rewarding in that the products teachers develop are the successful careers of young culinarians.

Entrepreneur: Many chefs are taking an entrepreneurial approach to food service. After years of experience, either with their own money or with outside financing, chefs are taking on the role of owner and operator. In this way, chefs have complete control over the entire operation and can infuse their personality in all aspects of the business. Chef owners are able to create concepts that please both their own egos and their potential customers' needs and desires. Having the pride of ownership and pride for their craft, chef owners can become some of the more competitive operators in the world today. Chef ownership requires great stamina, years of experience in food service, knowledge of business structures, law, and accounting, people skills, public relations skills, savvy and nerve.

Gourmet Retail: A new trend in the food service industry found in grocery stores, independent retail shops and retail outlets linked to restaurants is the trend toward gourmet retail, or gourmet carry-out. Customers want the flexibility of being able to choose a variety of prepared specialty foods and carry them home for a more relaxed dining atmosphere. Grocery store chains are among the leaders in this area, since people are already drawn to them for their everyday groceries. They are hiring chefs as consultants for their deli selections, their seafood departments, and meat departments, where fully and partially prepared foods are made in the store for consumer carry-out. Some chefs are opening their own retail gourmet shops with catering capabilities, linking both the individual gourmet carry-out trade with wholesale accounts. Menu planning, recipe development and organization are essential skills for the chef to become successful in this arena.

Hotels: The diversity in hotel properties and chef responsibilities is also very great. Independent hotels, chain hotels, franchised hotels, resort hotels, international hotels, conference hotels and casino hotels all offer challenges to the young as well as the experienced chef. The size of the property is the differential that determines the scope of responsibilities for the chef and for the organizational structure. Hotels offer the widest range of levels of kitchen jobs when compared to most other properties. The complexity of the operation is balanced by the strength of the brigade system. Chefs who work for national or even international hotel chains usually have the flexibility of being able to move from one location to another, from city to city, state to state, or even to another country. What a great opportunity for young culinarians who would like to travel and work in some of the world's finest properties! Becoming the executive chef of a hotel is usually a much longer process than becoming a restaurant or club chef, since many hotels offer a higher complexity of food service, from restaurants to catering to room service.

Institutional: Institutional food service operations are those found on college campuses, in factory buildings, bank buildings, prisons, and other such settings. These are operations which have a captive audience (people forced by circumstance or convenience to eat on a regular basis in the same establishment). Menus have to be exciting and ever changing to keep the interest level of the patrons high, while inventories remain small and versatile to help control costs. Chefs in this field require special talents in organization, costing, and menu planning.

Private Chefs: From Hollywood to Washington, D.C., there is an ever increasing need for chefs to work in a single household. Parties, and most especially food, have again become a status symbol for the rich and famous. Who would not like to be the private chef aboard the Budweiser Yacht, which summers in the Great Lakes and winters in Florida? Or the chef of a famous movie star, or of a state governor? Private chefs have small staffs and do a lot of the work themselves, but there is great flexibility in creativity allowed, if not expected, in many cases.

Chefs are not limited to food preparation and service jobs for their careers. There are a number of related fields which require the expert eyes and hands of a trained chef without the actual hands-on approach. Purchasing agents for large hotels and conference centers, catering sales, sales people for food manufacturers and food distributors, brokers, restaurant equipment sales people, restaurant design engineers, architects and consultants all benefit from a culinary background. Food writers, editors and educators are also viable positions for the modern chef.

Here are some testimonials from professional chefs describing their climb up the career ladder and the skills it takes to perform the jobs they have obtained. While by no means are they at the point of retirement, and may change jobs again, they will give you some valuable insight into just a few of the many culinary career paths you may embark on one day.

Private Country Club Chef
Reimund Pitz, CEC, CCE, AAC
Executive Chef, Orlando Country Club, Orlando, Florida

The career at a country club for culinarians and professional chefs provides tremendous opportunities which are not realized in most restaurants and hotels today, from the utilization of the finest ingredients not often affordable in the standing restaurant or casual dining rooms across America, to the freedom of creativity that is almost expected of club cooks and chefs. However, club careers also provide enormous challenges.

For example, if you are employed at a private club owned by the membership you will answer to everyone who is ultimately your boss. At any time any one of them could have unique dietary requirements that you must cater to. Recipes are altered on a daily basis to suit everyone's personal tastes and needs.

Attention to detail is extremely critical to the success of the club cook and chef. Perfection is expected and anything less is scrutinized with great fervor.

The rewards are both financial and educational. Financial because private clubs are not afraid to pay top dollar for quality cuisine and service; after all, that's why members pay so much to join the club and participate in its events. Education is keen because of the exposure you can gain dealing with the most expensive and exotic foods and ingredients money can buy; these foods become standard and expected fare. The fabrication of wild game, fish and meat is commonplace, whereas it is almost a lost art in most establishments. The utilization of exotic ingredients like white and black truffles, fresh abalone and sea urchin are just some of the items found on daily menus.

Yet let there be no mistake about it—the demands of the club's members and managers are enormous, requiring a lot of extra time, labor and detail. Patience is also a golden attribute to have in one's own portfolio. It will be tested often.

A successful club chef must be versatile in all forms of cuisine, including American regional, classical and international. The club's membership is very affluent and well traveled; they expect the best, and it is your job to provide it.

Spa Chef
Cary E. Neff
Executive Chef/Director of Food and Beverage
Woodloch Resort and Spa, Chicago, Illinois

So you want to be a chef—how about a career as a spa chef? It's a fun, challenging, engaging and a rewarding way to cook that not only provides you with an opportunity to create great tasting foods—you can help improve someone's life through your food. A spa chef specializes in the use of whole sustainable foods that are delicious and healthful, creating nutritionally balanced meals.

I've always considered it a blessing that at the early age of 16, I was determined to pursue a career in culinary arts. Almost 30 years have passed since I began my career, and I remain as enthusiastic and honored to don my toque and chef's jacket as I was when I first began my career.

I now preside over my own consulting company, I've authored two cookbooks, and continue to work as the executive chef of one of the country's top rated destination resort spas. I reached this point in my career not by design but by making myself open to new opportunities. And one glorious thing about the culinary profession is its boundless opportunity. At no time during the first twenty years of my profession had I desired to become a spa chef, creating health conscious fare. Nor had I envisioned that I would have created a new food style, written two books on the subject and

consulted to some of the country's largest and most respected food service establishments on the benefits of healthy cooking.

What prepared me for my current position, and what continues to set me apart from my colleagues, is my desire to learn multiple food styles, which has allowed me to be employed in various types of establishments. Another trait is a desire to offer my guests the coming "next best thing," which has kept me ahead or abreast of culinary trends. These attributes allowed me the opportunity to take on the duties of a nationally top rated fine dining restaurant at the height of its success. Building on this success, I responded to the growing desire of my guests to receive foods that were delicious and lighter, indulgent and still healthful. It was there that I began to make a conscious effort to make all of my food lighter and to reduce and eliminate the use of added calories and fats. It wasn't low fat or low calorie foods that I sought to make, but good food that was created with my patrons' wellness in mind. That was 1993, two years prior to opening Miraval Resort and Spa in Tucson as the Executive Chef and Director of Food and Beverage. Within the next two years I led my food and beverage staff and helped Miraval achieve the ranking as the number one spa in North America—also number one for its cuisine and diet plan.

I now concentrate my daily efforts on creating health conscious foods, in a food style that I call Conscious Cuisine®— a food style that awakens the senses to new possibilities by embracing conscious efforts in selecting, preparing and serving foods. Conscious Cuisine makes a mindful attempt to create meals with whole foods that are least processed, retaining an abundance of flavor and nutritional value. The basis of this food style is now widely used in spas across America, providing spa chefs with a platform on which to create the next best thing.

If you're ready to create the next best thing as a spa chef, here are some traits that should provide benefit to you and success in your career.

- Desire and ability to build a culture within your staff that supports and challenges one another
- Desire to learn more about the nutritional components of food and suggested dietary guidelines for balanced nutrition
- Desire to expand your knowledge of whole foods and unconventional ingredients
- Desire to learn different diets and illnesses, such as macrobiotic, vegetarian and ayurvedic diets and foods to remedy illnesses such as diabetes and coronary disease
- Willingness to obtain additional education and training for yourself and staff members
- Thorough knowledge of traditional and fundamental cooking methods
- Highly developed communication and organization skills to conduct cooking demonstrations

These are the skills required of a spa chef that are beyond the daily expectations of the executive managerial duties of supervision, purchasing, budget management and menu development. Attention to these traits can foster a rewarding career in the ever expanding venue of spa and nutrition cookery.

Catering Chef
Dan D'Angelo, CEC, AAC
D'Angelo's Summit Restaurant and Caterers, Philadelphia, Pennsylvania

Whether you serve fifty or five thousand people, the first meal served must be the same as the last. This is the pledge of the catering chef where you cook from your heart as much as with your hands.

As a banquet or catering chef, you have much more control over the meal periods you are about to serve than in any other area of food service. You know the menu weeks in advance; you know exactly how many people to prepare for; you know what time they are coming and how long they are staying; and most important, you know how much they are going to pay for the meal and service. Sounds like a restaurateur's dream, but it is a caterer's legacy.

To be a good caterer, you must have strong people skills as well as impeccable organization and planning skills. Catering, whether it is off premise at a client's house or in a great hotel banquet room, is by definition a party catered to the particular needs and wants of the customer. The caterer, or banquet chef, must become intimately acquainted with these needs and desires in order to assure the success of the event. In catering, the client's background, religion and even age play some part in designing a menu and theme for a particular affair. Often the chef has to work side by side with the customer in planning the menus and setting the theme. It is the pride of a caterer when they can realize that they made a special event a memorable one through their food and hospitality.

In catering, we cater to our customers' special requests. This is where they can feel important and proud when handled with respect and courtesy. Special requests such as dietary needs, religious restrictions, and personal choice restrictions (like vegetarianism) set the tone for many affairs. The caterer's ability to react and adapt to special needs becomes their legacy and strongest asset.

Remember, cook with your heart as much as you cook with your hands.

Chef Educator

James W. Paul II, MS, CCE, CSC, FMP

Chef Director, Culinary Arts, The Art Institute of Atlanta, Atlanta, Georgia

What makes a good culinary educator? First and foremost, passion and compassion for the student. You've got to remember what it is you're there for, regardless of how busy you are. Your job, every single day, is to touch the lives of the students and to help them on their way. I am fortunate enough to come from a large family where many people have worked in the field of education, so I learned early on how rewarding a field it can be, and how deeply you affect the lives of the people you help. I think the most important thing you can do as an educator is to always keep that in perspective. If you do that, you'll make the right choices for yourself and your students.

But, that passion needs to go hand in hand with a solid base. Being in the world of education means that it helps to have a solid education yourself. Certainly in this specialized industry, a culinary degree is essential. You have to be able to speak the language, know the ins and outs of the kitchen and let students know why each and every thing they're doing is important. Of course, it helps to have real world experience so you can share all those things you've learned the hard way. But, I think having advanced degrees has really helped me better understand and function well in the world of education itself. I know what it's like to be a number, and to have to fend for yourself on a big campus. I know how crazy it can be to juggle school, work and personal life. I think experiencing the education process was just as valuable to me as the technical knowledge I gained. And, going beyond my Bachelors Degree to the Masters level is what really helped solidify my abilities as both a chef and an educator. Without my educational experience, I don't think I would have the base I need to be truly effective in my job.

As rewarding a field as I find culinary education to be, there are some challenges. For me, the biggest one is working in an environment where a sense of urgency isn't part of daily life. In the industry, everything is done in a hurry. In the world of education, especially in an artistic environment, you realize that immediacy of execution just isn't as important in every field. A painting might be finished in a week or in a decade. A dinner has to be served right here and right now. It's important to adapt the skills you use in a fast-paced kitchen so they work for you outside that high adrenaline environment. Also, being in the world of education means that you are no longer on the front lines of your industry. It's easy to be out of touch with the latest trends if you're not careful. But, the trade-off is that you are the one who is influencing the next generation of culinary artists, so you are actually helping to create the new front line.

One of my favorite expressions is an old Chinese adage that says the highest level a soul can achieve is that of teacher. Touch just one life, and you'll get a taste of what that means. To me, that is true joy of being a culinary educator. And with passion, compassion, flexibility and a solid base, you should have the building blocks you need to experience that joy for yourself.

Hotel and Conference Center Chef
Thomas J. Macrina, CEC, AAC
Desmond Hotel and Conference Center, Media, Pennsylvania

Being an executive chef in a hotel kitchen is one of the most rewarding experiences one can have. Many hotels, unlike freestanding restaurants, have several outlets. A large hotel could have as many as five or more restaurants within its confines. The executive chef of a hotel is like a captain of a ship. He or she must always be in control of everything that is going on. This means that they must have excellent, well trained individuals working under them as well.

Usually, there is an executive sous chef and sous chef for each independent food outlet, and a banquet chef in larger hotels, all under the direction of the executive chef. In most cases, the executive chef writes all the menus and puts the systems in place to make sure recipes are followed correctly and his or her own production standards are being met. This requires great organization and leadership skills.

The executive chef meets with the food and beverage director on a daily basis, and must work well with other hotel departments such as maintenance and housekeeping. The executive chef has a wide range of responsibilities, from controlling all kitchen labor and food cost to helping the catering sales staff give presentations.

It is very difficult to be bored in a hotel. There is always something going on. You might have several different theme restaurants appealing to various types of clientele. One menu may include hamburgers and hot dogs, and another caviar and foie gras. This keeps the executive chef very busy trying to keep a variety of menus up to date with new and exciting choices, while maintaining an expanding and diverse inventory of goods, controlling food costs, and training the staff for the ever changing menu items. Sometimes you may even have a celebrity or other important guest staying at your hotel who requires special attention and consideration. Special guests often expect foods, presentation, and service to be exceptional, placing extra pressure on the abilities of the chef to perform. These special guests may even include dignitaries from foreign countries who expect to have their own traditional foods prepared and served with the same elegance and finesse as other menu items. The executive chef must have a large repertoire of menus and cooking styles to draw from at a moment's notice. A combination of personal experience and an extensive collection of various recipe books help make these experiences a huge success.

Once the executive chef has achieved a level of consistent expertise, he or she will have a following of hotel and walk-in customers that will return time and time again. When guests return, they expect the same perfection every time.

Chef Owner/Operator
Nancy Longo
Chef Owner, Pierpoint Restaurant, Fells Point, Maryland

While being a chef owner of a restaurant may seem like a dream for many, for me it has meant a great deal of sacrifice and hard work. From my twenty plus years of experience owning and operating, as head chef, a relatively small restaurant in the outskirts of Baltimore, I have worked pretty much all holidays, most weekends, and for the first seven years practically twelve to sixteen hour days, six to seven days a week.

But I will tell you I love the freedom of being my own boss. If you are your own boss you have more creative freedom, and can choose the level of quality you want for your menus and service. On the down side, as owner and operator you don't get as much vacation time as a regular employee might, and there's no such thing as calling in sick. I have to plan my vacation around the time of the year that I can afford to close my restaurant, which is usually the coldest part of the winter when business would be slow anyway. Because I close the whole restaurant everyone takes vacation at the same time. I post the closing weeks ahead of time so not to offend any of my regular customers; after all they are what really make the restaurant succeed.

In order to be an owner operator it takes more than just knowing about food and good service. It also takes a good mind for business since that is what you are really doing, running a small business. Your capital and business plan have to be in sync, which takes a lot of research, organization and planning. For capital investment, for example, you need to research exactly how much it will take to open your restaurant and cover your basic fixed costs for up to a full year (fixed cost being your rent, utilities, insurance and licenses: everything it takes to run the restaurant whether or not you have any customers sitting at your tables). Without a solid business plan and sufficient capital, a restaurant can not succeed no matter how good the food is, or how widespread your reputation.

In short, owning and operating your own restaurant can be a great joy but a lot of hard work. If you think you want to work hard for yourself and be creative, go for it.

Large Scale Restaurant Foodservice
John Zehnder, CEC, AAC
Zehnder's Family Restaurant, Frankenmuth, Michigan

Growing up in a family owned restaurant, doing the volume that we do sometimes numbs one to the reality of how large we really are and how complex our operation can be to an individual who comes in from the outside. We call it the "deer in the headlights" reaction because what we do is multi-tasking taken to an extreme level. As one of my former chefs who now works in Las Vegas told me, Zehnder's is a "dog year" operation. He told me that working one year at such volume level (5,000 to 6,000 covers a day) and with a staff of over 500 front/back of house is like working seven years in any "normal" operation.

So . . . what we do is different than most operations and the specific set of skills required tends to focus on a solid understanding of good cooking basics plus a good understanding of the interplay

of human relationships. The first thing I tell a newly hired chef is that as a volume operation, consistency is our primary objective. Our first dinner of each year and that last plate prepared on New Year's Eve must be consistent. It is, in my opinion, as difficult to prepare food consistently day after day for one million guests as it is to produce fine dining meals in a country club setting.

Consistency goes one step beyond the culinary into management style and adherence to the policies/ procedures of the company. No other factor brings down morale and causes more problems than inconsistent application of rules and policies. One can be strict or lean toward being more lenient, but whatever path is chosen is the path that one must follow every time.

So let's take a look at what skill sets have proven to work over the years. Culinary skills are important and I require that all my cooks and chefs have a good basic understanding of cooking techniques. I prefer an associate's degree, but will accept experience of ten years or more. For lead positions on my culinary staff, a bachelor's degree is required along with chef certification from the American Culinary Federation.

Because my staff includes a number of chefs, the specific levels of skill vary from chef to chef. Some are great cooks with average management skills while others are average cooks with great management talent. A common requirement, however, is a high level of understandable communication. Communication is key to success in volume operations—constant, clear and specific. This includes both verbal and written communication skills. I remind my chefs that every chef is a teacher and there is an expectation that teaching and sharing one's knowledge is a prerequisite for employment.

As Executive Chef my role is to oversee all these differing levels of culinary skill and to be the most knowledgeable culinary team member. Multi-tasking is the name of the game, and my biggest frustration with newly hired chefs is their inability to meet pre-determined deadlines and timelines. Time management and the ability to see the overall picture, developing the steps from start to finish on a project therefore become critical to the overall success of the volume chef—it's easy to get distracted by petty items and personal issues.

One needs to keep focused on the task at hand, to break down tasks into their most basic steps and follow those steps in progression. And . . . to do all of these things properly, the volume chef must have a high level of mental and physical energy. When I interview prospective chefs I'm always looking of that "wiggle factor"—the internal energy level that makes one a bit "antsy." A volume kitchen requires someone with an above normal energy level and stamina, both physically and mentally. Big kitchens require standing, walking, lifting, and physical activities beyond what most people imagine.

In our operation we practice management by walking around. It is a physical job with a high stress level. The stress level alone can wear one down to the point of having health issues. The ability to handle high levels of stress is mandatory. From the Human Resources/"people" perspective, a chef working with a large staff needs to be a good listener, first and foremost. The ability to listen and see the other side of any issue is critical to the credibility of the chef. Staff members want to be a part of what's happening, and in a volume operation it's easy to get lost and to feel insignificant in the overall scheme of things. I've also found that most all of the solutions to any issues confronting an operation can be found internally if you just give staff the opportunity to express themselves.

There is no place in the volume kitchen for a chef with an ego, hot temper or one prone to foist one's opinion on others. With so many different personalities comprising a large staff, the "dictator" style of management simply doesn't work. Inclusion is the route needed—not divisiveness. The ability to properly delegate tasks and to know who can/can't perform those tasks is the second "people" skill one needs to develop.

Volume operations quickly destroy a chef who is a micro-manager. It is critical to get your work done through other people's efforts and to give those individuals credit for properly performed tasks. By delegating tasks and including staff in the decision-making aspects of the work, you tend to develop a working team that "owns" the decision and is much more likely to implement and follow through.

Finally, one must be a diplomat—solving problems and making compromises for the betterment of the entire organization. There are the typical front-of-house, back-of-house turf battles emerging from time to time, and interpersonal personality clashes. A good diplomat must remain above the fray and give the appearance of being neutral in matters relating to staff relationships.

If you tend to be an adrenaline junkie and truly enjoy sensory overload, juggling six balls at the same time, then the high volume kitchen is the ideal work environment for you to succeed in.

Culinary Administrator
Barbara Hulick, CEC
L&M Produce Company, Jessup, Maryland

Who would have known the heart shaped meatloaf I made at age eight would lead to where I am today: a graduate of the CIA; a private chef for the elite; an executive chef in health care; a chef in the R & D kitchen of a Fortune 500 company; the Quality Assurance and Food Safety Director for a regional produce company; and presently the Operations Manager and Director of Quality Assurance of a fresh cut produce processor. The possibilities and opportunities have always seemed endless.

Forty years after the meatloaf, and I look back on all my experiences; it has been an interesting journey. I am a firm believer that my New York City temperament got me half the way here, and a great culinary and academic education did the rest. Education should always come first; I can't believe I am writing this, since I remember being nineteen years old too, and books and studying were the last things on my top ten list. However, I did finish college with a B.A. degree, and landed a cook's job in the Virgin Islands.

My first chef job was in health care. I had the production manager every female can relate to, but shouldn't have to. He was determined to show me where he thought I belonged in the food chain, and it wasn't at the top. My first test came in the form of two legs of veal for an upscale luncheon that was planned for the next day. It was the veal, a sharp boning knife, and me, yet I was determined to succeed. I just did as I was taught—thank you, Chef Biscardi and Mr. Nick. Further tests came daily, then weekly, and then after a while I became the tester instead of the testee. Patience and confidence have been two of my greatest assets.

The test kitchens at Marriott Corporation were another turning point in my career. I had just earned my certified executive chef status through the American Culinary Federation, and was ready for new challenges. I found that proper communication is the answer to a lot of problems we face in the busy culinary industry, and the method(s) we choose are what determine our success or not. This is the greatest lesson I could possibly share; it does not mean a thing unless what you want to achieve is communicated, received and understood. This business is definitely a team sport, and everyone needs to be in the same game.

I am currently working on my Master's degree in food safety. It is challenging to have the bureaucrats determining food safety and security systems for operations they know little about. I thought by getting involved myself, perhaps I could try and change that. Wouldn't it be great if a chef helped to decide the safe and sanitary means of running a kitchen? I think so; it should be cooperation between the scientist and the chefs, not arbitrary rules and control.

I may not cook as much as I like anymore, which I miss, but I have a great staff who will cut any vegetable or fruit by hand or machine any way anyone could possibly want it. I remember that heart shaped meatloaf well, and all the people who have come along since then. The people make this business great. Good luck!

CHAPTER 3

The Structure of Kitchen Organization

When you complete this chapter, you should be able to:

- Describe the purposes of a well defined organizational structure.
- Describe the relationship between the level of business and the complexity of the organizational structure.
- Describe problems inherent in businesses that are run by monarchical leaders.
- Describe some of the studies and accomplishments of Frederick Winslow Taylor.
- Describe Escoffier's design of kitchen organization by tasks, and discuss how it led to the classical brigade system.
- Describe Escoffier's brigade system and the responsibilities of each station.
- Describe modern kitchen positions and their similarities and differences with Escoffier's brigade.
- Develop an example of modern kitchen organizational structures for simple and complex establishments.

VALUES IN ORGANIZATIONAL STRUCTURES

Organizational structure is the topic of many textbooks and collegiate journals in the United States and around the world. It presents the first line of authority and the first and most direct line of communication for staff and managers to follow. It describes who has the authority to answer questions and direct production, and with whom the responsibilities for large and small tasks reside. Without a well planned and executed organizational structure, authority is questioned, tasks are altered or altogether skipped, and responsibility including praise and criticism is hard to place.

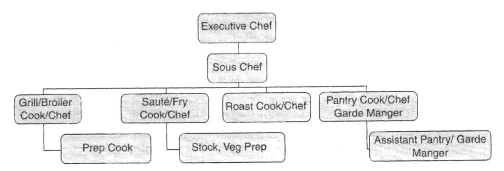

FIGURE 3–1 Organizational Chart Small to Medium-Sized Restaurant

Figure 3–1 shows the organizational structure of a small to medium-sized restaurant:

Having and following a solid organizational structure can not be over emphasized. It is critical for employees, supervisors and managers to know their exact place in the operation's hierarchy. By doing so they can rely on the work of others to accomplish their jobs well and know that what they do affects the work of others.

It is also important that the structure of the organization fit the size and complexity of the operation it directs. A simple description of job responsibilities may be adequate for small mom-and-pop operations, while a detailed delineation of responsibilities and tasks may be required for larger, more complex organizations.

In professional kitchens, organizational structure has not always been the clean, direct and hierarchical structure it is today. Before Escoffier's time, kitchen organization could have been classified as a free-for-all. Chefs and cooks worked alongside each other, preparing completely unrelated components for the evening's meal. Many cooks prepared the same items as orders came in from the dining room. Tasks were often repeated by different cooks and consistency was difficult, if not impossible, to obtain or guarantee.

Food service was not the only business that lacked organizational structure. Solely owned businesses, as restaurants generally were, followed a simple, direct line of authority from the owner to the staff. The owners took the role of master of ceremonies and the workers were the performers and artisans. Whatever the owner believed to be the best course of action was directed to the workers to be carried out without question.

This simple monarchical approach to organizations may work in small businesses with fewer than a dozen workers, especially those that supply single services or products. As a business grows in number of workers or complexity of services, however, it becomes nearly impossible for one person to manage and control everything. Without the owner present to personally direct every task, work is often duplicated or left undone, and productivity drops.

As businesses grow, owners must make sure that tasks are done properly and on time whether they are present or not. This becomes the role of management, and with management comes the beginning of an organizational structure.

DESIGNER TASKS AND RESPONSIBILITIES

Formal organizational structures were not common practice in American businesses at the turn of the twentieth century. The usual model had only two levels of authority: the owners and the workers. Either the owners led production by direct interference, or hired highly trained workers as foremen to manage and supervise the work. In both cases work got done, tasks completed and products made, but as businesses became even more complicated and competitive, owners needed more assurances that things were being done properly and that both production and profits could be guaranteed.

The manufacturing and service industries, including everything from the steel industry to professional food service, were susceptible to inefficiencies in production and management due to the unprecedented amount of expansion they experienced through the nineteenth and early twentieth centuries. Steel was being made, products manufactured and great meals served, but were they produced and delivered in the most efficient ways possible? Were production and costs being controlled while delivering a consistent product? Were customers satisfied with their products and services, ensuring repeat business during a time of exploding competition? And most important, could the operators and managers guarantee those needed profits owners and investors were looking for to continue building and expanding their businesses and financial security?

To complicate the matter more, the expansion of businesses required an increased number of skilled workers to perform the high levels of production that were demanded. Unfortunately there were more jobs than skilled workers to take them, and dependence shifted to hiring untrained workers and on management to supervise and control production.

Everyone who wanted to work could find a job no matter how much education, skill or experience they had. In fact, labor shortages began to plague expansion efforts so much by the turn of the century that the immigration of foreigners to American shores was encouraged rather than denied by the U.S. government, which relaxed many quotas and restrictions, allowing them to fill the growing number of jobs.

Complex organizations, a diverse work force and added competition fueled the need to redefine organizational structures for the sake of improving corporate efficiencies, but in what form would they emerge and how would they be administered?

The same problems that Escoffier faced in late nineteenth century French kitchens trying to put together an organizational structure for cooks and chefs were challenges of other industries world wide. While he was designing his brigade system defining kitchen positions based on tasks and responsibilities, and the authority structure in place to manage them, an American engineer, Frederick Winslow Taylor (1856–1915), was helping define tasks and responsibilities for steel and ball bearing companies in Pennsylvania and America's northeast. Across the ocean, both innovators would soon reshape the industries they worked in and set in motion new designs in task design and then organizational structures, which would become the models for everyone to follow.

Task engineering and management were new ideas in business and industry during this stage in their evolution. Jobs were worked, tasks were completed, but there had never been a deliberate attempt to define individual tasks with exact sets of rules or specifications and the process for managing them until Taylor set his eyes on improving efficiencies for some of America's booming industries.

Frederick Taylor was born in Germantown, Pennsylvania (now part of Philadelphia), the son of two Quakers who were both well educated and disciplined individuals. His father was a Princeton graduate and lawyer and his mother a spirited abolitionist who was said to have run an underground railroad station for runaway slaves. Both parents believed in high thinking and plain living.

Frederick Taylor (c. 1911)

At age twenty-five, Taylor earned an engineering degree at the Stevens Institute of Technology in New Jersey, and soon afterwards began working for the Midvale Steel Company, where he started out as shop clerk and quickly progressed to machinist, foreman, maintenance foreman and chief draftsman. Within six years he advanced to research director and then chief engineer at one of the largest steel companies in the area.

While working at Midvale, Taylor introduced the concept of piece work in the factory. His goal was to find the most efficient way to perform specific tasks, and breaking them down into individual components seemed the most natural way to begin the evaluation process.

Taylor left Midvale to begin a successful consulting career and was soon hired by many leading industries to help them improve their processes, reduce labor and increase profits. While retained by the Bethlehem Iron Company (later Bethlehem Steel Works), Taylor conducted a series of studies which evaluated the efficiency of workers in various work situations. He discovered a direct relationship between the efficiency of production and the number of complicated tasks assigned to individual workers. Taylor also observed that the more complex a job assignment, the greater the need for educated, trained workers.

It was for the Bethlehem Iron Company in 1895 that Taylor began his now famous study on the design of equipment (in this case, shovels) and the work that could be accomplished by establishing production quotas based on having the proper equipment to do the job, the hours established to accomplish work and the number of people employed. After making thousands of precision observations where Taylor scrupulously recorded the amount of work a single person could produce given specific directions and equipment, he was able to deduce that the employee was not the only person responsible for the amount of work done. There were other factors involved which either helped or impeded production, and it was management's job to correct the problems. By focusing his engineering background, keen observations and analysis on the process of shoveling coal for the huge furnaces, Taylor was able to improve production while reducing the number of people actually shoveling the coal by more than half.

Taylor was the first to advocate time-and-motion studies to find the most effective way of completing each task in a project. Thus, the entire project would be assembled as a collection of the many completed parts. No one person worked on the whole project; instead, each worker contributed to the whole by specializing in one part. This led to a highly motivated work force that was excited by its accomplishments. Taylor's studies had created hundreds of short term goals that were easily achievable by a diverse work force. Job satisfaction was up, and so was productivity.

In 1911, Taylor published his now famous book *The Principles of Scientific Management*, where he laid down his theories on the structure of tasks and hence the structure of organizations which would be required to implement and manage them. Taylor's theories were based on these four objectives he established for management:

1. The development of a science for each element of a person's work
2. The scientific selection, training and development of workers
3. The development of a spirit of hearty co-operation between workers and management
4. The clear division of work between workers and management

These new objectives required a formal organizational structure to implement and measure their effectiveness, which Taylor defined by the following set of principles:

- Clear delineation of authority
- Clear declaration of responsibilities
- Separation of the work of planning (management) from production
- Instituting an incentive scheme for workers, including promise for promotions and pay equal to the level of production accomplished
- Identification of specialized tasks
- Identification of specific management goals and responsibilities

Taylor's theories were not immediately accepted because they placed credit and blame for inefficient company processes on management, whose job it is to supervise and improve production. The worker's job is to follow directions of management. The fall of the monarchial boss was foretold by Taylor when he made this claim:

> The old fashioned dictator does not exist under Scientific Management. The man at the head of the business under Scientific Management is governed by rules and laws which have been developed through hundreds of experiments just as much as the workman is, and the standards developed are equitable.

The newly formed business strategy lay the foundation for advancements in many of America's industries, and was the impetus to developing the mass production systems that revolutionized the automobile, textile and food canning industries. This revolution in business manufacturing created the greatest supply of goods the world had ever seen. American businesses had the lion's share of the world's markets because of the mass production of acceptable goods.

ESCOFFIER'S TASK DESIGNS

When Auguste Escoffier was head chef of the Ritz–Carlton in London, he implemented a system of task design and production which he had developed through an in depth investigation of the fundamental techniques of food preparation and service. He knew that the organizational structure of professional kitchens in the hospitality industry could work well only if there were also very specific task and production standards that everyone could understand and follow, for which he was in full support. Chefs could no longer keep their secrets of cooking, but had to pass them on to those around them and to those who would surely follow.

Escoffier first identified specific tasks leading to quality food production and service, then organized those into groups of related tasks. He labeled the specific realms of techniques as sauté, roasting, grilling, fish cookery, vegetable cookery, cold food production and pastry production. By doing this, Escoffier laid the foundation for the mass production kitchen brigade system which is used throughout the world today.

The classical kitchen was organized into several independent, yet interdependent, stations where specific tasks were performed in the preparation of a meal. Chefs de partie (of the station) were responsible for each of those stations, or posts. This method allowed chefs to specialize in a particular area of the kitchen. It also streamlined production into a team effort, with each player dependent on the others for completion. It allowed for easy supervision and correction, since the responsibilities were delineated to specific areas and individual people. The executive (head) chef was the line inspector who made sure the stations functioned properly and that the final meal was presented according to the establishment's standards.

For Escoffier, this accomplished the same for restaurant kitchens as Taylor's experiments had done for American industries: Projects were broken down into simple tasks easily mastered by one or two experts assigned to concentrate on those tasks. The results were a more consistently high-quality product, produced in a faster and more efficient process. What this also created was a very strong brigade system of linear management, from the executive chef down to the commis (apprentice) chefs, with no crossing of the authoritative lines.

The emphasis in management went toward the assessment of the processes. Were there more efficient ways of delivering the same products or services at the same or higher levels of quality?

ESCOFFIER'S BRIGADE SYSTEM

Escoffier introduced the idea of a brigade system of authority for the kitchen, designed from the military system he had served under in the French army. He implemented a clear delineation of authority and responsibilities so that everyone knew their superiors, their co-workers, and their specific duties. This system, as shown in Figure 3–2, solved centuries of kitchen chaos.

At the top is the chef. Sometimes called the executive chef, or chef de cuisine, this person is responsible for the entire kitchen operation. The size of the establishment dictates to what extent those responsibilities are delegated to others. Virtually all decisions on food purchases, storage, prep and service are controlled through the chef's office. Hiring, training and promotion of kitchen personnel also rest finally upon the chef's decisions.

The second in command is the sous (pr. *sue*) chef, which translates literally as under the chef. The sous chef is usually the one who more directly supervises the production of the line chefs while the executive chef plays more of a

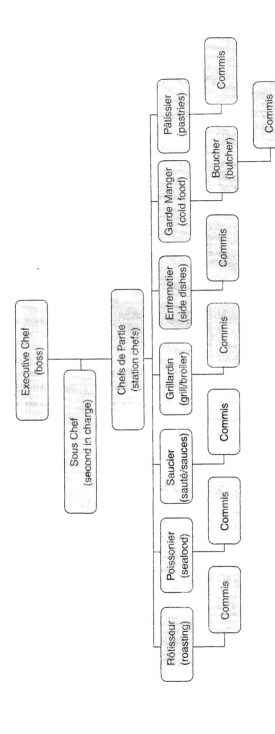

FIGURE 3–2 Classical Brigade System

manager's role in the kitchen. The sous chef's strong culinary skills and people skills play equal roles in maintaining a well motivated and well trained crew. During service hours, the sous chef may assume the role of the saucier (*sos seè aý*), or sauté chef, who is the controlling position for the whole cooking line, or of the aboyeur (*ah bway eŕ*), or expediter, who is the last person to see the food before it leaves the kitchen.

Chefs de partie (*par-teé*; party, station chefs, or line chefs) are the working chefs on the production line. Depending on the size of the kitchen, the number of stations will vary, as will the responsibilities at each station. Here are the typical stations found:

Chef saucier (*sos see aý*): Responsibilities include the sauté station and the preparation of most of the sauces used in production. In traditional kitchens, this station is often considered the most difficult and demanding of all positions. It requires a skilled and experienced line chef, usually the chef just below the sous chef in the hierarchy of the organization.

Chef grillardin (*gree yar de:ñ*): Responsible for all grilled and broiled foods and their accompanying sauces. This station is gaining popularity in modern kitchens because of the trend toward low fat cooking methods, especially regarding seafood and poultry.

Chef rôtisseur (*rô tee see eŕ*): Responsible for all roasted items and their accompanying sauces, including the jus and jus lie (pan drippings and pan drippings slightly thickened).

Chef poissonier (*pwas son ee aý*): Responsible for all fish and shellfish items, including their preparation (dressing, filleting, etc.), their accompanying court bouillons (poaching liquids) and sauces. It has usually been considered one of the more specialized stations because of the delicate nature of the items prepared. Today the responsibilities of cooking seafood usually rests with the station with the appropriate cooking method (i.e., saucier for sautéed fish and shellfish items, grillardin for grilled or broiled items).

Chef entremetier (*ãtreh met eeaý*): During the age of Taillevent (fourteenth century), the term entremet signified items served before and between main courses. In the modern kitchen, this station produces all hot appetizers, and usually takes on the responsibilities of the legumier (vegetable/starch/pasta cook) and potager (soup cook), as well as the preparation of all egg dishes.

Chef tournant (*toor noñ*): Literally the "turning" chef, this chef fills in at any position where he or she is needed. This chef might be assigned to assist a chef de partie for large productions or to fill in when a chef de partie is absent. This is traditionally the position in the kitchen brigade between the commis (apprentice) and chef de partie.

Chef garde manger (*gard´māj;*): Responsible for all cold appetizers, hors d'oeuvres, salads, salad dressings, and other cold sauces. This station also prepares cold food items such as patés, gallantines, gravad lox, and decorated pieces for buffets.

Chef boucher (*boo shaŷ*): "Butcher" is the station where all meat, poultry, and fish fabrication takes place before service. It may also be the station where sausages are made (charcuterie [shar coo tay rée]), and is often part of the garde manger station.

Chef pâtissier (*pat ee see aŷ*): This station is responsible for all baked items and sweets. This is usually a separate station from the rest of the kitchen brigade because of the special equipment and production schedules necessary for the work.

Chef aboyeur (*ah bwa yeŕ*): Sometimes called the announcer or expediter, this position controls the orders coming into the kitchen from the dining room and going out of the kitchen to the guests; it is an extremely important position. In many cases, the sous chef takes on the role of the aboyeur during service so that he or she can supervise the production of the food and its presentation at the same time.

Chef commis (*coe meé*): The apprentice chef plays an important role in any professional food service operation. Young culinarians learn the tricks of the trade from experienced chefs in a live work situation. Today the chef commis is as likely as not to have formal educational training. The emphasis is moving toward culinary education to speed up the process from novice to commis.

The brigade system can be customized to fit any size and type of organization. The hierarchy of authority will always trickle down from the chef, or kitchen manager as he or she is sometimes called, yet the chef may play a more active production role in smaller establishments.

Apprentices find smaller operations a great learning arena since they are given a greater variety of tasks to accomplish. They may be assigned to help break down meat and poultry (boucher), make sauces (saucier), soups (potager), prep vegetables (entremetier), and prepare appetizers and salads (garde manger). Young chefs must be willing to do any job assigned to them to strengthen their skills and their confidence.

MODERN BRIGADE SYSTEMS

In American kitchens, the modern brigade system looks very similar to the classical model, with the ultimate authority emanating from the head chef downward to sous chefs and beyond, yet there may not be as many stations and they may have American titles like first chef, lead chef and first cook instead of the French titles Escoffier used.

Often classical terms still appear in modern kitchen brigades—like chef, garde manger and sous chef—mixed in with more modern terminology. A lot of operations are moving completely away from the classical names, substituting words like kitchen manager, cold station cook or assistant kitchen manager in their places.

There aren't as many individual stations in the modern kitchen brigade because new cooking equipment and kitchen designs allow procedures like roasting, broiling, deep fat frying and sautéing to occur along a single production line. In the old kitchens of Carême and Escoffier, each station had to be separate from one another due to the extreme heat generated from the burning coal or wood used in the huge brick and wrought iron ovens and open fire pits. With the advent of mechanical hood and ventilation systems and enclosed stainless steel ovens, ranges and grills the size of kitchens began to shrink and work stations got moved closer together. Now it takes fewer people to do the same tasks as before, since they don't have to move from one position to the next to change tasks, but simply one piece of equipment to another.

Then the combination of stove tops and deck ovens simplified the need for separate roast cooks and sauté chefs in the same brigade. One chef could be roasting large pieces of meat and poultry while at the same time preparing stocks, sauces or any variety of stove top preparations without moving two or three feet to either side. Broilers with salamanders and oven compartments replaced another two or three positions with one work station: broiler chef seafood chef (for baked and grilled seafood items) and vegetable chef with anything that needed glazing or browning (gratinée) could be performed by one person without stepping more than two or three feet in any direction.

Modern brigade systems, as seen in Figure 3–3, are based on the complexity of the menu produced and the amount of business the operation has for each meal period. Large operations with complex menus require large work areas, multiple pieces of cooking equipment and the corresponding number of trained staff to work them; smaller operations require much less. Usually the larger the operation, the more specialized the positions and the smaller the operation, the more multi-tasked each kitchen position becomes.

Here is a list of some of the modern names used to describe kitchen brigades and what their general responsibilities might be:

Kitchen Manager/Food Service Director: The executive chef, or the person in charge of the food service operation; could include expediting, butchery and other highly skilled tasks.

Assistant Manager/Assistant Food Service Director: The second in charge of the food service operation who can replace the kitchen manager/food

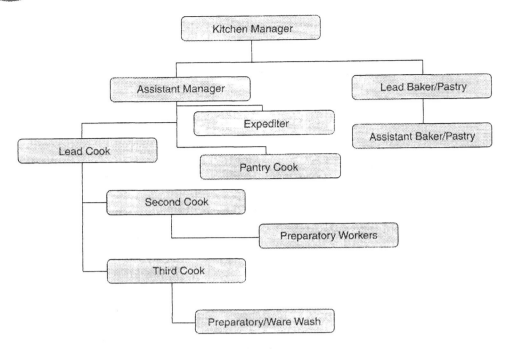

FIGURE 3–3   Modern Kitchen Organization

service director when needed; could include high level skill production and direct line (production) responsibilities.

Lead/Head Cook: Could be a shift manager, expediter or main cook on the production line. In cases where the menu is based primarily on one cooking technique, such as deep frying or broiling/grilling then the cooks in those positions are usually also the lead/head cook, often responsible for daily specials, including soups in addition to their station responsibilities. May have low supervisory responsibilities.

Second Cook: Usually assigned to the second most popular form of cooking for the particular establishment they are working in; could be the lead fry cook, sauté cook, or cook assigned to carving and plating large roasts and birds; often have mise en place preparatory responsibilities for more than one station; may have low level supervisory responsibilities over preparatory cooks and/or ware wash personnel.

Third Cook: Often the lead preparatory cook responsible for the bulk of the higher level mise en place items, including the daily vegetable and starch preparations or kitchen setup responsibilities in preparation for service; may have low level supervisory responsibility over other preparatory workers; often assists in receiving deliveries and placing stock into proper inventory.

Pantry Cook: Responsible for all cold food preparation, including cold sauces, dressings, appetizers, specialty condiments, salsas and other cold accompaniments; often is responsible for all salad preparation and plating, but may depend on other preparatory workers for basic salad ingredients.

Butcher: Where they exist, responsible for all meat, poultry and seafood fabrication; may be responsible for the ingredients to be used in all charcuterie (sausages, pates, terrines) items on the menus as well as stock and fumet bones; may make sausages and any smoked or cured items on the menu.

Lead Baker/Pastry Chef: Responsible for all baking and pastry items used in the kitchen and served in the dining rooms; often responsible for breads, rolls, biscuits and other table accompaniments in the baked dough or pastry categories; may be responsible for all high level pastry production and display decorations; often has supervisory responsibilities over one or more pastry workers.

Baker/Pastry Worker: Assist the lead baker/pastry chef in whatever capacity is needed; often is responsible for all baking/pastry mise en place, including making dough, fillings and frostings; usually has sole responsibility over low level baking/pastry production such as rolls, muffins, pies, sweet buns and Danish pastries.

Expediter: Usually acts as the middle person between the dining room staff and the cook's line to ensure that the foods ordered and recorded by the wait staff are prepared properly, plated and served according to acceptable quality standards (i.e., the different types of garnishing or plating styles between a steak house and a private club dining room); often responsible for setting up the service or food pick-up areas, including soup wells and bread stations.

Section 2

MANAGING FOR QUALITY IN FOOD SERVICE OPERATIONS

Business owners and managers in the hospitality industry are faced with a great challenge today. They must learn to survive in a marketplace where the consumer's perception of quality and value is constantly changing, competition is becoming more intense day by day, and the supply of trained and educated workers entering the industry is not keeping pace with the steady increase in job openings.

Problems associated with employee turnover, increasing competition, and an shrinking bottom line affect every level of hospitality, from the very exclusive to the family- or value-oriented operations. The business of food and hospitality has become a complex international industry.

CHAPTER 4

Foundations in Quality

When you complete this chapter, you should be able to:

- Discuss the influences that challenge traditional organizational behavior and management theories.
- Discuss the influences that led Shewhart to move from quality inspection to improving the processes themselves.
- Discuss the tenants of Shewhart's system of Statistical Quality Control (SQC).
- Discuss Shewhart's cycle and its primary purpose.
- Apply Shewhart's cycle to food service and hospitality industry examples.
- Explain how quality standards in food service changed when Escoffier and Ritz expanded their dining rooms and menus to accommodate the common person.
- Explain why managers are becoming more flexible in their management styles and versatile in the products they deliver.

TRADITIONAL THEORIES CHALLENGED

Frederick Taylor's goal was to turn diverse groups of workers into efficient production teams by eliminating barriers to work and increasing motivation. His scientific management theories challenged the basic theories of his day and founded a new philosophy of organizational behavior.

Some companies embraced Taylor's theories and others did not. While they proved to increase production and reduce labor they also took authority away from the domineering owners and autocratic managers and placed more control in the hands of the line supervisors and workers. They created a give and take scenario that not all companies were willing to accept.

Traditional philosophies of management continue to be challenged on a daily basis as chef managers try to cope with their expanding responsibilities. The hierarchical approach to food service management, established by the grand chef Auguste Escoffier, brought order to the organizational chaos found in the kitchens of nineteenth century France, England and throughout Europe, but may not be enough to cope with an increasing demand on quality products and services placed on operators by customers of today.

WALTER SHEWHART ON QUALITY

Walter Shewhart (c. 1935)

Walter A. Shewhart (1891–1967) is often referred to as the grandfather of Quality Management Theory for it was his early studies into the statistical analysis of processes and the quality of products they produced that influenced the theories propounded by quality gurus Edward Deming and Joseph Juran, who both worked with Shewhart when he was with Bell Labs in the early 1930s.

Shewhart graduated from the University of Illinois with bachelor's and master's degrees, and he received a doctorate in physics from the University of California at Berkeley in 1917. He taught at the universities of Illinois and California, and briefly headed the physics department at the Wisconsin Normal School in LaCrosse before his death in 1967.

Most of Shewhart's professional career was spent as an engineer at Western Electric from 1918 to 1924, and at Bell Telephone Laboratories, where he served in several capacities as a member of the technical staff from 1925 until his retirement in 1956.

Shewhart didn't share all of the visions and ideas of Frederick Taylor either, but did agreed that it was paramount to the success of businesses to continuously improve the systems and processes of production based on new technologies and new market demands. Shewhart made this observation in his book *Economic Control of Quality of Manufactured Product*, published in 1931:

> Both pure and applied science have gradually pushed further and further the requirements for accuracy and precision. However, applied science, particularly in the mass production of interchangeable parts, is even more exacting than pure science in certain matters of accuracy and precision.

The problem with Taylor's model was that the line workers became so caught up in their individual assigned tasks that they could not see whether the products as a whole were being assembled properly. They could not see the whole picture. The result was a dependence on quality inspectors placed at various locations throughout the production line to ensure inferior products did not get passed along the line to the customer. That was the standard, albeit very costly, means by which mass production companies could ensure that only quality products were made and sold.

Shewhart was a quality inspector, but also a trained statistician. As an inspector, Shewhart's job was to pull substandard items off the assembly line so that only products meeting the company's quality standards would be completed, packaged, and sold. Standing on the production line day after day, pulling item after item off of the line, began to raise questions for Shewhart on the efficiency of the production systems themselves. It was not enough to have inspectors checking for quality; Shewhart decided to look at ways of improving the production processes to assure less deviation from quality standards.

As a trained statistician, Shewhart was able to track the total quantity of inferior products and calculate their numerical relationship to the total number of manufactured items. He could also study the frequency in appearance of inferior products on the line and relate those figures to production quotas, which is a relationship of production quantity and time. As a manager, Shewhart began to ask what costs could be associated with the rejected products. He looked at the cost of reworking them to meet standards and the possible cost, or loss of business, from unsatisfied customers.

Shewhart focused his studies and then his management theories on the quality control of products in the system which Taylor said was the role and responsibility of management. However, Shewhart believed that quality could be protected at various stages of production by people other than managers and supervisors through detailed statistical analysis and directed supervision and management. By measuring the effect of certain production steps or procedures on the overall quality of the product, charting (using quality charts) the results in such a way that the average worker could evaluate progress at various stages in production, then quality could be protected at each step of production. The workers themselves could see that standards were not being met and could change or fix things to get them back on track. He labeled this system Statistical Quality Control (SQC).

Shewhart's quality charts detailed every step in production and the quality standards assigned to each so that average workers could become in-line inspectors, placed strategically throughout the production and service processes. They would, as a part of their assigned task, pull from the production line parts or products that did not meet the standards outlined in the charts without interrupting the production line itself, eliminating the need for additional and expensive inspectors.

Shewhart had to consider the cost of people like him—quality inspectors—who were paid to prevent inferior parts or instruments from making it through the production line to the customer. It was not only an expensive way to ensure quality, but it was also an inconsistent method: Poor quality products still found their way through the production line to the customers. It was an imperfect system that cost a lot of money to maintain.

Shewhart would eventually ask this question on all Bell processes: What could be done to produce higher quality products in the first place, and lessen the financial liability of running an imperfect operation? If quality standards could be met consistently through proper procurement, design and production then the dependence on inspectors to prevent inferior products from getting through the production line would lessen, allowing them to do more direct supervision and management, or be eliminated altogether.

Shewhart's notion was that many people along the flow-of-goods line from buying to selling could take on a partial role of in-line inspector. He was the first person to promote publicly the concept of empowerment for employees so that they could take on judgment roles as well as production. The workers would be empowered to make decisions on quality throughout the process and fix the problem themselves before passing it on to the next person in the production or service process.

This was a revolutionary idea since management and direction had always devolved from the owners to upper managers, middle managers, and finally to the on-line managers who might be able to effect change. Shewhart would say that everyone on the operation had a part in controlling the quality of the products and services the operation offers, an adage which has since carried over into the professional food service industry.

The premise of Shewhart's program was to assess management's role in the determination of quality standards and the processes to meet them in production and service. For the first time, management was asked to evaluate their own performance based on measurable employee production and customer satisfaction goals. Workers alone could not be blamed for poor quality if they were managed and supervised through inferior methods. To improve quality, Shewhart had to change the entire concept of worker and employer relationships and then implement the notion that the customers, and not the owner, were the most important people involved in determining quality. Shewhart's process for the first time in modern history intertwined the roles of management, worker and customer into one symmetric goal of quality assurance.

SHEWHART'S CYCLE

Shewhart believed it was far better to deliver quality than to ask forgiveness for poor quality (which for manufacturing usually meant costly guarantees and warranties). He was determined to design a system of statistical analysis that could increase the predictability of quality products and ultimately the customer's overall level of satisfaction. This included investigating procedures and processes for the procurement of parts, inventory procedures to ensure adequate supplies and step by step procedures for manufacturing, packaging and distribution (selling) to ensure quality procedures were implemented and protected each step of the way. Then, Shewhart would say, when you've examined all the parts, made adjustments to improve quality, and measured your success then it is time to start over again with new information, new improvement plans, and even higher levels of sustainable quality.

Shewhart designed his management program to assess constantly and forever the efficiency of the processes in order to improve those processes. The more efficient the processes in relation to time, motion, employee satisfaction, and the availability of quality parts, the higher the quality of products. This in turn would reduce the cost of re-working items pulled from the line by the inspectors, reduce the cost associated with returns when inferior products made it to market and therefore improve customer satisfaction. Customer satisfaction, Shewhart would argue, turns into praise for the workers and managers, which helps translate into higher employee morale and job satisfaction. Then, Shewhart predicted, even more efficient processes would evolve from this rejuvenated work force leading again toward improving quality. This prescription for continuous study would later be called Shewhart's Cycle of Quality Management.

The cycle is begun by first establishing a "quality team" comprised of managers with authority to make changes and workers directly involved in the particular process being examined. By combining managers and workers, Shewhart hoped to get both sides to buy into the changes that were inevitable as part of the process. If direction continued to come down from the managers to the workers then the workers would be less likely to embrace any changes; if, however, the workers themselves had input into the changed processes then the success of those projects would be come a measure of their own success, which they were eager to improve.

The quality teams would break the whole process of phone production (which was the business of Bell Labs) into individual tasks, much as Taylor had done for the steel industry, and assess the efficiency and predictability of each task. Efficiency would be measured by the quantity of quality parts made per hour per employee, and predictability by the level of consistency in the system.

Shewhart identified four distinct steps to his quality cycle: plan, do, check and act. These steps (commonly referred to as the PDCA cycle) Shewhart believed ultimately lead to total quality improvement (see Figure 4–1).

Before starting a new PDCA plan you first have to identify all the operational procedures that lead to or protect quality of the products and services, and under what priority they should be investigated.

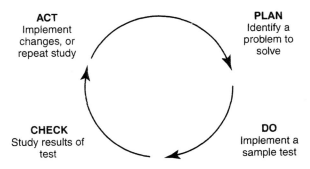

FIGURE 4–1   Shewhart's Cycle of Continuous Quality Improvement

Here is what you do for each stage of the cycle:

Step 1: Plan to improve your operations first by finding out what things are going wrong (that is, identify the problems faced), and come up with ideas for solving these problems.

Ask these questions:

1. What change might be demonstrated by altering an existing procedure or adding a new one?
2. What data are available to measure the existing status, and will it be sufficient to measure success under the newly implemented procedures?
3. Are new observations needed? If so, create the tools to collect and measure them.
4. What effect might the proposed changes have on other related processes and procedures?

Step 2: Do what the team decides is the best solution to the problem on a small or experimental scale first. This minimizes disruption to routine activity while testing the effect the changes have or have not made to the process.

Do these things:

1. Create a small task group of workers, managers and supervisors to lead an experiment of the proposed changes.
2. Implement the changes in a controlled test utilizing the selected task group.
3. Allow the processes to continue until measurable results become reliable and predictable, whether positive or negative.

Step 3: Check whether the experimental changes are achieving the desired result or not. Also, continuously check related processes to identify any new problems should they arise. Check the effect of the changes:

1. Did the process become more consistent?
2. Did quality improve?

Step 4: Act to implement changes on a larger scale if the experiment is successful. This means making the changes a routine part of your activity. Also act to involve other persons (other departments, suppliers, or customers) affected by the changes and whose co-operation you need to implement them on a larger scale, or those who may simply benefit from what you have learned (you may, of course, already have involved these people in the do or trial stage).

Note: If the experiment was not successful, skip the act stage and go back to the plan stage to come up with some new ideas for solving the problem and go through the cycle again.

You have now completed the cycle to arrive at "problem solved." Repeat Step 1 with the new information you collected, or move on to the next process.

Shewhart's quality teams would systematically evaluate each process of production that had an effect on the final product. The use of statistical analysis enabled management to make some reasonable decisions with hard numerical evidence toward improving processes. Statistics alone, however, did not make Shewhart's theories revolutionary; it was his insistence that quality control become an ongoing assessment that began to change the way some managers would think.

Quality, according to Shewhart, was an ever-changing standard based on the demand of the customers and the ability of the company to produce new products and services. Therefore quality improvement had to be a continuous process involving the workers, managers and customers. This notion set Shewhart's theories apart from other scientific management theories, which tended to be finite in scope and still devolved from managers to workers. The continuing aspects of Shewhart's theories involving employees as well as managers and supervisors laid the foundation for other quality standard theories to come.

An initial problem with the acceptance of Shewhart's theories by management in America was influenced by the entrepreneurial attitude that had led American business leaders for centuries. Many business owners and leaders believed an autocratic style of management guaranteed long-term success. They were the leaders who directed their operations toward success; workers were merely tools to get the job done. But that was then.

SHEWHART'S THEORIES APPLIED TO FOOD SERVICE

In the hospitality/food service industry, the in-line inspector system can also be used as a quality control technique when the operation promotes the use of standardized recipes, standard operational procedures and the staff is comprised of well trained employees. While the total responsibility for quality of foods produced and served fall to the chef, the sous (second) chef and, if the restaurant had one, the expediter, preparatory workers, line workers and servers share the responsibility at every step of production and service along the way. If food received is inferior, or deteriorates too quickly under refrigeration, then the preparatory cooks can decide not to proceed and notify lead cooks and/or the chef when discrepancies to standards occur; if a stock, soup or sauce is not finishing properly, it is up to the line cook/chef preparing it to seek ways of improving the product or starting completely over, and all of this long before the product gets to the expediting line, where it is carried out to the customer. By checking the quality of products before cooks get started, and providing quality checks along the way (tasting to measure and adjust seasonings is one of the best quality checks a cook could apply), quality of foods served can become a consistently achievable goal.

Wait staffs are also, in effect, inspectors since they deliver the finished product to the table and get immediate feedback from the customer. They must make sure the food meets their customers' perception of quality because they are the ones delivering the product. They are the direct link of communication from the customer to the kitchen staff and the managers. This is where the bulk of the customers' perception of quality and value can be assessed when properly cultivated and measured.

A measurement of the restaurant's level of quality can be taken directly from the customer without asking any questions. Perception of quality can be taken at the trash can by the dish room. How much food is left on the plate? What categories of foods are left—appetizers, soups, vegetables, potatoes, entrées or desserts? If food is taken away from the table and disposed of as opposed to being taken away by the guest to eat later, then the customer's perception of quality has already been ascertained. However, by that time the customer's perception of quality may be permanently swayed in the wrong direction.

Shewhart's cycle can be applied to food preparation and service processes with the same level of critical research that is done by the manufacturing industries. In food service, the tasks can be broken down into many parts.

For example, consider the process of receiving food from the vendor and apply Shewhart's cycle to assess its contribution to product quality.

Task: Receiving

Workers involved: The chef and other kitchen employees

Plan:

1. **What change might be demonstrated by altering an existing procedure or adding a new one?**

   If you could limit the number of times a particular vendor had to make deliveries, it would help control the amount of time it took to process deliveries and aid in the inspection and storage of those foods for later use in a more efficient manner; already stored foods would then be rotated by experienced workers to assure that the freshest foods are used first.

2. **What data are available to measure the existing status, and will they be sufficient to measure success under the newly implemented procedures?**

Purchase orders, food requisition sheets, and inventory logs contain the purchasing quota and food specification information.

3. **Are new observations needed? If so, create the tools to collect and measure them.**

Time charts and schedules are needed to determine how long it takes to handle each order as it comes in, and how many staff it takes to do the receiving and storage.

4. **What effect might the proposed changes have on other related processes and procedures?**

They would affect all preparatory, cooking and service procedures, depending on the items being received. When done efficiently, the new procedures would ensure that there would be adequate food and sundry supplies to run the operation.

Do:

1. **Create a small task group of workers, managers and supervisors to lead an experiment of the proposed changes.**

Receiving clerk, preparatory cook, line cook and sous chef can make up an excellent team to help conduct the study.

2. **Implement the changes in a controlled test utilizing the selected task group.**

Choose one of your product categories that now have multiple deliveries made each week, like produce or dairy. Order enough of the product to last a normal week's worth of production (based on past inventory counts).

3. **Allow the process to continue until measurable results become reliable and predictable, whether positive or negative.**

Run the experiment for one full month, keeping track of the progress or interference it may have on production.

Keep a written log of receipts for the same time period, noting the time the truck pulls up to the receiving area; the time it takes to check in the order (does the driver have to search for items or is everything clearly marked and stacked?); the time it takes to get fresh and frozen foods stored; and the time it takes to get the dry goods, paper, and other supplies stored. Finally, measure the overall time it takes for each employee to return to regular duties.

Check:

1. Did the process become more consistent?

Create a chart showing, by vendor, the number of items meeting company standards and compare those to the number of items returned for not meeting standards. Compare total number of items received against total number of items ordered; this tells you how efficient the vendor is in complying with your purchasing needs.

2. Did quality improve?

Keep a log book detailing the amount of time it takes to receive and store supplies in relationship to the total number of items ordered. Then create a chart detailing the day and time of delivery, the length of time for each delivery, and the amount of time for the proper storing and rotation of supplies.

- We can learn which vendors do a better job of loading their trucks, meeting our own specifications for food and non-food products and completely filling orders. It also is a measurement of how well trained the delivery worker is.

- We can learn if there is any pattern of lateness or inefficiency from the vendor, in which case we might want to look for additional vendors.

- We may learn that we are receiving too often during a single day or week, taking too much independent time away from other work that has to be done. Perhaps it is better to concentrate orders to fewer vendors to reduce the number of deliveries. We may decide to do this even if the cost of the product is comparatively higher, because of the savings in labor and work interruption.

- We may also learn that it takes too long to store frozen and fresh foods because the person doing it is involved in other critical tasks at the same time. We may want to reassign the receiving function to someone who does not have other critical tasks to perform in the same time. We may find that selecting one or two people to perform the task on a regular basis may also speed up the process and make it more efficient.

Act:

Train certain staff people to perform this function, rather than pull people from the line who, by chance, are available at the time of the delivery.

Restrict purchases to fewer vendors to see if any time is saved in receiving and storing, or we may decide to wait two or three weeks to see if patterns emerge.

Track receiving and storing times again to compare results.

Once satisfied that the receiving function is running as efficiently as possible, turn your attention to other functions in the kitchen. One by one, each process, from food receiving and storing to food fabrication and cooking, can be analyzed for efficiency using the same method. While it will take time to administer this quality assessment of processes, the efficiency it creates will save future time in production and service and give operators better control over the level of quality produced and served.

Inspection of the processes is a new approach to quality control in food service and hospitality operations. Applying Shewhart's philosophy of continuous assessment and evaluation to the daily operations of professional kitchens, dining rooms and hotels will take a lot of work and dedication. The results will be better efficiency, greater consistency and higher quality standards for the industry.

Through Shewhart's in-depth analyses and improved processes, quality has finally become an obtainable standard rather than a percentage of overall production. Based on the level of customer satisfaction, employee motivation and management commitment, quality has become the primary goal in business.

CHAPTER 5

W. Edwards Deming's Fourteen Quality Points

OBJECTIVES

When you complete this chapter, you should be able to:

- Describe events that lead to W. Edwards Deming's trip to Japan and a revolutionary new style of management.
- Describe features inherent in the supply of food service and hospitality services that force managers to look for new management philosophies and operational strategies.
- Describe the overall strategy behind Deming's fourteen quality points.
- Describe the best way to create a constancy of purpose for any organization.
- Discuss steps needed to make the quality process an official part of the organization.
- Describe a strategy to make all workers their own in-line inspectors.
- Describe the benefits of selecting vendors based on quality first.
- Explain the process of continual assessment.
- Describe steps to assure proper on-the-job training.
- Describe the role of leadership in motivating and stimulating employees toward achieving quality.
- Describe problems inherent in motivation through fear.
- Explain the need to break down barriers in food service and hospitality operations.
- Discuss the negative influence of slogans.
- Describe why management by quotas is not effective.
- Explain how by concentrating purely on numerical objectives, quality can suffer.
- Describe how managers can improve a worker's feeling of self-worth and pride in workmanship.

- Explain some problems with awarding employees with production-based incentives and bonuses.
- Explain the importance of continuing education to improve quality.

W. EDWARDS DEMING

W. Edwards Deming
(c. 1980)

W. Edwards Deming, born in 1900 in Sioux City, Iowa, earned his bachelor's degree in physics from the University of Wyoming and his doctorate in mathematical physics from Yale University. Directly out of Yale, he took a job with the U.S. Census Bureau and used his statistical background to help formulate new techniques for conducting the 1930 census. Not completely satisfied with the processes or the results of the 1930 census, Deming was convinced he could do better.

By 1938 Deming had heard of another statistician who was conducting statistical quality research for Bell Laboratories and made it a point to meet Walter Shewhart. Deming quickly became a devoted follower and grasped wholeheartedly the statistical quality control techniques Shewhart had formalized for manufacturing systems.

For the 1940 census, Deming adopted some of the techniques that Shewhart had already proven in manufacturing. The 1940 results were reported to be the most accurate census ever taken in U.S. history. Deming was given all the credit.

On December 7, 1941, the evolution of American industries came to a standstill when the United States was brought into World War II. When Japan bombed Pearl Harbor, forcing the United States into the most devastating war in the history of the world, she triggered the beginnings of the greatest war machine the world had ever seen. The manufacturing companies within the United States had already been moving at full speed, and, with few adjustments and little retraining, the same companies that built household appliances were able to produce guns, ammunition and military vehicles at an astounding pace. Millions of human lives were touched, whole natural resources depleted and quantity took precedence, once again, over quality.

After the war, a victorious yet tired America had to reverse manufacturing strategies once again. The demand for military supplies had completely controlled American industries for the duration of the war. By 1945 there were very few washers, refrigerators or personal cars or trucks to be bought in American markets, while the need for them had grown exponentially. In addition, the war had given rise to many new technologies which made much of what was already being used by the public obsolete. Industrial gears shifted again, workers were retrained, and washing machines, radios and cars were again being mass produced by American industries. Unfortunately, the emphasis was once again on quantity.

In the meantime, post-war Japan found herself devastated. The most important items were food, water, and shelter. Most of what they had in homes, hospitals, shops and manufacturing was destroyed by the war.

Likewise, the entire political structure was demoralized. Leadership was reduced to fragments of what had previously existed. No one could predict Japan's future, but no one doubted the tumultuous changes that had occurred in her very framework as a nation.

As Japan was picking up the pieces, the government realized that her population demographics had completely changed. Large cities were destroyed and practically wiped off the maps, and new towns had sprung up all over the island. Therefore, one of the tools Japan's leaders needed to help them direct supplies, when they did become available, would have to be an accurate census. But who would take such a census and how accurate could it be?

The supreme command for the allied powers' main objective was to help Japan become self-sufficient when they asked W. Edwards Deming to go there in 1947. They knew the Japanese desperately needed a census, and America had already seen Deming's work with the U.S. census in 1930 and 1940. They didn't know that through Deming's work in Japan, the Japanese would learn to be one of the strongest manufacturing work forces in the entire world.

Deming did aid the Japanese in taking their census, but he did much more than count people; he also changed the way they thought. The Japanese were eager for the change.

On his 1947 trip, Deming happened to be meeting in the same building as the Union of Japanese Scientists and Engineers (JUSE), which had organized to aid in the reconstruction of Japan's industries and businesses. What better timing; Deming wanted to take the opportunity to introduce to JUSE the statistical quality control systems that Shewhart had developed and that he himself had used. He found the Japanese leaders hungry for this advice, particularly Kaoru Ishikawa, the founder and then president of JUSE. They had nothing to lose, and everything to gain.

The Japanese were willing to try anything to get back on the road to recovery. Deming's promises of world recognition as a manufacturing giant were almost too good to believe, but what inspirations they had become.

In the modern hospitality and food service industry, owners and managers are beginning to feel the same way the Japanese felt at the beginning of their reformation campaigns. They feel a need to change the very foundation of their management and operation philosophies in light of the growing diversity of the workplace and the educated demands of the customer. When chefs realize that the need for change is greater than their need to rule the kitchen autocratically, they can begin to be successful in the modern food service industry.

Working with the Japanese gave Deming the chance to organize and test his ideas as they were being developed. It was a mutually beneficial relationship.

FOURTEEN POINTS

Over the next few years Deming organized his ideas of management for quality into fourteen points:

1. Create constancy of purpose toward improvement of product and service with the aim to become competitive and to stay in business and to provide jobs.

2. Adopt the new philosophy. We are in a new economic age. Western management must awaken to the challenge, must learn their responsibilities, and take on leadership for change.

3. Cease dependence on inspection to achieve quality. Eliminate the need for inspection on a mass basis by building quality into the product in the first place.

4. End the practice of awarding business on the basis of price tag. Instead, minimize total cost. Move toward a single supplier for any one item on a long-term relationship of loyalty and trust.

5. Improve forever the system of production and service to improve quality and productivity, and thus continually decrease costs.

6. Institute on-the-job training.

7. Institute leadership. The aim of supervision should be to help people, machines, and gadgets do a better job. Supervision of management is in need of overhaul, as well as supervision of production workers.

8. Drive out fear so that everyone may work effectively for the company.

9. Break down barriers between departments. People in research, design, sales, and production must work as a team to foresee problems of production and those that may be encountered with the products or services themselves.

10. Eliminate slogans, exhortations, and targets for the work force asking for zero defects and new levels of productivity. Such exhortations only create adversarial relationships, as the bulk of the causes of low quality and low productivity belong to the system—beyond the power of the work force.

11a. Eliminate work standards (quotas) on the factory floor. Substitute leadership.

11b. Eliminate management by objective. Eliminate management by numerical goals. Substitute leadership.

12a. Remove barriers which rob the hourly worker of his right to pride in workmanship. The responsibility of supervisors must be changed from sheer numbers to quality.

12b. Remove barriers that rob people in management and in engineering of their right to pride of workmanship. This means abolition of the annual or merit rating and of management by objective.

13. Institute a vigorous program of education and self-improvement.

14. Put everybody in the company to work to accomplish the transformation. Transformation is everybody's job.

Although revised often since he first went to Japan, Deming's fourteen points stand as the basis of his proposals for management. Following them faithfully, he advised, you will increase business and save money simply by concentrating all your efforts on the control of quality.

Back in America, however, businesses had once again grown accustomed to quantity production. Most manufacturing companies worked off quotas and numerical goals, and were led by hierarchical organizational structures. When Deming returned, he returned as an unsung hero; only the Japanese knew of his great accomplishments.

Japan absorbed Deming's ideas with great fervor and dedication. What made the Japanese so successful, Deming believed, was their level of commitment. Without this commitment, the system would fail.

The Japanese redesigned their industries from the ground up. Using the standards that Deming had promoted as guides, they incorporated quality into every aspect of production. By the late 1950s and early 1960s, Japanese products began to make it into American stores. Not only were they of consistently high quality, but in many cases they were cheaper than the American competition. Although there was some resistance on the part of the American public to buying Japanese products at first, resistance was slowly worn down by a steady supply of quality automobiles, radios and televisions. Some Japanese products even seemed more advanced than their American counterparts. Japanese companies seemed more flexible in dealing with the increase of technology of post–World War II and beyond.

What Deming had started was the beginning of a series of improvements to manufacturing industries, and even to management systems in general. Others, like Joseph Juran, Philip Crosby, Kaoru Ishikawa and Armand Feigenbaum, would add their own contributions. Sometimes at odds with Deming, sometimes in support of him; Their theories all lead to one goal: quality.

DEMING'S QUALITY POINTS APPLIED TO HOSPITALITY AND FOOD SERVICE

While Shewhart and Deming were concerned only with management in manufacturing companies, their theories can be applied to the service industries too to improve quality. Here is one way Deming's fourteen points could be interpreted for the food service and hospitality industries:

1. **Constancy of purpose:** The best way to create constancy of purpose in any organization is by developing a company mission statement that is embedded with the planned outcomes and supported by upper management. An example used for a food service operation could be:

   To provide the highest quality food service that meets the time and value demands of our market. To create and maintain a quality workplace for our employees and managers.

   These, however, are just words unless the components are defined in real terms, and standards by which to measure compliance are set.

   In this mission statement, quality is further defined in relationship to time and value demands of a particular market. Restaurants in all markets could adopt a similar mission statement, yet each would be courting a different level of quality based on their particular market.

   Whereas the customer defines quality, the employee defines quality in the workplace. Quality management practices labels employees as customers of the organization, for in effect, they are buying job security, the chance for good pay and regular schedules, and job satisfaction with their commitment to the job and their loyalty to the organization. If the organization gives the employee the quality of work that they desire, the employee can pass the atmosphere of quality and cooperation on to the paying customer. Organizations that do not allow for job security, that keep workers at minimum wage levels and force employees to work split shifts that constantly change cannot expect to attract and keep professional and dedicated workers. In return, these workers cannot be expected to pass high-energy quality standards on to the customer when they themselves do not feel gratified by their jobs or their immediate working environments.

2. **A new philosophy:** Writing the mission statement is only the first step. To fully adopt the new philosophy will require implementation of organizational changes to include the quality teams in Deming's plan, and the

training sessions necessary to bring all employees into the quality planning and improvement processes.

The change in the organizational structure must be made formally and communicated to the entire staff from management to bus people and ware-washers. The Quality Council has to be seen as an active role of upper management, and one that has the highest priority. Quality Improvement Teams have to be empowered to investigate fully any and all processes within the boundaries of the organization, and have their suggestions implemented and tested.

We are indeed in a new economic age. The working environments of nineteenth-century France, where Escoffier first adapted his militaristic linear line of authority in the kitchen, and of early twentieth-century America with its abundance of untrained immigrant workers, no longer exists as we cross into the twenty-first century. Levels of customer expectations continue to change, and so must our management styles and products change to meet the new and evolving marketplace.

Take on leadership for change by placing the emphasis on change for the sake of better quality. Every process becomes suspect. Even those processes that have been practiced for decades and proven to work may no longer be appropriate, given the demographics of the kitchen and dining room staffs and the sophisticated demands of an educated customer.

3. **Cease dependence on inspections:** In many food service establishments, the executive chef and/or sous chef have become the in-line inspectors whose task it is to taste the sauces, soups, and marinades before the cooks complete the final touches and prepare the items for service. When the emphasis is placed on the inspection process to catch the flaws and inadequacies of the recipes or procedures, then the cooks are less likely to take ownership of the quality of the food. Likewise, employees are reluctant to bring criticism on themselves and may try to hide or push inferior products out into the dining room. In-line inspectors on small assembly lines like restaurant kitchens can inadvertently place blame on a worker's performance as easily as they can point out products that don't meet their company's standards of quality.

    By hiring skilled workers and implementing a strong training program for others, you are ultimately producing a better mechanism from which higher quality products can be expected throughout the process. Employees become their own in-line inspectors. They have the knowledge and skill to evaluate their own products based on a well communicated level of quality, and can make their own decision whether to pass an item along the line for finishing and serving, or pull it back for reworking. Trained workers who also have the responsibility for judging the quality of their own work ultimately become their own best critics.

The process of self-evaluation combined with an atmosphere of pride in the job encourages workers to strive for improvement. Improving the quality of their work will reflect an improvement in their own self-worth, making them motivated and loyal employees.

4. **Move toward a single provider:** It has been a long-term practice in food service to shop around for the best price when it comes to buying food, paper and sundry products. Many purchasing textbooks promote the idea of comparison shopping as a way of saving and forcing purveyors to compete for business by lowering their prices. Quality of product and quality of service often do not have as high a priority as price, and this alone can jeopardize the entire quality assessment and improvement processes.

    Deming was referring to manufacturing suppliers when he wrote this recommendation, but analogies can be drawn to the food service arena. An example Deming might have given is machine bolts. If you buy bolts from a variety of vendors based on price alone, then you cannot guarantee the quality of any of the bolts once they're used in the production process. Machines made with good strong bolts will work well, while others made with inferior bolts will break down. When the machines fitted with inferior bolts break down, you may not be able to identify the exact problem of the malfunction. Therefore, you can never improve the process. By keeping to only one bolt manufacturer for your supply, you can guarantee consistency in the bolts purchased, and subsequent success in the operation of the machines.

    In food service, examples may not be as clearly relevant, but the outcomes of shopping by price alone can produce similar predicaments. Produce, for example, can be purchased from dozens of suppliers in almost every market in the country. By shopping around the vendors for the best price of carrots, potatoes and lettuce, you may find the best price comes from a vendor who buys seconds. A "special" price for a case of lettuce might reflect the vendor who over-purchased lettuce in the first place and needs to move the product quickly before having to throw it away.

    By selecting a produce vendor based on quality of product as the highest priority, quality of service second, and price third, you can better predict receipt of fresh produce resulting in higher yields and a longer in-house shelf life. By concentrating on quality and service, your vendor will work harder to meet your quality standards because they know you will not accept inferior products regardless of price. You build a business relationship with your vendors whose success is partially a result of your own success. The better the produce, the better the finished product, the happier the customer, and the more often the customer will return. The more business you do, the more business the produce supplier will do; it is a congenial relationship where both parties can benefit.

Price comparisons are often suggested as a way of keeping purveyors honest in their pricing policies. However, if you question your vendor's honesty in pricing policies, how can you not question their honesty in delivering quality product? It is better to choose reputable vendors in the first place, and build a relationship with them.

5. **Improve systems forever:** Referring to the example given in Chapter 4, use Shewhart's cycle to begin the process of quality assessments and quality improvement. Then extend the cycle analogy to other production and service processes. Once the cycles of assessment are set in motion, they continue until the process is improved. Then, once you have improved all the processes, go back and start over again.

By improving the processes of production and service, you will automatically be reducing the cost of poor quality. The cost of poor quality for restaurants includes the cost of product that is thrown away, the cost of trimming of inferior products, and, more gravely, the cost of losing customers because they were served an inferior product. The cost of losing a customer is the most grave because one dissatisfied customer can prevent dozens of potential customers from ever entering your establishment. The adage "Good news is silent, and bad news spreads" is never more appropriate than in situations in food service.

6. **On-the-job training:** On-the-job training is not a new concept for food service operations. No matter how experienced a new worker is, there is still a period of transition that all employees go through, comparing past work habits and routines to the different standards of the new establishment. Recipes and formulas used in the past are replaced by new ones, operational responsibilities vary, and new styles of management have to be learned. When there is a well established plan to train new employees on the job, it becomes the best mechanism to predict a smooth transition from new employee to team member.

A plan to train employees on the job includes:

- A fully executed job description for the position, including an organizational chart

- Pairing new employees with experienced employees during the training period

- Developing a training schedule that allows new employees to learn different aspects of the operation

- Reviewing training schedules and goals with the new employee, the partnered experienced employee, and the supervising chef

- Reviewing progress on a daily basis

With the high turnover of food service employees, some establishments feel the pressure of being constantly short of staff, so they bypass formal training plans to fill positions quickly. Ultimately, new employee training consists of on-the-job training, but without structure or review. New employees are often put directly into production and are expected to perform their duties and meet their responsibilities based solely on their past experience. This practice, although defended by a few managers as a practical test of a new employee's abilities and stamina, is a short-term solution to the long-term problem of employee turnover. Unfortunately, test or not, this practice contributes to the turnover problem, and is usually not a cure at all.

7. **Leadership:** Supervision and direction cannot, in themselves, motivate employees; leadership is necessary. Supervision can make sure employees do the work properly, and managerial direction can tell employees what to do and when; however, neither can challenge employees to constantly improve nor challenge them to insist on quality. Leadership is an aggressive activity that attacks the behavioral aspects of job performance, job loyalty and job satisfaction.

In traditional food service establishments, leadership is an attribute associated with ownership. Owners have a personal interest in the success of their business. Not only is their interest financial; it is also one of reputation. The success of their business speaks to their own ability to succeed and be recognized as an accomplished entrepreneur. Failure in business may also reflect the owner's inability to meet the pressure of a demanding market and an insensitivity to market fluctuations. Therefore, owners always maintain high visibility in their operations. They spend an inordinate amount of time at the establishment to meet the guests, direct the staffs, and supervise the supervisors in the performance of their jobs. Owners become the foundation of the success of their business. Owners with great personalities and great vision, and who understand and administer hospitality to their guests and employees, can assure success. In the absence of ownership, leadership has to be instilled in the management and staff to supply the same levels of inspiration and vision.

In many food service establishments today, owners are not as visible as they once were. Ownership, instead, may be represented by a corporation which is directed by a board of directors and investors. There is no entrepreneurial personality to infuse inspiration into the establishment, no one to offer a private hand of hospitality to the guests. Other privately owned restaurants and hotels may be run by absentee ownership where owners may only come by periodically and leave the day-to-day operation to managers and supervisors. In both cases, the establishment loses the personal commitment to maintaining the reputation associated with owner-operated organizations.

An owner's pride and respect for personal reputation can be infused into these operations when leadership is infused in management and key personnel. Leadership is a reflection of multiple behavioral attributes that are geared toward motivation and inspiration. These attributes include morale-building insights, channeling energies toward success, and team cohesion. A close analogy would be that of a sports coach whose role is to motivate and guide the team into winning situations.

Leaders in food service are supervisors who have earned their workers' respect and can turn that respect into loyalty to the organization. Leadership can be inherent in some individuals, but can be learned by others. More on leadership will be covered in Section 4.

8. **Drive out fear:** Fear inhibits a workers' ability to perform effectively. Fear of losing a job, fear of retaliation, and fear of embarrassment are all counterproductive elements in a poorly run organization.

   Some managers try to motivate through fear. They use screaming tactics and they criticize employees openly as a means to improve production speed. Then they use a strong-handed management style to ensure that production meets company standards. However, any gains perceived by these managers are only short-term reactions to the tactics themselves. An employee's need for self-protection will cause many to react to those confrontations with militaristic obedience. Then, as soon as the mechanism of fear is gone, this apparent obedience will likely turn into apathy and discontent.

   Some strong-willed employees will not subject themselves to this form of abuse; they leave the company altogether. Fear of losing their job is not as great as their sense of self-worth and self-respect. Those who remain will at first perceive those tactics as a reflection of a manager's efforts toward perfection, and may be motivated to try to meet those goals. Where fear is used as a motivation tactic, however, company goals are never satisfied. Eventually morale breaks down and fear of being reproached takes control over speed of production and quality.

   When fear tactics are replaced with praise for good work and supervision takes on a supportive rather than a disciplinary role, then managers and workers can concentrate on quality of production and not quantity or speed of production. Fear also breeds stress, and where there is stress, even quantities and speed of production suffer. In the absence of fear, stress becomes minimal and workers can perform more effectively and consistently.

9. **Break down barriers:** In food service there are two main departments: production and service. It is easy for cooks to criticize wait staff for slow

service, irregular timing of courses, and unyielding demands. It is likewise easy for wait staff to criticize the cooks for improper cooking and plating of food, jeopardizing the speed of service and being insensitive to the customers' demands. All of this is counterproductive, and the customer is usually the one who suffers the consequences.

Under the new definition of quality as defined by the customer, and proper training of both kitchen and dining room staffs, the entire organization works as a team, each contributing to the success of the other. Wait staff's demands translate into customer demands, and timing is a reflection of the customer's prerogative.

Both cooks and wait staff must work together to satisfy customer demands and pamper their idiosyncrasies. When the staffs are properly coached, they fully understand and appreciate the complexities of each other's jobs. The wait staff learns that quality food cannot be rushed and that direct communication with the kitchen staff can expedite orders. The kitchen staff learns that there are no unreasonable requests from wait staff, and within the framework of quality production, exceptions can become options.

10. **Eliminate slogans:** In food service the dangerous slogans, exhortations, and targets take the form of food cost percents, money-back guarantees, and customer check averages. In effect, these are management concerns that should not be placed in the hands of the production and service employees.

Food cost percents, after all, are a reflection of management's ability to purchase foods under concrete specifications, produce menu items within the capabilities of the staff and equipment, and sell the items at a reasonable rate within the dynamic marketplace. Cooks and wait staff do not need to be concerned with controlling these costs, for that is the role of management. Food cost percents are prescribed by the process. Lowering food costs is not the issue; rather, controlling food cost percents is a measurement of the company's efficiency.

Money-back guarantees, in food service, take away from the real issue of customer satisfaction. Slogans like "Your meal is free if you are not completely satisfied" are not perceived as a customer benefit, but as a pacification of discontent. Where quality food and service are given top priority, customer satisfaction can be the guarantee. This should be the goal. Customers do not want money back; they want a good meal, good service, and good value.

Customer guest check averages are not a reflection of good service, but a direct reflection of market demands. Suggestive selling is a trait of properly trained staffs, while overselling is an abuse of customer relations. Supervisors warn wait staff that guest check averages affect their tips;

therefore, the incentive to raise averages becomes a personal money gratification issue. If customer satisfaction is the one and only key issue, then tips will reflect that satisfaction more than the average of the check itself.

11a. **Eliminate quotas:** Work standards or quotas used to measure an employee's effectiveness encourage speed of production rather than quality production. Employees who see these quotas as a determination of their wage and job security see only the numbers. How many steaks can be cooked in an hour? How many guests can be served in an hour? In a properly trained, efficient operation there are control and design issues that affect these quotas rather than employee performance. How many cooks are on the line at one time? Is the equipment adequate for production needs and versatile enough to meet changing demands? How many wait staff are on the floor at busy times? How many tables are in the dining room and how are they spaced apart? These are management issues and are a part of the overall plan. To force employees to stretch appropriate production amounts based on arbitrary quotas will challenge the employees to cook and serve foods faster than the equipment, staff and space was designed to do. Quality must suffer.

11b. **Eliminate management by objectives:** Management quotas have a negative effect on quality. Chefs and dining room managers are constantly challenged to lower food, beverage and labor costs. What is really needed are accurately forecasted food, beverage, and labor costs based on accurate costs, well executed recipes, properly trained staffs, and menu item sales. Meeting those numbers is the only way of measuring management's effectiveness. Lowering them challenges managers to take shortcuts and reduce staffs to subminimum standards.

Food, beverage and labor cost percents that come in higher than projected are a reflection of the process, not of the employees' or manager's efficiency. It is the process that has to be evaluated, tested, and changed. Overburdening an already weak or inefficient process with superficial objectives will also have a negative impact on quality. Quality must be top priority. To ensure this, equipment has to be adequate, staff levels have to be consistent with sales, and cost percentages have to be a reflection of the plan instead of a reflection of the owner's desire for profits.

12a. **Remove barriers:** Employees' pride in their own workmanship can further develop their loyalty to the organization as they develop a deeper sense of self-worth and commitment. People who feel good about the work they do and know that their contributions affect the company as a whole are more willing to work hard over a consistently longer period of time. Workers who don't ever see their work finished, or the relationship of their work to the success of the operation, can lose motivation as their jobs become mechanical and unchanging.

In food service operations, each employee, from dish washer to line cook, can have pride in their work when they feel that management is committed to them as people rather than as a part of a living machine. Here are some suggestions to help foster this positive approach to personnel management.

- Managers should institute an open door policy to hear employees' concerns, listen to their comments, and heed their suggestions.

- Managers should take the time to meet with each employee periodically to allow for the exchange of ideas and to give positive criticism on the employee's work.

- Managers should greet employees by name and take the time to learn about the employee's personal goals and aspirations.

- Each employee should be given tasks that can be completed during their shift.

- Each shift should have a beginning and an end, allowing employees to complete their assigned tasks, clean their areas, and make their areas ready for the next workers.

- Employees must be able to make their own quality assessments and their own decisions.

- Employees must be able to work at their own pace to assure quality; speed will come with confidence and experience.

- Managers should look for reasons to praise employees for their work; too often, only criticisms are heard.

- Employees should hear customers' positive comments.

- Managers should share the company's plans with every employee, and the financial health of the company should be common knowledge.

- Managers should strive to give employees a schedule that fits their personal needs.

- Managers should always thank employees for their work at the end of their shifts.

When quality of food and service is top priority, then quality of the work environment must also be guaranteed. When employees are properly trained, adequate in number and morale is high, then quality can be a predictable outcome.

12b. Pride of workmanship: While managers are higher up the organizational ladder, they are people too. They have the same needs and desires as their hourly employees, which includes the need for a feeling of self-worth.

A lot of organizations, food service and non–food service, practice a merit raise or bonus system which is rewarded to managers upon meeting production and budgetary goals. When management meets those objectives set by the owners, they are given additional compensation. In time, managers begin to expect those bonuses and become dependent on them as a part of their regular pay.

Many managers will do whatever it takes to make the production and cut costs in order to get the extra money. They begin to place priority on obtaining bonuses instead of on quality. They begin to see the bonus as a measurement of their own abilities to perform their jobs. However, the next quarter they are still under the same pressure, and the cycle continues.

Managers and workers should receive fair compensation for the work that they do. Promising bonuses as a means of raising one's income does not make people work smarter or harder over periods of time. There is only so much work any individual can do. To force them to work faster than they are capable will sacrifice quality.

Managers under this pressure may cut employee labor by eliminating positions and force everyone else to work harder. They may send workers home as soon as business slows and call them back when business rises again. They reduce food cost by buying inferior products, or shortening portion sizes. Although cost of labor and cost of product may go down, so too will quality of food and service, and the cost of poor quality will go up.

Bonuses could be given, but should be based on the company's overall profits and not on numerical goals. Treat managers and employees like stockholders in the company, sharing the profits, and they will take on a sense of ownership, pride and extreme loyalty to whatever the company sets as its goals. When those goals are customer satisfaction then everyone will benefit.

13. **Education and self-improvement:** We already addressed issues of training and evaluation of new employees, but what of the veteran employee? They need the same level of personal commitment as the new employee, yet their basic needs have already been met.

Company-sponsored continuing education programs are a way of keeping the veteran employee challenged and inspired. They too need to be motivated toward constant improvement.

Education can take the form of continuing education courses sponsored by a local culinary school or hospitality management school. It could also come from an internal cross-training program where employees are trained to do more than one job. In both cases, the employee and the company benefit.

The employee benefits because of an increase in self-esteem and future job security. The more they know and the better they can perform their jobs, the better they feel about their contribution to the company. This increased self-esteem can then lead to better positions within the same company and to opportunities for advanced positions in larger operations.

The company benefits as a result of the increased motivation, the increase in skills and knowledge, and the greater consistency in quality production. Even when the highly trained employee leaves an establishment for a better position, the parent company still benefits. The company continues to benefit through an increase in inspiration for everyone remaining on the team to do better and through the edge it gives them in hiring new employees. A company with an aggressive personnel development plan has a better chance of attracting motivated new employees looking to build a career in food service and hospitality.

14. **Transformation is everybody's job:** Most of what has been described in the previous thirteen points goes against normal practices in the militaristic framework of modern food service and hospitality organizations. The move from classical organizational structures and management practices to the new Total Quality Management system will take a complete transformation for most establishments. This will be neither an easy task nor a quick turnaround. It will take time, devotion, commitment to the final goal of quality improvement and an aggressive implementation plan.

The large number of untrained and diverse workers that seek food service and hospitality jobs makes it difficult for managers to maintain high quality standards without total commitment from employees, management and owners. The transformation to quality management will affect all employees, and therefore must involve everyone's participation in order to succeed.

These examples only begin to address the issues of quality management in hospitality and food service. This is the starting point. Organizations that adopt the quality management system of management can begin with these steps and let the process itself help them to investigate further the other avenues to quality planning and control.

CHAPTER 6

Joseph Juran's Trilogy and the Pareto Principle

OBJECTIVES

When you complete this chapter, you should be able to:

- Discuss the relationship between Shewhart, Bell Labs, Western Electric and Joseph Juran.
- Describe Juran's contribution to the quality management movement in the 1950s that turned it into a Total Quality Management program.
- Describe Juran's interpretation of Shewhart's definition of quality as it relates to controlling the number of deficiencies in proportion to the total number of possible deficiencies, and why he felt quality in fact is always changing.
- Describe Juran's two different frames of reference for defining quality and what they represent.
- Describe Juran's Trilogy for quality planning, quality control, and quality improvement.
- Discuss the Pareto principle and how Juran adapted the Italian economist's theory of economic distribution to quality management.
- Discuss ways of adapting the Pareto principle to normal business operations.

SHEWHART MEETS JOSEPH JURAN

In 1926, a team of quality control experts from Bell Laboratories, operating under Walter Shewhart's direct supervision, brought the new quality management program they had been developing for Bell Labs to the Western Electric Hawthorne Works plant in Cicero, Illinois, just outside of Chicago. Working at the Hawthorne plant at that time was a young mathematical scientist named Joseph M. Juran, hired as a statistical engineer.

The Western Electric Plant was owned by Bell Labs and was responsible for making many of the parts Bell needed for its phone service and operating equipment. Its efficient and consistent operation was therefore critical to the overall success of the expanding telephone company.

The quality improvement program Shewhart and his colleagues had been developing in theory was being implemented for the first time in American history by a large manufacturing plant employing over 40,000 workers. Needless to say it required a lengthy training program to indoctrinate everyone into the new system, and Juran was chosen as one of the first twenty to go through the process.

Although Juran was very young, and new at the Hawthorne plant, he was nevertheless impressed with Shewhart's and the committee's insights into quality improvement and protection. They would become two themes of Juran's own philosophy on quality management which he would develop over the next seventy-plus years of his extensive career.

A year later, the National Research Council (NRC) of the National Academy of Sciences began to conduct a study of employee productivity to try and determine what effect a worker's environment had on their level of productivity. The lengthy studied continued from 1927 through 1932.

The Hawthorne study, and the work Dr. Elton Mayo did to condense the information and analyze the results, will be discussed in more detail later in this book. Here it is mentioned because the results of the Hawthorne experiment lead managers to believe in the power of the employee to control productivity and their dependence on the worker to getting the job done properly and efficiently. He was the first to incorporate this human factor into the process of quality management, making it a Total Quality Management program, for it then involved everyone and everything (everything can be always improved).

Although his own interpretation of quality management would not come for several more years, Juran had clearly been baptized by the tenets of research, study, analysis and statistical studies that complemented the engineering degree he had earned from the University of Minnesota a few years earlier. Thanks to Shewhart and his statistical control approach to quality management and the Hawthorne experiments on human productivity, Juran was drawn into what became his life's study of quality planning, improvement and management.

JURAN GOES TO JAPAN

As early as 1928, Juran had written his first pamphlet on quality management for Western Electric which he entitled "Statistical Methods Applied to Manufacturing Problem." The pamphlet attempted to apply Shewhart's theory of statistical control to actual manufacturing

Dr. Joseph Juran (c. 2000)

processes, and was so successful that it remains a part of Western Electric's operational manuals today.

By 1937, Juran had climbed the corporate ladder to become the Chief of Industrial Engineering, and moved to the Western Electric's home office in New York City, where he conducted his research. His work involved visiting other companies and discussing methods of quality management with them in order to bring back resolved plans to Western Electric and thus Bell Labs.

During World War II, Juran took a temporary leave of absence from Western Electric which stretched out to four years, while he served as an assistant administrator for the Lend–Lease Administration in Washington, D.C. The purpose of the organization was to aid in the delivery of critical military parts, fuel and provisions to overseas positions for America and her allies fighting in Europe, Russia and the Pacific.

He and his team were responsible for improving the efficiency of the process, eliminating excessive paperwork and thus hastening the arrival of supplies to the United States' forces and allies. This they performed with great success. When Juran finally left Washington at the end of the war in 1945, he didn't return to Western Electric, but chose to work as an independent consultant and devote the remainder of his life to the study of quality management.

By the end of the war, Juran had already become a well known and highly regarded statistician and industrial engineering theorist. After he left Western Electric, Juran became Chairman of the Department of Administrative Engineering at New York University, where he taught for many years. He also created a thriving consulting practice, and wrote books and delivered lectures for the newly created American Management Association. It was his time with NYU and the AMA which allowed for the development of his management philosophies, which are now embedded in the foundation of American and Japanese quality management programs.

Juran made many contributions to the field of quality management over a long and successful career. His book, the *Quality Control Handbook* (1951), is a classic reference for quality engineers and managers.

Juran followed W. Edwards Deming to Japan to help with that country's quality movement after the war, and in 1954 he began a series of trips to aid in what has become Japan's own form of industrial revolution. He helped to revolutionize the Japanese philosophy on quality management and worked to help shape its economy into the industrial leader it is today.

JURAN ON QUALITY

Juran is best known for his insistence on top management's involvement in the quality assurance process, his interpretation and application of what he labeled as the Pareto principle, derived from his studies of the twentieth century Italian economist Vilfredo Pareto (1848–1923), the need for widespread training in quality, the definition of quality as fitness for use and the project-by-project approach to quality improvement.

Juran carried the idea of quality to its highest degree. Where Deming had concentrated more on the role of management in producing quality products and services, Juran took a hard look at defining quality itself.

Juran once said of quality production, "Achieving quality involves a great deal more than what tools you use. It involves finding out what the customers need." Juran interpreted Shewhart's limited definition of quality to be:

$$\text{quality results when the frequency of deficiencies} \div \text{opportunities for deficiencies approaches } 0$$

Therefore, according to Shewhart, the predictability of quality products increases as the relationship of frequency of deficiencies to opportunity for deficiencies decreases.

The task of quality teams would be to assess both parts of the division. By finding ways to reduce the denominator—opportunities for deficiencies—the number of deficiencies would decrease proportionately. The degree of that downward trend could then be measured and charted as opportunities for deficiencies continued to decrease.

Then they could help control the frequency of deficiencies by buying quality materials in the first place, buying on quality instead of price. Together with having a properly trained staff to run and manage the operation, they would be able to directly affect the number of deficiencies produced.

Yet for Juran it was not enough to talk about decreasing deficiencies, but to think of quality as a standard which is set and measured, yet ever changing. Quality is measured by customer need alone, and customer need is constantly changing; therefore, the measurement of quality is also constantly changing.

Quality permeates every aspect of what a chef does, from the aspect of culinary art to total quality supervision. This must be driven by meeting and exceeding customers' satisfaction levels through quality food production and service. Quality is a continuous process, not a destination.

JURAN'S TRILOGY

To keep up with the changes in quality standards, management should follow what Juran calls the Quality Trilogy: quality planning, quality control, and quality improvement, which he publicized in his book. Through a vigilant commitment to these three managerial functions, quality can be predicted and preserved.

Quality planning entails the establishment of quality circles much like those Shewhart had pioneered for Bell Labs. These quality circles, comprising line workers and managers at all levels of the hierarchy, have as their primary responsibility the investigation and definition of quality for the products or services they produce.

Juran further defines quality in two different frames of reference:

1. One form of quality is income oriented and consists of those features of the product which meet customer needs and, therefore, produce income. In this sense, high quality usually costs more.

2. A second form of quality is cost oriented and consists of freedom from failures and deficiencies. In this sense, higher quality usually costs less.

Quality circles, therefore, must work on both descriptions of quality. The ultimate goal is to provide products of the highest level of quality from the customer's perspective, while controlling costs through reducing wastes, deficient products, and returns.

Determining the customer's needs and creating products that supply those needs are at the crux of quality planning. However, the first step is in identifying who your customers are in the first place.

Customers can be external as well as internal. External customers purchase your end products, while internal customers are employees in the production line who are dependent on a product from another department to do their own work. The quality of the product when they receive it will determine the quality of the finished product and affect the level of satisfaction for external customers.

Quality control is a look at the processes of production. Which processes produce the most consistent results, and which ones allow for the most frequent mistakes? Preserve the consistently productive processes and revamp the others. This too, for Juran, is an ongoing analysis.

Juran's third part of his trilogy, quality improvement, is the crux of his theory. Quality improvement must be made part of everyone's job description and be the first and last goal of every quality team.

Improvements can be made in the materials used in the process, each step of the process itself, the habits and proficiencies of the workers, and even in the packaging and marketing of the finished products. No part or process is left untouched. Then, once a thorough analysis is complete, it is time to re-evaluate and start over again with new information, new goals, and a new level of competencies. Reminiscent of Shewhart's cycle, Juran places this task of quality improvement at the top of his formula for successful management.

To make the trilogy work, Juran suggested following these nine basic principles of quality management:

1. Personally preside over the Quality Council, the top level council that coordinates the quality initiative.
2. Train in how to manage for quality.
3. Preside over the preparation of the vision statement and policies.
4. Participate in setting quality goals and deploying those goals.
5. Provide the needed resources for the initiative.
6. Participate in establishing new measures of performance.
7. Review those performances against the goals.
8. Be there when recognition is awarded.
9. Revise the award system to reflect the changes imposed by the quality initiative.

THE PARETO PRINCIPLE

Vilfredo Pareto (1848–1923) was born to an aristocratic Italian family living in Paris in 1848. At the age of ten, Pareto and his family moved back to Italy, where they enjoyed wealth and prestige. Pareto received his formal education at the Polytechnic Institute of Turin, Italy where he studied the classics, including Latin and Greek languages and philosophy, and engineering (very different disciplines). His career peaked with his appointment as Chair of Political Economy at the University of Lausanne, Switzerland.

Among many of his theories and studies, in 1906 Pareto used a mathematical formula to describe the unequal distribution of wealth in his country, observing that twenty percent of the people owned eighty percent of the wealth.

Juran studied Pareto and began to recognize that Pareto's ideas represented a universal principle which could be applied to many different situations. In an early work, Juran referred to this as the rule of the "vital few and trivial many" which stated that twenty percent of something is almost always responsible for eighty percent of the results. This soon became known as Pareto's Principle, or the 80/20 rule.

The 80/20 rule means that in everything a few (20 percent) are vital and many (80 percent) are trivial. In Pareto's case it meant 20 percent of the people owned 80 percent of the wealth, and for Juran it implied that 20 percent of the defects in manufacturing caused 80 percent of the problems. So if you concentrated on perfecting the processes that caused those 20 percent of the defects, then the entire operation would improve.

While the exact relationship of 80/20 may not always hold true, the theory of trivial many and vital few still remains, although perhaps at different values. How many times have you heard these statements?

- A few workers do most the work.
- A few volunteers run the organization.
- A few trouble makers spoil teamwork.

You can apply the 80/20 rule to almost anything in life, from the science of business and the mechanics of operations to social and political issues:

- Twenty percent of your inventory takes up 80 percent of your storeroom space.
- Eighty percent of your inventory comes from 20 percent of your vendors.
- Eighty percent of your sales will come from 20 percent of your menu items.
- Twenty percent of your staff will cause 80 percent of your problems.
- Twenty percent of your staff will provide 80 percent of your production.
- Eighty percent of your time is wasted on activities that produce only 20 percent of your production.
- Twenty percent of your workers spend 80 percent of their time avoiding making decisions.
- Twenty percent of your church's congregation contribute 80 percent of your church's collection.
- Twenty percent of your organization's members do 80 percent of the organization's work.

The value of the Pareto principle for a chef manager is that it guides you to focus on the 20 percent that makes the larger difference, and everything else should follow. For example, consider that 80 percent of your food cost comes from 20 percent of your menu items, undoubtedly the higher cost items. Then by concentrating on improving the quality, consistency and profitability of those 20 percent items, the entire operation will increase in sales and profitability. In the meantime, the processes you improved as a means to improve the cost of those high volume items will directly affect the cost control of other items as well, creating a ripple in quality improvement that affects every related process.

Another application of the rule can improve employee performance. By identifying the 20 percent of your employees who contribute 80 percent of the work (who are the most reliable and hard working) and by continuing to motivate and inspire them, then the rest of the staff will follow their example and also strive to increase performance. Instead of frustrating yourself with why some of your employees are motivated and the others are not, spend your energy on helping those who are motivated and hard working, reward them and the whole operation will become more efficient.

Consider that about 20 percent of your workload comprises high payoff, high priority items. Therefore to effect the greatest amount of positive change you should concentrate on those 20 percent of your total responsibilities. The first step would be to identify the 20 percent that has the greatest effect and then to concentrate 80 percent of your time on controlling them. You can then spend the remaining 20 percent of your time on the other 80 percent of tasks and by that concentrate on the few that create the greatest results and still work on the "trivial many" that remain.

By spending 80 percent of your time on the top 20 percent of your tasks, you can increase your productivity and improve your efficiency. By spending 20 percent of your time on the less important 80 percent of tasks, you are still able to affect significant changes overall.

THE PARETO CHART

A Pareto chart can be constructed to summarize graphically and display the relative importance of the differences between groups of data for a variety of business, social and economic situations. In this way, individual pieces of data can be evaluated to determine which one causes the greatest amount of problems and needs to be fixed first. Even Shewhart and Deming insisted that one of the main tenets of quality improvement was to concentrate on those parts of the problem that caused the greatest effect and in that way improving the greatest amount of products or services. The Pareto chart is a way of determining that priority.

A Pareto chart can be constructed by segmenting the data into groups (also called segments, bins or categories). For example, in food service operations, to investigate a problem with high food cost, you could group the data into the following categories:

- Percentage of meat entrees ordered from the menu
- Percentage of seafood items ordered from the menu
- Percentage of poultry items ordered from the menu
- Percentage of non-meat items ordered from the menu
- Percentage of dessert items ordered from the menu

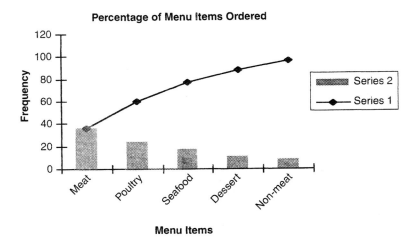

FIGURE 6–1   Sample Pareto Chart

The left-side vertical axis of the Pareto Chart (Figure 6–1) is labeled Frequency (the number of counts for each category), the horizontal axis is labeled with the group names of your response data; the columns represent the sum of the frequency of their use (purchases) for a given time period in descending order L-R, and the points in the curved line represent their cumulative averages in relationship to total use (sales).

You then determine the number of data points that reside within each group and construct the Pareto chart, but unlike the bar chart, the Pareto chart is ordered in descending order.

Once the chart is drawn, you can see the relationship of each category of menu item to total sales. Look for a break point in the cumulative percentage line which occurs where the slope of the line begins to flatten out. The items that fall below the steepest part of the curved line would be the first categories of menu items to investigate regarding purchasing price, any waste, returned items from the dining room, theft or any other thing that can affect food cost. If you can solidly determine that the food cost associated with the most used items are accurate and planned, then move to the next most sold items and begin your investigation over again.

The simplicity of the example, however, does not give enough information to work on since the three largest categories of foods on the menu fall under the steepest part of the curve. In this example, since meat items are clearly the largest number of menu items ordered, create a Pareto chart detailing the sales activities of the different types of meat entrees: i.e., what percentage sold were ribeye steaks; T-bone steaks; prime rib; tenderloin tips, etc., to identify the actual items that contribute to the highest percentage of costs. When the chart is re-drawn and you find out which meat items then fall under the steepest part of the new curve, start ensuring the proper food cost and control associated with those before moving on to the next.

CREATE A PARETO CHART USING MICROSOFT® EXCEL®

In Excel, set up a spreadsheet where the first column contains the categories of items being measured, the second column shows the percentage of those items to the total and the third column represents the cumulative percentages. Make sure the percentage of items sold is listed in descending order by going to Data, Sort, Percent, Descending, as depicted in Figure 6–2.

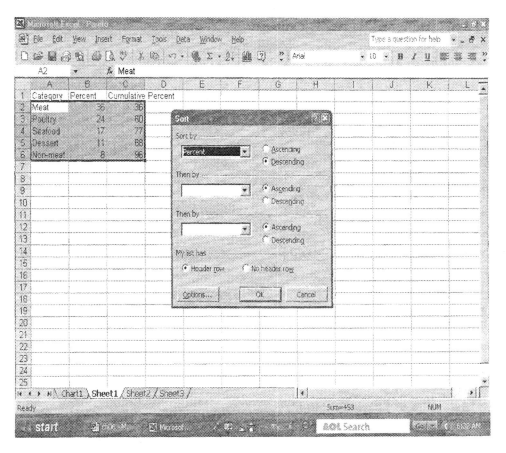

FIGURE 6–2 Setting Excel Parameters for a Pareto Chart

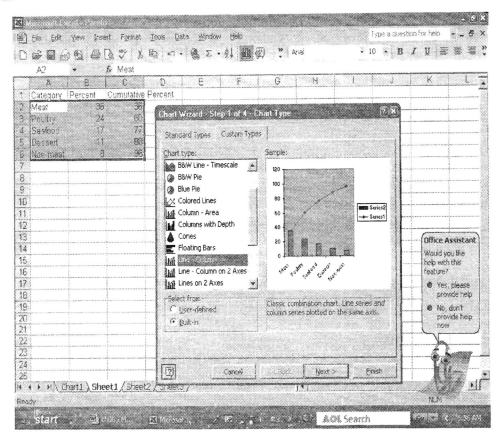

FIGURE 6–3 Plotting the Pareto Chart on Excel

Once that is finished, you are ready to create the Pareto Chart. First highlight the Category, Percent and Cumulative Percent columns. Go to chart wizard, select Custom Types, select Line-Columns and follow the instructions (Figure 6–3).

Using Excel to create Pareto Charts makes plotting the data easy and accurate. Once the charts are created they quickly identify the key areas to focus your attention when solving the problems at hand.

CHAPTER 7

Discovering Philip Crosby's Zero Defects

OBJECTIVES

When you complete this chapter, you should be able to:

- Describe Philip Crosby's novel approach to quality management.
- Discuss Crosby's fourteen points of quality control and any relationships that exist between them and Deming's fourteen quality points.
- Describe Crosby's definition of quality as conformance to standards.
- Discuss Crosby's Zero Defects philosophy for planning for and protecting quality.
- Explain the strategies for adopting a Zero Defects policy for food service.
- Discuss how the HACCP program for food safety embodies Crosby's theory of Zero Defects.
- Describe Crosby's theory that Quality is Free.
- Describe some of the costs of poor quality for food service/hospitality operations.
- Discuss Crosby's four absolutes of quality assurance.

PHILIP CROSBY (1926–2001)

Philip Bayard Crosby was born June 18, 1926 in Wheeling, West Virginia to Mary and Dr. Edward K. Crosby, a very successful podiatrist.

After graduating from high school in 1944, near the end of World War II, Crosby joined the U.S. Navy and became a corpsman on board one of its hospital ships, where he stayed until the end of the war in September 1945. After his discharge from active service, Crosby entered the Ohio College of Podiatric Medicine in Cleveland, following his father into the world of medicine.

With the outbreak of the Korean conflict (1950–1953), Crosby was recalled to military service for an eighteen-month assignment as a marine medical corpsman tending to wounded soldiers along the beaches and in the forests of

South Korea. Crosby was exposed to so much carnage and suffering that he decided when he left the service this time, he would change career paths and find something else to devote his life to.

In 1952 when Crosby did finally leave the military, he went to work for the Crosley Corporation (Richmond, Indiana) giving up his stethoscope and gloves for a position as a junior electronic test technician. Even as a junior member on the staff, his ability to assess situations and solve problems impressed his supervisors to such an extent that he was asked to join the American Society for Quality Control in Richmond, Virginia to represent the corporation along with other managers and supervisors. This is where his early concepts of quality and quality management began to develop.

CROSBY REDEFINES QUALITY

In 1955 Crosby moved to South Bend, Indiana, and went to work for Bendix Corporation as a reliability technician. At that time Bendix was under contract by the U.S. Navy to test and develop a new line of ground to air missiles that could be launched from the decks of fast moving cruisers. One of the missile types, the TALOS missile, was the one Crosby had a chance to observe and work with.

TALOS surface to air missile, US Navy

As a quality engineer, Crosby investigated the causes for any defects found by inspectors and those testing the missile in its early development stages. Although it was exciting work, Crosby's low level position did not afford him much authority to suggest or make changes, and after just two years he decided to leave Bendix for a job with Martin Marietta in Orlando, Florida.

Martin Marietta offered Crosby a job as a senior quality engineer with the aeronautics technology company and ended up staying with them for eight years. It was while working for Martin Marietta that Crosby developed his Zero Defects concepts, began writing articles for various journals, and started his public speaking career.

Under his direction, Martin's management and employees worked together toward developing new strategies for product development and manufacturing that would guarantee absolute quality for the Pershing Missile project which began in 1956 and continued for the next thirty-five years. These new strategies formed the basis of an innovative concept of quality protection he developed which would insist that things were done right the first time so that disasters with deficient parts of products could be avoided. He claimed that design features should ensure zero defects throughout the production and delivery process and raise the predictability for success to 100 percent.

According to Crosby, quality is conformance to requirements and is measured by the cost of non-conformance. Poor quality is, therefore, a contradiction in terms. Crosby preached that there is no reason for having errors or defects in any product or service. "Mistakes are based on two things: lack of knowledge and lack of attention." The title of Crosby's first book, *Quality Is Free*, sums up his approach to quality control and introduces his Zero Defects strategies in easy to understand language.

Crosby observed that people generally performed to the standard management set for them. As long as management asked for acceptable quality levels (AQLs) and not absolute quality levels (Zero Defects), they would receive products and services that may or may not meet the highest level of quality possible for those products or services. Wavering standards would produce costly inconsistencies in terms of returns, defects, and customer dissatisfaction.

ZERO DEFECTS

Crosby realized that the way to reach quality in production was to aim for the highest quality possible, all the time. He stated that quality was "conformance to requirements, not goodness" and that the policy should be Zero Defects, not AQLs.

The underlying fear of management, according to Crosby, was that to assure absolute quality, or Zero Defects, would be too costly to put in practice and would jeopardize the company's level of production and profits. Some companies would rather place their money in warranty programs and only deal with problems as they are brought to their attention. According to Crosby and his fellow quality gurus Deming and Juran, that was the worst scenario, because many times it was too late at that point to regain the confidence of the consumer. Rather, according to Crosby, it was the non-conformance to quality standards that costs a lot of money. Add up the costs of in-line inspectors, defective parts or products that are thrown away or re-worked, and the costs of dissatisfied customers and you have a major expense. Conformance to quality standards saves money by reducing waste, eliminating or streamlining inspection systems and by producing products that gain customer satisfaction.

Like Deming, Crosby promoted fourteen points (steps) for reaching Zero Defects and, like Deming's, Crosby's first step began with obtaining a commitment from management. Without management's support and direction, quality cannot be guaranteed. Management has to accept the concept of Zero Defects and drive every effort toward achieving the ultimate goal. Only then can quality be protected.

Crosby's 14 quality control points which may lead to Zero Defects:

1. Management is committed to quality—and this is clear to all.
2. Create quality improvement teams—with (senior) representatives from all departments.
3. Measure processes to determine current and potential quality issues.
4. Calculate the cost of (poor) quality.
5. Raise quality awareness of all employees.
6. Take action to correct quality issues.
7. Monitor progress of quality improvement—establish a zero defects committee.
8. Train supervisors in quality improvement.
9. Hold Zero Defects days.
10. Encourage employees to create their own quality improvement goals.
11. Encourage employee communication with management about obstacles to quality.
12. Recognize participants' efforts.
13. Create quality councils.
14. Do it all over again—quality improvement does not end.

In the hospitality industry, getting upper management and owners to buy into the Zero Defects philosophy is the biggest obstacle to overcome. Since the modern organizational structure is hierarchical in design, management must be in full support of quality controls in order for momentum to be carried down the ladder to the employees.

Crosby borrows his second step in quality control from Deming's mentor Walter Shewhart. Crosby equally promotes the concept of a quality improvement team whose whole purpose is to lay the foundation for a quality improvement program. This program must include aspects of Shewhart's cycle, that is, asking systematic questions on quality, gathering information about those questions, studying the implications of the information, making a change in the process, observing the effects of the change, and repeating the entire cycle over and over again.

Step 4 addresses the cost of quality. Crosby describes the costs associated with poor production, that is, scraps, re-working of products, warranties, etc., and lays the foundation for support of his Zero Defects policy.

The cost of poor quality for food service and hospitality operations includes the huge cost associated with negative publicity. Every satisfied customer is likely to tell three or four friends about a place, while for every single dissatisfied customer, ten or fifteen others are warned to keep away. In a highly competitive industry, a dissatisfied customer can have an enormous negative impact on the establishment.

Some operators will do just about anything to make sure the customer leaves satisfied. They may even resort to buying their meal or giving a free drink or dessert for any inconvenience in the meal or service offered. Free meals and free drinks are also a cost of poor quality.

In step 7, Crosby describes his concept of Zero Defects. "Zero Defects should be the standard on which all success is measured." Crosby's concept is that any standard less than a Zero Defects standard would be promoting "acceptable levels" of quality. There should be only one level of quality, that being zero defects, and everyone in the organization should strive to reach that goal.

The concept of Zero Defects is so different from other quality concepts in manufacturing that Crosby promoted a public relations plan for employees and managers to see it implemented. His step 9 promotes the idea of establishing a Zero Defects Day, a target day when everyone can celebrate the organizational commitment to zero defects, a celebration day to promote the company's change of philosophy and to launch a new level of employee participation in the decision making and quality control processes.

Finally, in step 14, Crosby joins Shewhart, Deming and Juran in the notion, "Do it over again." Even the standard of Zero Defects needs to evolve with customer input. As customer demands change, so must the standard. But in all cases, all subsequent standards will also be established under the principles of Zero Defects.

APPLYING ZERO DEFECTS
TO THE FOOD SERVICE INDUSTRY

A concept like Zero Defects may work for manufacturing and engineering industries which deal with parts and machines. It was a goal that was easy to adapt to missile design and manufacturing (e.g., the Pershing missile) because each missile launched could mean victory or defeat depending on its deployment and outcome. However, to adapt the same theories to the service industries, where each customer has a different perception of quality and value, Zero Defects becomes an enigma.

In a business where the customers' perception of quality is personally motivated, that is, steaks rare, medium-rare, food too salty, not enough salt, etc., is there any sense in adopting those high-end standards like Zero Defects? Wouldn't they ultimately demoralize workers when steaks keep coming back to the kitchen either undercooked or overcooked?

Zero Defects does not mean that things do not go wrong, or that all customers will always be satisfied. Both of those are not obtainable goals in a business where every individual person has a different appreciation for quality and a different expectation of the level of quality that is possible. Zero Defects means that the operation began with the premise of doing it right the first time, but also has put in place very specific rules and policies for reacting to and correcting deficiencies whenever and wherever they occur, thus ensuring no defects according to quality standards.

In food service and hospitality, the definition of quality is not as well defined as it may be in manufacturing industries where parts either fit or not, engines either run or not, and missiles either explode or not. In the service industries where each customer has a different slant on their interpretation of the words quality and value, then planning for Zero Defects in producing quality services becomes an undulating procedure. While service employees should always strive to meet the standards set by management, they must always remember that the customer is the ultimate person to be satisfied, and be able to adapt their policies, procedures and products to meet individual definitions of quality and value.

When quality is defined according to concrete and measurable standards, as Crosby promoted, then it is easier to plan to meet them and provide avenues for correcting variance. In food service and hospitality, whose standards should be used to set the mark for quality? One person may love the prime rib that a particular restaurant serves, and another may think it mediocre. They are all so different. If you are speaking about machine parts quality is easier to define than if you are talking about the doneness of a steak.

In a Zero Defects operation, everyone strives to achieve that ultimate goal, but realizing variables do exist they set aside procedures and policies for handling concerns and/or complaints should they arise. If the process of Zero Defects is working efficiently even when the steak does come back to the kitchen, as is likely to happen in any establishment from time to time, the mechanism to handle the situation has been rehearsed and perfected so that the customer is not inconvenienced by having to wait too long for the returned meal. In these cases, returned steaks become just another "expected" possible outcome, and the staff, waiters and cooks are trained to handle the situation in a timely and courteous fashion. Thus the system keeps working, frustration is minimal, and the customer walks away with a feeling of personal satisfaction on having his or her tastes catered to.

HACCP: A PROGRAM OF ZERO DEFECTS

In the early 1960s, when Crosby was building his Zero Defects policies for Martin Marietta, NASA (the National Aeronautics and Space Administration) was preparing for its first launch of a manned spacecraft aimed for a historic voyage to the moon and back. It would truly be an historical event should everything go well and the three men travel to the moon and return home safely; anything short of reaching those goals would have had grave affects on the continuation of the American space program.

One of the main concerns was the safety of the food that the astronauts would have to eat while in space, far away from any medicine chests, drug stores or doctors' offices should stomach problems, sweating or vomiting occur because of tainted food. NASA needed a system that would guarantee 100 percent safe food for these astronauts, and Crosby's Zero Defects model was the best thing around at the time to help them do so.

The Pillsbury Corporation actually designed HACCP (Hazard Analysis Critical Control Points) for NASA, utilizing the tenets of the quality control movement that had sprung roots in the manufacturing industries, adapting them to the food service industry for the first time. HACCP must involve everyone in the operation in order for it to succeed; it must gain upper management support to move forward and maintain itself; it must be an on-going program, one that reviews its progress through detail monitoring and comparisons to expected norms; and a program which changes as the information (statistics) that detects contaminants and protects food safety changes through the advent of new and more accurate science which identifies pathogens (harmful microorganisms) and means of preventing their spread and growth and for destroying them should they already be present.

HACCP is a program of food safety that predicts obstacles (hazards) to food safety from the beginning of the process to the end, has measurable statistics (critical limits) for ensuring food safety throughout the process, and has alternative solutions should dangers of food contamination become evident at any stage or step before the food gets to the customer. In effect, HACCP is a program to secure Zero Defects (food contamination) in the food being prepared and served to those astronauts thousands of miles above the earth, and has since spread to restaurants and other food manufacturers and suppliers here on Earth.

QUALITY IS FREE

In 1965 Crosby went to work at ITT Corporation's headquarters in New York, and spent the next 14 years applying his quality management philosophy to its huge internal network of planning, production and service personnel and processes. ITT at that time employed 400,000 people in 46 different countries. With Crosby's help, ITT soon became recognized as holding the standard for quality in their businesses, including their service operations like hotels and insurance companies. Crosby not only demonstrated that quality could be a consistent standard, but that the price of quality was a lot lower than the cost of poor quality or non-conformance.

Now that he had proven that working on prevention rather than detection and correction made an organization more profitable and reliable, Crosby decided to write a book that would help management understand its personal role in making quality happen and the changes that had to occur in operations in order to consistently achieve it. *Quality Is Free: The Art of Making Quality Certain* was first published in 1989 and explained in non-technical terms that management could take charge of quality. The book became a best seller, with over 2 million copies sold.

What drove the sales for the book was the acceptance of corporate executives of the idea that they could actually do something about planning and protecting quality standards. Until then, quality was an incomprehensible notion that was hard to speak of in concrete terms. Now they could see the results when defining quality as conformance to standards, and setting those standards as high as they could go. They could concentrate on helping establish clear requirements in planning, production, sales and service and insist that they be met every step of the way.

Crosby would often point out that doing things right the first time added nothing to the cost of the product or service. What costs, and costs dearly in terms of re-work, test, warranty, inspection and service after service, is doing things wrong.

In 1979 he founded Philip Crosby Associates, Inc. (PCA), headquartered in Winter Park, Florida just outside of Orlando, with the idea of writing and counseling on quality improvement systems for major corporations.

PCA went public in 1985 and produced films and workbooks to reach all the employees of the client companies in 17 languages around the world. Once PCA became established as a global company, Crosby began to popularize what he referred to as the four quality management absolutes which he said were needed to ensure total quality in whatever aspect of business you happened to be in:

1. Quality means conformance to requirements (customer values), not goodness (ethereal or personal values).
2. Quality is achieved by planned prevention, not appraisal (inspection).
3. Quality has a performance standard of Zero Defects, not acceptable quality levels.
4. Quality is measured by the Price of Non-conformance, not indexes.

Food service and hospitality managers can take lessons from the same four absolutes. Whether you deal with a large percentage of regular customers or transients, the true perception of quality comes from those customers. By defining quality by your customer's perceptions and planning for quality in the beginning, you can deliver quality at a high level of acceptability.

In recent years Crosby outlined what he believed to be the characteristics of all successful businesses, and what all others should strive to emulate. Does your organization embody these five characteristics?

1. People routinely do things right the first time.
2. Change is anticipated and used to everyone's advantage.
3. Growth is consistent and profitable.
4. New products and services appear when needed.
5. Everyone is happy to work there.

CHAPTER 8

Kaoru Ishikawa and Armand Feigenbaum

OBJECTIVES

When you complete this chapter, you should be able to:

- Describe Ishikawa's relationship with W. Edwards Deming and the Union of Japanese Scientists and Engineers.
- Discuss why Ishikawa demanded the implementation of a full customer service program to improve quality.
- Describe Ishikawa's adaptation of the Shewhart cycle.
- Describe some of the possible uses of the Cause and Effect diagram, also known as the Ishikawa or Fishbone diagram.
- Describe the process of constructing a Fishbone diagram.
- Apply the Fishbone diagram to an issue facing foodservice or hospitality operations.
- Describe Armand Feigenbaum's definition of Cost of Quality.
- Discuss the concept of Poor Quality Cost and why it is an operational factor that managers need to learn how to control.
- Discuss Feigenbaum's concept of Total Quality Control and both descriptions of direct and indirect poor quality costs.

KAORU ISHIKAWA (1915–1989)

Dr. Kaoru Ishikawa was born in 1915 in Tokyo, Japan. He was a graduate of Tokyo University, where he majored in applied chemistry.

In the 1950s, Ishikawa became involved in Japanese and international standardization. He was Professor at Tokyo University and founder of the Union of Japanese Scientists and Engineers (JUSE), a body which spearheaded the plans to rebuild Japan's industrial infrastructure after the war.

It was Ishikawa, on behalf of JUSE, who encouraged W. Edwards Deming to remain in Japan in 1947 after he had completed the Japanese census, and share his newly emerging strategies for quality planning and statistical controls. Ishikawa embraced the concepts and promises of quality control and was the leading proponent for its universal adaptation in Japan's industries and businesses.

Together Deming from abroad and Ishikawa from inside the Japanese revitalization movement worked hand in hand to rebuild the Japanese economy. They were quite successful, and the quality and consistency of Japanese made products soon found lucrative markets all over the world.

Ishikawa wanted to change the way people thought about doing work; he wanted to change workers into thinkers, not just doers doing the processes. He urged managers to resist becoming content merely with improving a product's quality. He insisted that quality improvement can always go one step further, reiterating Shewhart's and Deming's call for continuous improvement.

His notion of company-wide quality control included the implementation of a full program of customer communication and service. It was critical to Ishikawa's views that the customer be able to have a direct role in the production cycle. His innovative ideas meant that a customer would continue receiving service even after receiving the product, which was a novel idea for manufacturers in the 1940s and 1950s. Customer service would extend across the company itself in all levels of management, even beyond the company to the everyday lives of those involved.

With his cause and effect diagram (also called the Ishikawa or Fishbone diagram), Ishikawa made significant and specific advancements in quality improvement. With the use of this new diagram, the user can see all possible causes of a result, hopefully find the one or many that have the greatest impact on the result, and by concentrating on them, fix them forever.

Ishikawa believed in the importance of support and leadership from top level management. He continually urged top level executives to take quality control courses, knowing that without the support of the management, these programs would ultimately fail. Ishikawa stressed that it would take a firm commitment from the entire hierarchy of employees to reach the company's potential for success.

Another area of quality improvement that Ishikawa emphasized was the concept that quality should be protected throughout the product's life cycle, and not just during production. Therefore customers would remain satisfied for extended periods of time, continuing to buy and recommend the products and/or services to their friends and associates.

Ishikawa believed strongly in creating standards, although he felt they too should be constantly evaluated and changed. Standards are not the ultimate source of decision making; customer satisfaction is which is always changing and always has to be catered too.

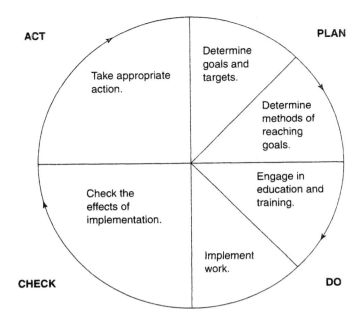

FIGURE 8–1   Ishikawa Cycle

Ishikawa expanded the Shewhart cycle's four steps into the following six (Figure 8–1):

- Determine goals and targets.
- Determine methods of reaching goals.
- Engage in education and training.
- Implement work.
- Check the effects of implementation.
- Take appropriate action.

FISHBONE DIAGRAM (CAUSE AND EFFECT)

The Fishbone diagram, also called the Ishikawa diagram or Cause and Effect diagram, is an analysis tool that provides a systematic way of looking at problems and the causes that create or contribute to them. It is a tool that is used best in a brainstorming session where key managers and employees begin to investigate the intricate policies, procedures, equipment and staffing matrixes for the purpose of improving efficiencies and quality of products and services.

Any idea is a good idea, and is placed on the diagram. When the same idea appears at multiple times in different areas of the operation, then the significance of that factor in improving overall efficiencies and quality gains importance.

The design of the diagram, with its pointed arrows and branched segments, gives a generalized impression of what might appear to be the skeleton structure of some fish. It starts out with a central backbone and thin segments (bones) stretching from it, giving structure and support to the overall diagram just as fish bones extend from their spines to their fins in systematic and symmetric patterns to give support to the whole body, head, sides and tails. It wasn't long before the Fishbone diagram became its more commonly recognized name.

The value of the Fishbone diagram is to assist management teams in categorizing the many potential causes of problems or issues in an orderly way, be able to identify the main or root causes and set about procedures to change or improve them for the collective goal of improving the consistent delivery of quality products and services.

When Should a Fishbone Diagram Be Used?

Does the management team . . .

- Need to study a problem/issue to determine the root cause?
- Want to study all the possible reasons why a process is beginning to have difficulties, problems or breakdowns?
- Need to identify areas for data collection?
- Want to study why a process is not performing properly or producing the desired results?

How Is a Fishbone Diagram Constructed?

1. **There are 3 Basic Steps:** First you need to define your problem. It may be a symptom of a problem, such as low customer counts during a particular meal period, or the whole problem itself such as being able to predict meal counts at a higher percentage of accuracy. Try to be specific; problems that are too large will have too many causes and sub-causes to investigate properly.
2. Write the problem on the far right side of your diagram and draw a long horizontal arrow pointing toward it. This becomes the backbone of the fish (problem to be solved). Figure 8–2 illustrates the first step.

FIGURE 8–2   Identify Problem to Be Solved

3. Label each bone of the fish with words that depict the major categories of possible causes as in Figure 8–3. The ones typically utilized by managers in manufacturing and service industries are:

   ▪ **The 4 Ms:** Methods, Machines, Materials, Manpower

   ▪ **The 4 Ps:** Place, Procedure, People, Policies

   ▪ **The 4 Ss:** Surroundings, Suppliers, Systems, Skills

Note: You may use any one of the four categories suggested, combine them in any fashion or make up your own. The categories are to help you organize your ideas, and from there be able to focus your attention on the major categories affecting the greatest amount of effect.

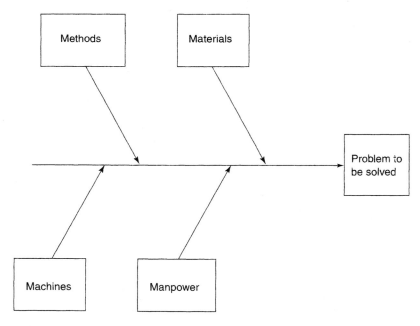

FIGURE 8–3   Decide What Will Be Measured

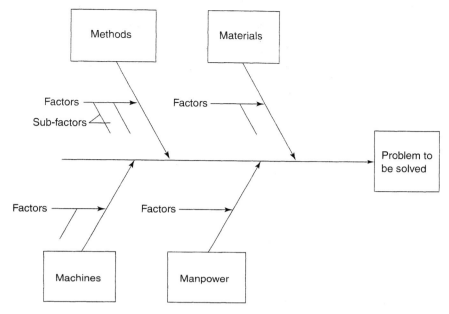

FIGURE 8–4 Fishbone Chart Showing Factors and Sub-factors

4. Now identify the factors within each category that may affect the problem/issue and/or effect being studied. These are attached to the category lines they apply to as shown in Figure 8–4.

5. Now identify those factors which may contribute to the major factors already identified; these become sub-factors. The attempt is to identify as many sub-factors as you can and therefore be able to focus on the causes in a great amount of detail before making any judgments about how to change them.

6. Continue until you have identified all major and as many of the minor causes as you can; the more factors and sub-factors you identify, the greater your ability to identify the ones responsible for the root cause, and therefore affect positive change.

7. Analyze the results of the Fishbone by looking for those items that appear in more than one category. These are the ones you should focus your investigations on in order to effect the greatest amount of change.

8. Next list them in order of importance based on how many times they were listed on the diagram. The assumption is that by analyzing and making positive changes in a sub-factor or factor that affects the most categories, the greater the overall impact will be.

9. Analyze each of those most likely causes one at a time, beginning with the one that appears, most frequent until positive results have occurred.

10. Apply strategies learned to existing processes and procedures and measure their affect.

FISHBONE DIAGRAM APPLIED TO FOOD SERVICE AND HOSPITALITY

The Fishbone diagram is a great tool to use when trying to identify the causes of problems related to food service and hospitality products and services because of the complexity of these industries, which rely on the ever changing mood of customers to determine their success. The Fishbone diagram allows chef managers and hospitality managers to examine the whole problem associated with a particular situation rather than parts that appear to be paramount in the process. In fact, the ones that appear paramount to the outside on-looker may end up being secondary in the exposed cause and effect models.

Let's use the Fishbone diagram to explore the problem of controlling waste in the kitchen and dining rooms. We'll use controlling waste as the backbone as shown in Figure 8–5:

FIGURE 8–5   Establish "Controlling Waste" as Problem to Be Solved

It's pretty easy to identify some of the key categories that have the greatest effect on controlling or contributing to waste: your staff is one—How experienced are they?; your supplies are another—How fresh were they when purchased?; methods including food and beverage preparations can definitely contribute to waste; and finally, borrowing one of the four Ps, policies, we need to examine company policies regarding portioning, comp meals, discounted pricing, etc.

Let's look at our diagram so far as shown in Figure 8–6:

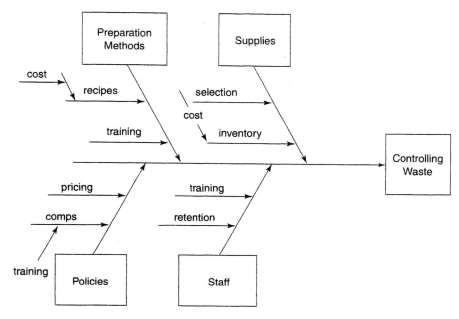

FIGURE 8–6   Expanding Fishbone Chart

This diagram is only starting to take shape, and you can already see some duplication (training and costs).

ARMAND FEIGENBAUM: COST OF QUALITY

For years, management in American manufacturing businesses generally believed that it was too expensive to provide high quality products and service to customers. They believed they were doing the best that they could, and that ought to be good enough for the consumer.

Often companies would use this excuse to build customer service departments, saying that servicing the customer after the sale, including the offer of warranties and returns, was a high

Armand Feigenbaum
(c. 1980)

priority. They were betting that most buyers would be satisfied with their purchases, that others would accept what they purchased as the best they could get, and only a few would actually return the products for re-working or refunds. It was a gamble that often failed, leaving Americans with a taste that American made products were inferior by design and opening the door for foreign products in U.S. stores and on U.S. roadways (Toyota, Honda).

To help offset this, Armand V. Feigenbaum (1920–), while working at General Electric Company's Schenectady Works Plant in New York in 1943, developed a system called Cost of Quality. Dr. Feigenbaum's system examined all the costs related to developing a quality production and inspection system, as well as the cost incurred when the product failed to meet customer demand. He then provided management with a report that was based on actual dollars spent and not on hyperbole; it was a language that top management and owners could understand. The Cost of Quality system was adopted during the following year by GE's Jet Engine Group in Massachusetts, and a few years later by all of GE U.S.A.

Dr. Feigenbaum first published a brief view of Cost of Quality in the American Institute of Electrical Engineers Magazine in 1945, then again in 1951 in his book, *Total Quality Control.*

His concept divided the cost of quality into the following four categories:

1. Prevention cost
2. Appraisal cost
3. Internal defect cost
4. External defect cost

POOR QUALITY COST (PQC)

Unfortunately, the term cost of quality had a negative impression that reflected the thinking of the 1950s, when many company managers still believed that quality products cost much more to produce than the inferior products that consumers were willing to accept. Given the change in management attitude toward quality, and the new dimensions that had been added to the original concept, Feigenbaum started using the term poor-quality cost (PQC), which seemed more appropriate to budget minded managers.

The purpose of a poor-quality cost system is to provide management and employees with data that can be used to identify improvement opportunities, optimize the effectiveness of the improvement efforts, and measure the progress that is being made to improve continuously.

Poor quality costs the organization money, while good quality saves the organization money. Unfortunately, many organizations did not measure the cost of poor quality, and by not measuring it they couldn't control it. Feigenbaum made managers realize the importance of measuring the cost of poor quality as though it were an integral part of the company's profit and loss statement, and therefore bring attention to the numbers and their relationship to overall costs. By doing so, Feigenbaum would conjecture that companies would soon realize the magnitude of the problem and by sheer diligence begin to find ways of lowering those costs.

Poor-quality cost is defined as all the cost incurred to help the employee do the job right every time (this includes process designs that have non–value-added activities included in them) and the cost of determining if the output is acceptable, plus any cost incurred by the organization and the customer because the output did not meet specifications and/or customer expectations.

With today's focus on the external customer and on business process, it is imperative that operators report and consider the impact poor quality has on customer satisfaction and the amount of money wasted on external customer related activities such as warranties, guarantees and returns. These two factors require organizations to re-evaluate the way they measure poor-quality cost; it is much higher than they previously could have imagined.

TOTAL QUALITY CONTROL (TQC)

Feigenbaum later went on to develop the concept of Total Quality Control, emphasizing that quality requires a total effort of management—not only the inspection department—to make sure inferior products do not make it to market. Feigenbaum has summarized his ideas about Total Quality thus:

I. Direct poor-quality cost
   A. Controllable poor-quality cost
      1. Prevention cost
      2. Appraisal cost
      3. Non–value-added cost
   B. Resultant poor-quality cost
      1. Internal error cost
      2. External error cost
   C. Equipment poor-quality cost
II. Indirect poor-quality cost
   A. Customer-incurred cost
   B. Customer-dissatisfaction cost
   C. Loss-of-reputation cost
   D. Lost-opportunity cost

Feigenbaum's work centered around the notion for a systematic or total approach to quality planning and control. He argued that total approach to quality required the involvement of all functions of the quality process, not only manufacturing. His idea was to build in quality in the early stage rather than inspecting and controlling it after the processes had been completed.

Dr. Feigenbaum believed companies needed to move away from the technical aspect of quality control and change their focus of quality control as a business method, including administrative and human relation functions.

Feigenbaum saw Modern Quality Control (MQC) as the stimulating and building up of operator responsibilities and interests in quality. Feigenbaum also argued that all levels of quality need to be emphasized. For quality control to achieve the specified results, there is the need for complete support from management. The quality control program must develop gradually from within the organization.

QUALITY IMPROVEMENTS FOREVER

The backbone of the quality movement is the notion of continuous change and improvement. Since change is inevitable, the quality movement must also change to meet the new demands set before it. Ishikawa and Feigenbaum both accepted the tenets of quality planning and control, and added their own interpretations and guidelines to the ever increasing multi-dimensional framework of statistical investigation, subjective analysis and strategic implementation that had been evolving ever since it was started by Walter Shewhart.

Whether the Fishbone diagram or financial discussions of the cost of quality are used by chef, hotel and dining room managers when dealing with the idiosyncrasies of individual customers or not is not as important as their basic understanding that quality can be achieved through systematic observations and measurements, the development and implementation of standardized procedures, proper training and supervision.

CHAPTER 9

Implementing Quality Management Programs

When you complete this chapter, you should be able to:

- Define TQM and explain its processes.
- Describe the first step necessary to implement a TQM strategy in management.
- Describe the role of upper management in the TQM process.
- Describe reasons why it may not be possible to integrate TQM into all operations.
- Write a mission statement for a business, including a commitment to the TQM strategies.
- Describe the rationale for involving middle management in the decision to implement a TQM plan.
- Describe the function of quality control teams.
- Describe some of the steps needed to properly train staffs for TQM implementation.
- Explain how to select the first processes that need assessment under the new TQM guidelines.
- Describe steps to ascertain the customer's perception of quality.

CHANGES IN QUALITY FOOD SERVICE

The perception of quality and value in food service is constantly changing; therefore, management's ability to meet those standards is constantly challenged. The chef manager can stay competitive by recognizing the need repeatedly to evaluate production and service processes in order to keep pace with customers' changing attitudes about quality and value.

The classical standard of food service quality was determined by how much money patrons wanted to spend for their dining experience. When only the ultra wealthy dined away from home, quality was easy to establish by using only the most expensive and most exotic foods available. Neither price nor speed of service were considerations; only extravagance and uniqueness of food ingredients and preparations defined quality.

When Escoffier and Ritz began their "new wave" of food service and lodging strategies, and invited the general public into their hotels to dine, those quality factors had already changed. Consistency of food preparation and presentation and speed of service became standards of quality.

Escoffier's brigade system and his commitment to establishing standardized recipes and procedures guaranteed consistency in food and service. Speed of the service also improved with the new organizational structure and the training of cooks to perform specific tasks. Ritz's commitment to pleasing the customer in the dining room complemented what Escoffier was doing in the kitchen. Together they created an atmosphere of ideal hospitality service for their patrons. This ideal reigned in kitchens around the world for many decades.

World War I, the American Depression and World War II each in turn had a lasting effect on the state of world hospitality services. Among the rebuilding of world cities and the restructuring of economies, there emerged a larger and stronger middle class of people who soon looked to share in the services offered by the hospitality industry. While the ultra wealthy still clung to their private clubs and exorbitant hotels for the luxuries they afforded, the new class of citizens began to make their own demands on products and services that operators could not ignore. Many operators were challenged to change their policies, menus, and even prices to attract these new customers and keep their dining rooms and hotel beds full.

There was a surge of new restaurant and hotel openings to meet the demand for the increased business in the post–World War II era. With competition on the rise, consistency and speed gained greater importance in defining quality.

Customer loyalty, defined by the frequency with which patrons choose to eat at a particular establishment, was easier to nurture when there were only a few restaurants and hotels around. The more choices a customer has, the more difficult it is to garner the same levels of loyalty. Operators have to discover new ways to attract customers to their doors and to keep them coming back.

Competition offers many choices for consumers and consumers have learned to use this to their advantage. Customers are more demanding of quality and value than ever before and are not afraid to speak out. In hospitality, the adage "the customer is always right" has never before been so hard to follow.

Competition, high employee turnover, and demanding customers fuel decisions to tighten up on operational controls while at the same time expanding customer services. Lines of authority emanating from the executive chef on down are being tested on a daily basis. Specific realms of responsibilities with performances measured on abstract values like food and labor cost percents have become suspect in light of down-sized organizational structures and computerized accounting systems.

Managers are learning to be flexible in their management styles and versatile in the products delivered in order to stay competitive. Success is achieved by aggressive operators who assess consumer needs, predict future trends, assess processes and implement changes that may affect the very foundations of their businesses. Operators who are not willing to change struggle to survive.

Food and other hospitality services have heretofore been measured purely by the bottom line. The food and labor cost percents, guest check averages and customer turnover ratios had taken priority in the decision making process. Consistency of service had been the number one underlining standard of quality. An entire fast food industry had spun off from a perceived need for speed and consistency of product with "acceptable" quality. But acceptable to whom? is the real question. At another extreme, managers of "white tablecloth" restaurants staked their companies' reputations on the service given at the table. These managers believed that two or three servers per table gave quality service simply by the volume of service. But was this an accurate assumption? Service was being measured by quantity, not necessarily by quality.

Some kitchen managers and chefs share the same notion: The more people you have behind the production line, the more consistently you can predict the outcomes. What this portrays is a compromise fostered by a lack of quality trained employees. Managers guided by this belief think they can protect consistency in production by creating simple tasks using convenience products, and by over-staffing the production lines. The more hands you have contributing to the same tasks, the less likely something might go wrong or be neglected.

Although prevalent in hospitality, this management style does not address the real issues of motivation, teamwork and leadership. In some cases, over-staffing can contribute to the apathy and carelessness it tries to avoid.

The greatest challenge facing managers in the food service/hospitality industry is learning to deal with the diversity of their staffs and to lead an otherwise dissimilar group toward common quality goals. While they may have great technical skills, many chefs and managers have little or no training in people skills to help them achieve this goal. This deficit can be overcome with education, practice and patience.

For many untrained managers, it is easier to deal with people the way they deal with inanimate objects, with concrete sequential precision, but they soon find out this does not work. People need more care and nurturing, and less discipline and precision, to be effective workers. Dissonance between management and employees can result when human issues are ignored. The consequences are felt by employees, management and customers alike.

Employees come from many backgrounds and experiences and are asked to produce an acceptable product in a quick and efficient process. It is the job of management to define those standards and motivate their employees consistently to meet them. Unfortunately, management often settles for inferior products for the sake of speed and cost-cutting measures. Quality has, in some cases, become a pliable standard.

Modern chef managers cannot afford to be complacent if they want to be successful at their craft.

A COLLECTIVE VIEW

The unifying philosophies of Shewhart, Deming, Juran, Crosby, Ishikawa and Feigenbaum—which constitute the Total Quality Management (TQM) movement in business—can and should be adopted by service industries as well as manufacturing industries. Here are a few key points that all of these quality engineers agree on:

1. Let the customer set the standard.
2. Examine the processes.
3. Get the workers to join in the decision-making processes.
4. Chart information to look for trends.
5. Choose one problem at a time to investigate.
6. Apply changes in controlled settings and measure results.
7. Start all over again.

Owners and managers in the food service and hospitality industry need to consider adopting these key points for their workplaces. Customers and workers are more demanding today than ever about their needs and personal wants. Businesses, manufacturing or service oriented, need to concentrate their management efforts on customers and workers first, and product success will be almost guaranteed.

Food service and hospitality businesses must actively seek customer input and conduct real research into dining and lodging trends within their market. Satisfying the customer—especially in the hospitality industry, which relies heavily on word-of-mouth advertisement—is the best guarantee for consistent business and steady growth.

The main point of TQM is shared by all the gurus of innovative management styles: Quality improvement is a continuous project. It's like painting a bridge or resurfacing a road—when you finish, it's time to start all over again. This is especially true in the service industries, which are so directly affected by the changes in customer needs and wants, and where products, value and quality are all evolutionary concepts. Therefore, even if you were accomplishing everything perfectly and had Zero Defects in your particular products or services, you would still need to change in order to keep up with changing customer demand and improved technologies.

This philosophy of management takes into account the diversity of the workplace, the complexity of the job, and the demands of the customer when planning changes. Owners and managers must be willing to change even the fabric of their management styles in order to be successful in the modern business arena.

In a busy work environment where many things are going on at the same time, it is better to concentrate investigative and corrective measures on one problem at a time. Decide a set of problems to be worked on, then prioritize those problems, but work on one at a time. Once that problem is fixed, it will stay fixed for a long time. You are not just putting out fires; you are helping to prevent future fires as well.

TQM

Total Quality Management is a simple three-word phrase that depicts a complete philosophy of management. Each word represents a complete set of ideologies that, when combined, become the foundation for an aggressive plan to assess and improve quality production and services.

The word *total* reflects the tenets that everyone in the organization plays a role in the success of the business: management, employees, and consumers. *Quality* reflects the edict that the customer represents the market and therefore sets the standards by which quality is measured. This is a shift in the definition of quality standards from the supplier to the buyer. Once, classical quality standards were set by management and the professionals who produced the products; the customer was expected to accept these standards as quality. *Management* supplies the leadership and direction that the organization needs to set goals and the parameters within which to meet those goals. Employees are the means by which management can transform their goals into productivity and efficiency. Consumers define quality, and by virtue of their patronage, are the measurement of the organization's ability to meet those standards.

TQM asks the customer to define quality and challenges the employee and manager to meet their standards. Management reflects that TQM is a process of review, controlled studies and validation. TQM is not a system of management, but a philosophy that analyzes processes in a continual and cyclical fashion.

THE FIRST STEPS

There is a series of steps that must be taken in order to fully adopt a TQM philosophy of management. Every facet of the operation will be challenged and tested, and every person will have a new role to play. The success of TQM will be determined by the level of commitment and measured through increased efficiency and teamwork.

The first step is to obtain commitment from senior management to proceed with the strategies and practices of TQM. In a successful program, senior managers will have an integral role to play, from approving the costs associated with initiating and protecting the process to giving direction, guidance and counsel.

Inevitably, there will be costs associated with the implementation of the quality control processes that senior management will have to approve. These costs produce no immediate profits, but must be considered investments for the future.

The cost of improved quality includes the cost of training and of product used during testing and evaluation. The cost of allowing workers and managers time away from production and service to review processes and test for quality must also be approved and defended. Unfortunately, in shrinking budgets, the cost of labor is usually the first item managers look to for reduction. When a TQM process is established, labor cost must be protected through good and lean times.

Senior management must take on the responsibility of leading the quality control teams; it is their vision and inspiration that workers will look to for guidance. Senior management defines the mission of the business, and ultimately makes the decisions to change or evolve that mission to meet changing consumer demand. They will become the steering committee from which guidance and evaluation for the quality control teams will come.

The second step is to measure the organization's readiness to begin the TQM process. To initiate a TQM process while the organization itself is unstable will doom the effort from the beginning.

Once upper management has committed to the process and the cost associated with it, then the stability of management must also be assessed. Is there likelihood that management will remain in place? If TQM is promoted as a last chance for management to succeed, then the likelihood is that there will not be enough time to show success, and management will change. If the organization is targeted for sale or restructuring, then it is not a good time to begin a process that, by definition, must be continuous. Also, if there is some looming crisis, such as shrinking markets, intensified competition, or a possible total change of the organization's market and therefore its mission, then it is best to hold off implementing TQM until the organization has returned to normal operation. TQM is not a quick fix or an immediate answer to shrinking profits; rather, it is a long-term commitment to quality prediction and control.

The next major step is to define a new company mission statement that clearly places the emphasis on TQM and the quality controls that implementation of the process will dictate. It will no longer be adequate to have a mission statement that seeks only profits and a share of the market. Those organizations based solely on profits and market share will continue to be satisfied as long as customers keep coming in the door. A mission statement centered around the concepts of TQM will never truly be satisfied, but will always strive for more customers and a more loyal customer base.

Let's examine closely the TQM based mission statement proposed in Chapter 5:

> To provide the highest quality food service that meets the time and value demands of our market. To create and maintain a quality workplace for our employees and managers.

Measurements that the mission is achieved include:

- Increase in the number of customers for every meal period offered
- Increase in the number of repeat customers
- A balanced menu mix, where all items are ordered at a regular rate
- Employee turnover decreased because of a rise in employee morale

INVOLVING MIDDLE MANAGERS

Depending on the complexity of the organization (see Chapter 3), middle management can be defined as the sous chefs, line chefs, expediter, purchasing agent, dining room manager and personnel manager. In many food service operations, the chef has the purchasing and personnel responsibilities. In these cases, involvement of the accounting officers may also be necessary for the TQM process to work.

Involving middle management in the TQM planning stages will assure its success. These are the people who are accountable for production and service, and are the direct links of communication to the line cooks, prep cooks, warewashers and service staff. In manufacturing businesses, these workers are called line workers. Enabling middle managers to have an active role in planning and executing the TQM process will give them partial ownership of the newly formed mission statement. The people they supervise are the direct links between management and the customer. No matter how committed the upper management is to quality control and management, without a strong connecting link to the workers who perform the duties and serve the customers, the message will not be carried through and TQM cannot be achieved.

Some middle managers may not be able to comprehend or appreciate the values of the TQM process. You may have to perform a few immediate quality control cycles to demonstrate the benefits of this new program. Choose the processes that affect the middle managers directly, like purchasing, staffing or menu planning. When it is demonstrated that the TQM process will directly benefit the quality of the work environment and, consequently, the quality of the products and services, then middle managers will be more likely to accept the changes in attitude and procedures dictated by the TQM process.

ORGANIZING FOR TQM

Traditional organizational structures will have to change before implementing TQM processes into the work environment. The hierarchical approach to management will have to be modified to allow middle managers and line workers a share in the decision-making and evaluative processes that will ensure TQM's success.

Upper management, including the executive chef, executive sous chef, general manager, and shift managers, will take on the role of the Quality Council. They will act as the steering mechanism that will guide the rest of the process. They are also the people who will evaluate the conclusions drawn from an investigation of the processes, and who will put the results into action. Noting upper managers as part of the Quality Council on the organizational chart will provide assurances to middle managers and line workers that the organization itself is dedicated to the new processes being proposed and to the long-term commitment that is needed to see it succeed. Without this, many will not be willing to make the commitments necessary to see the processes through.

Middle managers should be renamed as Quality Improvement Team Leaders, where the emphasis is placed on leadership as opposed to supervision. The teams themselves, comprising representatives from various organizational departments, will test and evaluate the processes. In this way, both stand-alone and cross-functional processes can be tested and measured by the same team of people. Workers will learn to appreciate the relationship of each department to the organization as a whole. Workers should be willing to make suggestions regarding all organizational functions, even those outside their area of expertise.

Not everyone on the staff will be willing to take part in the quality improvement system. These are the workers whose motivations are short-term oriented and who may not have a commitment to the organization as a whole. This by itself does not make them bad employees; they are simply motivated by other factors that may be too big for them to conquer. You cannot force people to act with positive and motivated behaviors. All organizations have workers who are interested only in a paycheck and the security of going to work every day. This may be the only motivation they need to function efficiently and get the job done. In time, they will either learn the effectiveness of the team's efforts and decide to take part or, at the least, they may accept the results of the team's studies and recommendations, and become the workers to incorporate the changes. If these workers do not accept the positive atmosphere that TQM processes foster, then after an extended time, they may decide to leave the organization or be forced to leave because of peer pressure.

TRAINING FOR QUALITY

Training is essential to a successful implementation of the TQM process. Traditional methods of production and service will be challenged and workers' job descriptions will be changed to meet the new guidelines of quality improvement. Whenever change is imminent, then training must be initiated to alleviate all of the human frustrations associated with change.

Training for TQM should include:

- An explanation of the change in the organization's mission and upper management's commitment to the new focus on quality, not quantity
- An explanation of the need for improvement as a continual and necessary function of aggressive businesses; that it is not to fix problems, but to promote benefits
- Development of a common language for addressing quality, testing and assessment issues, in many cases redefining already accepted definitions
- An explanation of the process of quality improvement, including the assignment of upper management to the Quality Council with their function defined, middle management to Quality Improvement Leaders and their new roles and the assignment of each participating worker to their own Quality Team
- Clarification of everyone's responsibilities and the way the process will proceed
- Provision of the tools workers need to manage the quality of their work, including the authority to make their own decisions regarding quality issues

Training, in itself, is a process that needs to be tested, evaluated, and redone given new information. Like all other processes, training must also be revisited with follow-up training sessions that can take advantage of total organizational input.

WHERE TO BEGIN BUILDING QUALITY

Once you have decided the organization's strength and commitment, developed a new organizational structure, involved middle management in the process, and begun training the staff, then you have to decide what processes need to be assessed first in a series of evaluations and experimentations. The Quality Council will most likely identify the first series of processes that need to be assessed. As the process of assessment begins, the Quality Teams will be able to prioritize other processes until the whole organization is dissected into tangible and achievable goals.

The first plans should be targeted to the processes that will produce a great amount of action for the organization as a whole. These should address system-wide problems which will affect all facets of the organization. By starting with these organizationally global issues, every person in the organization can have input, become part of the testing group and realize the first benefits of the new strategy.

One initial task could be to identify the customer and begin to define the customer's perception of quality. In this way, upper and middle management, dining room and kitchen staffs, and the customers themselves become involved in the assessment process. Senior management will identify the sought after customer group by virtue of the restaurant concept, design and service style. Middle management will analyze the customer demographics that currently exist by conducting customer surveys aimed at collecting quality, value and timing standards. Dining room staff can begin to assess the customer's level of acceptance to current standards of quality, while the kitchen staff can assess the customer's perception of the menu and the food itself by analyzing the categories of sales and the amount of food that is returned unconsumed or for re-cooking or exchange. The customers will automatically be involved and will soon realize that quality, as they define it, has become top priority.

Let's examine how the HACCP program for food safety, which we discussed as a Zero Defects program, embodies many of TQM's guidelines and strategies.

As an applied sanitation inspection system, HACCP asks operators to assess the safe handling of food during its receipt, storage, preparation and service, that is, the flow of goods. At each point that food is handled or stored, there exist potential hazards that could lead to product contamination. Broken packages, inadequate temperature control, improper thawing techniques and interrupted cooking times are all examples of potential hazards that could affect the wholesomeness of foods. Critical control points are those specific times and events where these hazards become possible and where proper intervention could assure safe handling practices. HACCP is a system of analysis that asks operators to assess the safe handling of specific foods through the flow of goods to prevent these types of hazards from occurring.

A HACCP worksheet, shown in Figure 9–1, is designed to offer guidance to food handlers when confronted with potential hazards or contamination.

**Hazard Analysis Critical Control Point
Product Worksheet**

Recipe name _____

Potentially hazardous ingredients_____

Procedure/operation	Temp.	Time begin/end	Comments

Critical control points: Record observations or directions

State at delivery	Storage	Thaw
Preparation	**Cooking method**	**Hold for service**
Time to service	**Cooling procedures**	**Cold storage**

Reheating	

Date of report _____

Name of preparer _____

FIGURE 9–1   HACCP Worksheet

Only one specific food item at a time can be evaluated for safe practices, since hazards may change depending on the food and the food application being studied. Crabmeat used for crabmeat cocktail, for example, has a slightly different set of potential hazards than crabmeat used for crab soup.

Temperature readings are taken during each critical control point because maintaining safe food temperatures (below 41°F or above 135°F) is one of the most effective ways of assuring food safety. Then observations and specific instructions can be given for each critical control point to assure that proper handling takes place.

Both potentially hazardous foods (foods containing animal proteins) and nonhazardous foods should have HACCP worksheets developed for their protection. Once this is done, quality assurance is given a higher percentage of predictability.

With the new Total Quality Management plan in effect, well defined and integrated into the organization, the cycle of quality planning, improving and management will have begun. By initiating the first process assessments, everyone will get involved in the evolution of the organization. Soon, a status quo operation can become a vibrant community based on quality products and service with a culture based on cooperation and dedication to success.

Section 3

MANAGEMENT AND SUPERVISION

Chapter 10
Personnel Management

Chapter 11
The Chef Supervisor

Chapter 12
Communication

Chapter 13
Managing Diversity

Building a quality work environment is key to quality food production and service. The greater the level of efficiency and teamwork in the staff, the greater the chance to predict quality outcomes. It is the predictability of quality that defines consistency, and the consistency that builds business.

Management and supervision take on a new light in the wake of Total Quality Management. No longer isolated to control and discipline issues, management and supervision must now address issues like team building, motivation and diversity in the workplace. Where machines are made of bolts, chains and gears, care and maintenance are critical. In food service and hospitality where people are the tools and the parts that keep the machine working, care and maintenance on the human plane is also critical to the success of the operation.

Managing staffs and supervising production are processes that TQM asks us to question, test and verify. Quality in the workplace is defined by the employees, for they are a company's internal customers.

CHAPTER 10

Personnel Management

When you complete this chapter, you should be able to:

- Describe the importance of the worker to the success of the operation.
- Describe the role of formalized education to worker preparedness.
- List some of the key factors that people search for when applying for new jobs.
- Explain the benefits of hiring from within.
- Explain the relevance of culinary/hospitality schools and professional associations when seeking new employees.
- Describe the makeup of the perfect classified ad.
- Describe the processes and importance of organized orientation and training.
- Describe what constitutes a Total Quality Culture.
- Define empowerment and enabling in respect to personnel management.

DISCOVERING THE SOCIAL WORKPLACE

General Electric, already a major manufacturer of light bulbs in 1920, wanted to prove that better illumination of the workplace actually improved productivity in an attempt to sell more light bulbs, especially to major corporations. In cooperation with the Bell Labs Western Electric Hawthorne plant located in Cicero, Illinois, one of GE's biggest customers at that time, GE funded the National Research Council (NRC) of the National Academy of Sciences to conduct an impartial study to determine if there were any effect of lighting on productivity. This was during the time that Joseph Juran worked for the Hawthorne plant. Beginning with this early test, the Hawthorne Experiments were a series of studies on worker productivity beginning in 1924 and ceasing in 1932.

Illumination Studies, 1924–1927

The first experiment was conducted by the NRC with engineers from MIT (the Massachusetts Institute of Technology), who actually performed the activities. The study would end just three years later with the NRC abandoning the project because of a lack of positive findings.

As commissioned, the group examined the relationship between light intensity and worker efficiency. The hypothesis was that greater illumination would yield higher productivity. Two work groups of female employees were selected for control and for experimental groups. By comparing the changes in worker productivity by manipulating lighting in the experimental group with the production of the control group, the researchers could validate and measure the impact of lighting on productivity. The study, however, failed to find any simple relationship as poor lighting and improved lighting seemed to increase productivity. Indeed, in the final stage, when the group pretended to increase lighting, the worker group reported higher satisfaction.

The preliminary findings were that behavior is not merely physiological but also psychological. This was a break with the Scientific Management theories that Frederick Taylor propounded which identified work productivity as "mechanical," and led to the decision to learn more about worker behavior. George Pennock, Western Electric's superintendent of inspection at that time, suggested that the reason for increased worker productivity was simply that the researchers interacted with the employees; this was the first time any one had shown an interest in the workers. Basically, the workers were trying to please the researchers by continuing to increase their output and report satisfaction in the study, no matter what the intervention was. Later, the phenomenon of a researcher corrupting an experiment simply by his presence would be termed the Hawthorne effect.

Relay Assembly Test Room Experiments, 1927–1929

When the NCR left the project in 1927, Western Electric continued the project, drawing on support from Harvard researchers including Dr. George Elton Mayo. Mayo and his colleagues established an experimental group of five young women from the Relay Assembly room of the plant for the next phase of productivity experiments. The experiments involved the manipulation of a number of factors, to include pay incentives, length of workday and workweek, and use of rest periods, to measure impact on productivity and fatigue. Again, the relationship among pay, incentives, rest and working hours seemed to have little effect on productivity, even when the original, more demanding conditions were re-implemented.

Five Women at Work at the Hawthorne Works in Chicago

Mica-Splitting Test Group, 1928–1930

Disturbed by the inconclusive evidence that rewards and incentives improved worker performance, a second experiment was conducted to look only at this relationship using workers in the Mica-Splitting Room. In his experiment, the workers' piece wages were held constant while work conditions were varied. Productivity increased by about 15 percent. The researchers concluded that productivity was affected by non-pay considerations. Members of the research team began to develop the theory that social dynamics were the basis of worker performance.

Plant-wide Interview Program, 1928–1931

As early findings indicated that concern for workers and willingness to listen affected productivity, Western Electric implemented a plant-wide survey of employees to record their concerns and grievances. From 1928 to 1930, 21,000 employees were interviewed. This data would support the research of the Harvard team for years and lead them to conclude that work improved when supervisors began to pay attention to employees, that work takes place in a social context in which work and non-work considerations are important and that norms and groups matter to workers.

Bank Wiring Observation Group, 1931–1932

The final Hawthorne experiment was conducted studying 14 male workers assigned to the Bank Wiring factory. The objective was to study the dynamics of the group when incentive pay was introduced. The finding was that nothing happened. The work group had established a work norm, a shared expectation about how much work should be performed in a day and stuck to it, regardless of pay. The conclusion: Informal groups operate in the work environment to manage behavior.

Importance of the Hawthorne Plant Studies

Despite modern criticism that the research was flawed and that incentives played a larger role in improving worker productivity than the Hawthorne plant researchers concluded, these studies changed the landscape of management from Taylor's engineering approach to a social sciences approach. Worker productivity would, henceforth, be interpreted predominately in the United States in terms of social group dynamics, motivation, leadership and human relations. The practice of management could not be the aloof technician of Taylor's Scientific Management, designing the job, selecting and training the "right" worker, and rewarding for performance. The manager was an immediate part of the social system in which work was performed, responsible for leading, motivating, communicating and designing the social milieu in which work takes place.

Mayo's reporting of the Hawthorne experiments became the most influential in that he laid out a programmatic interpretation, which would be called the Human Relations approach to management that dominated management thinking until the 1950s. Mayo's views lead to the interpretation of manager as a leader supported by knowledge and skills to build social cooperation.

MAYO'S CONCLUSIONS

Mayo organized his findings into eight general concepts of employee motivation:

1. Work is a group activity
2. The social world of the adult is primarily patterned about work activity.

3. The need for recognition, security and a sense of belonging is more important in determining worker morale and productivity than the physical conditions under which they work.

4. A complaint is not necessarily an objective behavior; it is commonly a symptom manifesting disturbance of an individual's social status.

5. The worker is a person whose attitudes and effectiveness are conditioned by social demands from both inside and outside the work environment.

6. Informal groups within the working environment exercise strong social controls over the work habits and attitudes of the individual worker.

7. The change from an established society in the home to an adaptive society in the work environment resulting from the use of new techniques tends generally to disrupt the social organization.

8. Group collaboration does not occur by accident; it must be planned and developed. If group collaboration is achieved, the human relations within the work environment may reach a cohesion which resists the disrupting effects of adaptive society.

Mayo's conclusions led to many new management theories on human productivity and the social environment of workers that were later expounded by motivation theorists Abraham Maslow, Frederick Hertzberg and Douglas McGreggor.

A Modern Application

Many of America's corporations and businesses came to agree that the key to their success lay with its workers. They are the mechanics of production and the lifeblood of the organization. With a properly selected, trained and motivated work force, businesses can place themselves in a strategic position to succeed in a busy marketplace; without one, the business can be consumed by the competition.

Personnel management is a critical aspect of quality management. Even well planned quality improvement programs cannot meet their goals without a quality work force, including well directed supervisors and managers and highly motivated, dedicated employees. The success of a business is dependent on the strength and stability of its people.

Personnel management is a foreign concept for a lot of chefs because of their lack of management education. Some chefs and restaurant managers take employees for granted and react to them in the simplest of terms. The management of personnel is a complicated task and one that takes a great deal of time, energy and planning to achieve.

There are no easy resolutions to the difficulties encountered in personnel management. It is a complicated task that takes planning, time and energy to accomplish. The chef manager who focuses time and energies on improving the workplace for employees and makes it a special project to consciously recruit, train and utilize skilled employees to their maximum potential will also be the one to retain employees and build a quality team.

To build this strength and plan for stability requires an aggressive set of policies and procedures that focus on the worker, the team and the work environment. Each must be cultivated and nourished in order for the organization as a whole to work efficiently, with a consistently high level of quality.

THE WORKER

Attracting and keeping good workers is one of the most difficult jobs for food service managers. There is so much competition in the marketplace, and so few trained and educated potential employees, that the margin for job placement is almost always stretched to the limits. Downsizing that occurs in the hospitality industry is not because of advancing technology or sliding profits, as in other industries, but because there are simply not enough quality trained employees to go around.

Culinary education is itself a big business today. There are hundreds of post-secondary culinary programs around the country, graduating thousands of new workers for the hospitality and food service industry. The Culinary Institute of America, Johnson & Wales University, California Culinary Academy, Pennsylvania Culinary, The Art Institutes, Le Cordon Bleu Schools and dozens of other high profile culinary schools have built great reputations preparing a diverse student population for various career paths in the food service sector. These graduates are sought after by the most aggressive food service operations. Their solid training in the foundations of cooking, baking and kitchen management, and their commitment to building their career in food service, make them qualified and motivated employees. In recruiting, it is important to build a relationship with the culinary schools that will feed you new employees with a high caliber of skills and knowledge.

There is an untold number of individuals who studied on the job all their lives. With little or no formal education, their classroom has been the working kitchens and the busy dining rooms of restaurants and hotels around the world. These are tried and proven veterans of the industry. Their solid work ethic and varied experience make them coveted candidates for many new and existing positions.

However, the problem still remains that there are not enough culinary school graduates or veteran food service and hospitality employees to fill the vacancies in highlevel culinary and hospitality positions. Workers just starting to develop careers in food service and hospitality will take years to achieve the same level of skill and knowledge as culinary and hospitality school graduates or those industry-trained professionals. The fast growth of the industry is outpacing the growth of the employee market.

Attracting experienced workers continues to be a problem for all levels of food service and hospitality operations around the country. Keeping good employees has become a competitive business. Managers have to develop an aggressive plan to recruit and keep good employees.

Employees have many needs and desires when searching for new positions in the industry. Money is one issue; job security, upward mobility and a positive working environment are also key factors that can influence a prospective employee's decision to accept or turn down a job.

RECRUITING STRATEGIES

There are many ways to solicit applications for new and existing jobs. Everything from placing a sign in the window to soliciting the help of national placement firms (commonly called headhunters) can produce a good supply of applications, but the difficult job is in interviewing and selecting the right candidate for the right job. Your candidates must have all the skills and knowledge necessary to perform the job you've posted. They must be able to become a team player, handle stress, be honest and must be willing to make a commitment to you and your organization. If not, they won't be able to do the job they were hired for. They'll alienate themselves from the rest of the staff, they won't be able to keep up with the production, they'll steal, or they'll be lazy and then you'll just have to start over and do it all again. It's better to take your time, plan the steps you need to take and be discriminating about the people you hire.

Hire from Within

Existing workers should always be given the first chance to apply for open positions. A healthy job environment allows workers to advance within the same organization when they are ready to make a change. Otherwise, they may seek to advance somewhere else. Never force a worker to accept a different position on a permanent basis. They should be encouraged to do so, but if they're not ready for the challenge, they may soon lose their ambition, do a poor job, and leave because of discontentment.

Word of mouth is the best way to recruit new people for your team. Workers you already have should be encouraged to recommend friends and acquaintances for new positions. Your workers understand the complexities of your particular operation and the intricacies of the jobs that need to be filled. Being in the food service and hospitality business, your workers are likely to know other people who work in the industry—people who may be looking for a change from their place of work. It would be to their advantage to recommend people whom they feel will do a good job, work hard and be dedicated. They will not recommend people whom they think will not do good work, for it would be a reflection on them to the people doing the hiring.

Culinary and Hospitality Schools

Graduates and current students of local culinary and hospitality programs have made a time and financial commitment to working in the industry by virtue of having attended a post-secondary institution. They are likely to have a good foundation in basic skills and knowledge and to be willing to learn more and teach others what they know. With dedication and a foundation in basic skills and knowledge, they become the best candidates for new and existing positions.

Build a relationship with local schools and you will have the best chances over all of your competitors for the best graduates and students. Relationships can be fostered by allowing students to complete their internships or externships in your operation. Many schools required internship or externship, a curriculum-based experience that ties work experience to education, and need to solidify sites for their students to gain this valuable experience. By allowing student interns and externs into your operation, you've opened the door for a continued supply of seasonal workers (since these positions are usually short term) and workers to fill temporary vacancies. It is also a great way to test out potential new workers without making a large financial and operational commitment to them.

These relationships can further be enhanced by participating in a culinary and hospitality school's industry advisory committee. Schools seek industry professionals to help guide their curriculum development and assess the abilities of their students and graduates. If you play an active role in the school's own development, it will be to their advantage to do likewise for you and help place the most prepared students and graduates in your place of business.

Professional Associations

Membership and participation in professional organizations can also help in the recruiting effort. The American Culinary Federation (ACF), National Restaurant Association (NRA), and the International Association of Culinary Professionals (IACP) are all national associations of professional food service and hospitality workers. Each national group has many smaller local subgroups, or chapters, that are accessible to most chefs and restaurant managers. Joining these associations and participating in their meetings and activities will introduce you to many qualified people already proven in the workplace. Whether you are looking for a job yourself or recruiting people for your operation, these contacts can turn into job leads or employee candidates for your consideration.

Classified Ads and Placement Firms

Before placing any ad in the paper or seeking the help of placement firms to fill vacant and new positions, you must have a clear picture of the position that needs filling and the qualifications of the workers needed to do the job. Simple advertisements and window signs that say Help Wanted will generate a lot of leads, but unqualified leads. Unqualified leads are those that do not meet the minimum requirements of the job. While easy to obtain, they take time to review and can get more complicated in the interview sessions. In the end, you shuffle through dozens, even hundreds, of inappropriate applications, which is time consuming, frustrating and unproductive. A lot of operators simply hire the best of these unqualified applicants to fill the position and hope for the best. Unfortunately, hope does not make good workers; it is merely a temporary fix that will ultimately result in continued turnover of workers.

Job postings should be concise but descriptive of the needs and required qualifications. They should include:

- Title for the position
- Skills necessary for the position
- Experience requirements
- A description of part-time versus full-time positions
- A description of the hours or days that the worker will be expected to work: day shift, evening shift or weekend work
- A suggested range of pay, hourly or salaried
- A description of the operation itself

Advertisements for jobs need to be descriptive and appealing to potential employees. The descriptions allow the potential candidates to match their skills and experiences to the jobs that will best suit them and their career goals. They also allow the person reviewing applications to qualify them and quickly reject the ones that do not meet the needs of the job. To make an advertisement appealing, you need to use energized phrases like "expanding operation needs qualified persons seeking positive working environment and challenging position with the opportunity for advancement." The advertisement sells the job to potential candidates, who are undoubtedly wading through dozens of other job leads. A longer descriptive ad may be more expensive, but if it attracts the right applicants the first time, it is well worth the investment.

Internet Job Banks

In the twenty-first century one of the most popular places to look for jobs in all occupations, including hospitality and food service, is on the Internet. Technology has supplied operators and job seekers with vast numbers of opportunities to put employees and employers together through the vastness of the world wide Web.

Many companies offer their own Web sites, which are great places to host their own private job banks. Marriott, Hyatt Hotels, Sodexho, Ritz-Carlton, Ruth's Chris Steakhouse, Darden and just about every other major hotel chain and restaurant group have links on their home Web pages for prospective employees, both hourly and managerial, to search for job openings and apply on line. If you know the place you want to work, start looking there.

For those who are not sure of where they would like to work, and for companies who want to promote their job openings to a larger audience, then there is a slew of job banks to utilize. Careerbuilders.com, hcareers.com, foodservice.com and the mega site Monster.com are some of the more popular sites to use. These are great both for the employer seeking candidates and employees seeking jobs.

Internet job banks have become very sophisticated mechanisms, offering a host of services for both the employer and the prospective employee. Take a look at the American Culinary Federation's Career Center (found on the ACF Web page, www.acfchefs.org) to see how intricate job management has become. Here are the services offered both for employers and the many cooks and chefs who are looking for their next opportunity to succeed in business:

1. Post an anonymous résumé
2. View résumés
3. View jobs
4. Post a job
5. Receive job alerts that match your criteria
6. On-line interaction between prospective employer and employees
7. Manage your search
8. Store résumés and cover letters

These interactive job sites have become a great tool in recruiting and building a quality team of employees. While it opens the door for anyone to apply, it is fairly easy to pre-qualify applicants through the use of default parameters describing education, experience and/or certification requirements. But what it does the most is give both the employer and the prospective employee the largest selection of opportunities and refreshes itself at a click.

Qualifying Applications

Whether you ask for résumés to be mailed in or have people stop by to fill out applications, you can qualify potential employees based on whether or not they've met your basic criteria. Is their résumé or application completely filled out? Did they answer all of the questions and supply all the relevant information? Résumés and applications that are not comprehensive or neatly written are a clear indication of the person's inappropriate work ethic and poor work habits. While properly constructed résumés and neatly filled-in applications do not guarantee great employees, they do show some commitment to doing the job well, which can be translated into good performance on the job.

Résumés and applications that do not describe appropriate work experience and/or school requirements for a job can be discarded. The people who presented them did not even do the basic homework of matching their skills and knowledge to your requirements, or they have arbitrarily circulated their résumés to a large number of prospective employers. In either case, they have not made a commitment to work for you, and even if hired, would be most likely to leave as soon as another opportunity opened up elsewhere.

Interviewing Techniques

Interviews can give prospective employers valuable insights into an applicant's work habits, ambitions and experience when properly organized and administered. While not a guarantee that workers will succeed, properly conducted interviews can expose the behavioral profile of candidates as well as verify technical competence.

Identifying human behavioral patterns in prospective employees is critical to the selection process. When adding a new employee to an already established team of workers, it is important that the new hire share the same work ethic and dedication to quality as everyone else. Behavioral traits such as timeliness, friendliness, being a team player and the ability to concentrate and follow instructions can be partially measured through the interview process.

Timeliness can be measured by first witnessing whether or not the candidate is on time for the interview. No matter what the excuse, a person showing up late for an interview is often displaying a behavioral pattern of lateness that a well organized team of workers cannot afford to have infiltrate their ranks.

Friendliness in an individual is often displayed before or after the actual interview. During the interview itself, people are always on their best behavior, which may manifest itself differently on the production line or service team. A more incisive observation can be made by the receptionist, host or hostess who first encountered the applicant before the interview actually started. How pleasant or unpleasant was the applicant toward these first level employees? Were they courteous and polite or abrupt and standoffish? Behaviors demonstrated outside of the interview room often give a clearer picture of a person's personality than any battery of questions or tests could measure.

When conducting the interview, have prescribed questions ready for each position advertised. The questions asked can often solicit more information about a prospective employee than simply their knowledge and abilities. Answers to complex and relevant questions often give hints to a person's ability to work as a team player, concentrate on specific problems, and follow instructions. Figure 10–1 is a sample list of relevant interview questions that might be asked prospective cooks.

Concise, accurate answers to a set of well thought out interview questions are a true measurement of specific knowledge. Likewise, long, undulating responses are often indicative of uncertainty and lack of confidence. Applicants should not hesitate when answering questions and should openly admit when they do not know an answer rather than guess or fumble with a response.

While the accuracy of the answers are important as a measure of specific knowledge, the way the answers are given can often be indicative of the applicant's personality traits and behavioral patterns. Teamwork, for example, can be partially measured by the applicant's referral or non-referral to other employees they've worked with when describing past work experiences. A person's ability to concentrate can be witnessed if and when their answers match the complexity and depth of the questions. For example, a question such as "Explain the process of mise en place" asks for more than just a definition of mise en place. It asks for a complete description of the processes that determine an effective mise en place system. Does the applicant give full, complex answers or short, nondescript responses?

The ability of prospective employees to follow instructions is often demonstrated by how thoroughly they answer interview questions. Thorough responses also demonstrate a person's ability to think quickly, problem-solve, and make quick, reasoned decisions. These are all important factors that can help predict a person's success on a dynamic team.

1. Explain the practice of mise en place.
2. What are the five mother sauces?
3. What is HACCP and how would you help to assure its effectiveness?
4. Explain how you could help protect food from cross-contamination.
5. What are your career goals? How do you plan to achieve them?
6. Explain the braising method.
7. How can you determine the freshness of fish? Shellfish?
8. What is most important to proper plate presentation: portions, colors, or textures of food?
9. How do you make hollandaise?
10. How do you help others work as a team?
11. What is your favorite dish to prepare?
12. Explain the process for making your favorite vegetable side dishes.
13. How do you handle customer complaints?
14. How will hiring you improve our staff?
15. Why are you interested in working in our restaurant?

FIGURE 10–1　Sample Interview Questions for the Position of Cook

Trial by Fire

The best way to witness whether a potential candidate has the skills and knowledge required to perform the job is to administer a skill test in your working kitchen. Before or after a shift, have the applicant perform some cooking, baking or management task under your direct supervision. A cooking task might be as simple as making an omelet or baking some bread. A management task might be to have them structure a seating chart based on your dining room configuration and your staff. These tasks should represent activities they would likely perform if hired, as a way of testing their abilities before making a job commitment to them.

Be careful not to test someone in an activity not related to the job they are applying for. This can be construed as a discriminating way not to hire certain types, or groups, of people. Tests must be related to the job being applied for and can be appropriate qualifiers in deciding to make the final job offer.

AFFIRMATIVE ACTION/EQUAL OPPORTUNITY EMPLOYER

For many years, discrimination against minorities has dominated the hiring practices of many industries, including the hospitality industry. African Americans and women, for example, have had difficult times finding gainful employment. While many companies would hire minorities for menial, low-paying jobs, promotions and equal pay were rarely part of the plan.

The twentieth century has witnessed other minorities trying desperately to succeed in American industries. Southern California and Texas have had an influx of Mexicans looking for jobs, and Florida has become a refuge for many Haitians and Cubans seeking a piece of the American dream. While it is important to hire only American citizens or legal aliens (foreigners with a legal immigration status), minorities can contribute significantly to the success of many operations.

The U.S. Department of Labor represents American interest in providing equal employment opportunities for all Americans. Under its jurisdiction, all companies are scrutinized for hiring practices that discriminate against minorities. Some larger companies that employ many workers, and all government agencies, are given specific hiring guidelines to use when hiring new employees. These guidelines are often in the form of quotas detailing that a predetermined percentage of employees must be represented by minorities.

Affirmative Action plans are structured to assure that minority employee quotas are met and maintained by the participating company. Affirmative action refers to a deliberate plan to seek out minority applicants and award jobs to minorities when experience and skill levels are comparable to those of non-minorities. A classified ad that states that a company is an Affirmative Action employer testifies to the company's commitment to developing an ethnically and culturally diverse work force.

The term Equal Opportunity Employer (EOE) refers to a company that awards jobs solely on the basis of experience, skills and knowledge without regard to ethnicity, cultural background, sex or age. This is clearly a non-discrimination announcement. Attaching an EOE statement to a classified ad helps encourage minorities to apply for jobs that they might otherwise not even consider.

With a shrinking work force, it is often critical for operators to receive many applications for open or new positions. The greater number of applications a company receives, the more likely it is that they can identify and hire the right applicant for the job. Companies that promote themselves as Affirmative Action/Equal Opportunity Employers (AA/EOE) are more likely to receive the multiple applications they need than those who withhold making such a statement.

Making AA/EOE claims does not protect companies from discrimination lawsuits. There must be a measurable accountability that the company is earnestly trying to meet the standards of equal employment opportunities. Not only are these practices morally sound, but they help protect companies from potentially expensive and image damaging law suits. Before making the final decision to hire, operators must take into consideration the diversity of their existing work force and do everything possible to encourage and protect a well balanced team of workers.

ORIENTATION AND TRAINING

Once you've gone through the extensive effort to seek, identify and hire the right candidate for the job, orientation and training are required to assure that the new employee can function efficiently and cooperatively in the new working environment. No matter how experienced or how highly educated a new employee is, there is need for orientation and training. Orientation and training are based on your specific operation and are likely to be considerably different from the new employee's past experiences and expectations.

Orientation begins with an introduction to the team. New employees should meet all supervisors, managers and the people they are most likely to work with. This can be accomplished at a weekly staff meeting or informally, as you tour the new person around the facility. Touring, however, often does not offer the chance to meet all the key employees, since they may not be on duty at the time of the tour. It is important to make the new employee feel comfortable in their new work environment, and the first step is recognizing the faces and names of the key staff.

An official orientation to the organizational structure and introductions to key workers and managers can help position new hires as effective and cooperative employees. The organizational structure discussed in Chapter 3, The Structure of Kitchen Organization, details the hierarchical line of authority under which the worker must perform and describes the positions responsible for the various functions of the operation. When new employees are introduced to a formalized organizational structure, they have a clear picture of their role in the total operation and the effects their position may have on others.

Orientation to the specific job description for the position is also a critical step in new employee training. Employees must know exactly what is expected of them in the execution of their duties in order to perform them well. Only with proper instruction and detailed information can workers be properly trained and evaluated.

A well written job description (Figure 10–2) describes the position thoroughly. It states who the immediate supervisor is and whom, if anyone, the

AAA Hotel and Conference Center Job Description

Position: Saucier/Prep Department, Kitchen

Reports to: Executive Chef

Supervises: Prep cooks on shift

Position purpose: To ensure the quality production of menu items and specials following the guidelines of the executive and sous chefs

Examples of duties:

- Communicate daily with the executive chef and sous chef to determine preparation priority, style and quantity
- Assure all items meet production and quality specifications and are ready on time
- Prepare all hot sauces and daily soups
- Prepare mise en place for sauté station
- Prepare all sautéed dishes and accompaniments for daily production
- Supervise prep cooks
- Prepare daily employee meals
- Perform other duties as requested by executive or sous chefs
- Perform the duties of quality control team leader for prep staff
- Report any equipment problems or product shortages to sous chef or executive chef

Other:

- Regular attendance based on posted schedules
- Regular attendance at staff meetings
- Schedules may change depending on business; communicate special schedule requests to executive chef utilizing the schedule request form

Grooming: All employees must maintain a neat, clean, and well groomed appearance. Checked pants, white chef's coat, and hard leather shoes are required. AAA Conference Center will supply hats, aprons and side towels.

Employee Signature	Date

FIGURE 10–2 Sample Job Description

position supervises. It also details specific job responsibilities, general employee policies and issues such as dress code and grooming. When new employees are given exact details about what is expected of them, it is easier for them to meet those expectations and perform to company standards. When little or no information is given, chaos can ensue.

Orientation to the facilities may seem insignificant and perfunctory, yet it is key to the successful transition from new hire to team member. New workers should be shown the whole establishment, starting outside the doors and ending in the store rooms and mechanical rooms. Only when the new hire can see the whole operation from the point of view of the owners and managers can that person be expected to participate fully in the growth plans and vision of the company.

Training can be divided into two major categories: skill training and team training. Each plays a significant role in the success of the new employee and the maintenance of the functioning team approach to quality planning and control.

Skill training may be more or less extensive based on the complexities of the job and the skills and experiences the new employee brings to the job. Usually it entails learning new recipes or procedures in food preparation or service that are unique to the establishment.

Training may begin in a classroom-like setting where managers and supervisors review recipes, menu descriptions, preparation tasks and procedures with the new employees. Many operators administer a written test to assure that new employees are ready to begin their new jobs. Starting new employees in their jobs before proper training will affect the quality of production and service until the new employee learns the proper ways or leaves because of discontentment. In these cases, the customer suffers and the existing staff is forced to work harder and longer hours to produce the required levels of production or service.

Involve current employees in the training process, but do not leave it totally up to them. It is important that managers and supervisors control the training process to ensure the proper induction of company philosophies on production and service quality. Involving existing employees in the training process, particularly your lead employees, will help solidify the team building strategies you have developed so far. Existing employees then feel that they have an active part in the success of the operation and will be more likely to accept the new employee as a member of the team.

Team training begins with the involvement of lead employees in the skill training programs. Introduce these employees as team captains and describe the makeup of the team and the involvement of each player in the performances of the job. Allow the lead employees to conduct the parts of the training session that directly affect them and the other existing employees. Have them direct the new employees to do some simple mock tasks that will be duplicated on the job later. Placing these lead employees in important roles under the direct supervision of management gives the new employee a better understanding of the relationship between supervisor and staff, team leader and team captain.

TOTAL QUALITY CULTURE (TQC)

Giving extra attention to the needs of the workers is clearly defended by Joe Batten, author of *Building a Total Quality Culture.* Batten specifically addresses the need and the means for bringing about cultural changes in the workplace that will have a positive effect on employee motivation, production, and retention.

According to Batten, there is a great need for personnel-oriented management. The human dynamics of organizations are growing factors to contend with and managers must be trained to deal with the transition.

Organizations should plan for leadership development from within the organization itself. Everyone can participate in leadership assertiveness training, with one central person—the manager—being the guide. Managers and employees can help plan production criteria and quality standards together. Since the decisions become collective, the results become more realistic and success has a greater guarantee.

To further build a quality work culture, Batten addresses issues like empowerment and enabling, which are strategically related to the philosophy of TQM. Through these modern concepts of personnel management, employees take on a larger share in the success or failure of the operation. They have more input into the decision-making process and can make quicker decisions at critical control points without seeking the advice of management.

Empowerment

In traditional management structures, all decisions are made by the managers, supervisors and owners. Workers are expected to follow directions with little feedback and no hesitation. TQM enhanced with TQC has turned this around, and enlightened managers now actively seek employee ideas and criticisms.

Empowerment is a phrase that describes giving authority (power) to employees to make their own decisions, to try their own ideas toward improving production and service, and to openly express their ideas, aspirations and dreams. If every member of the team feels that their opinions and ideas are given equal credence to those of management, they will be more willing to accept the changes that quality improvement prescribes.

Empowerment can be broad in scope and affect the whole operation, or be specific to the area of work that each employee performs. The benefits of empowerment practices for the employee include:

- An increase in job awareness
- An increase in accepting responsibility
- Workers becoming more effective in their jobs
- Workers having a greater sense of job ownership

The benefits of empowerment practices for management include:

- Being able to concentrate on other tasks
- Having clearly marked lines of communication between employee and manager
- Guest satisfaction increasing due to a more energized staff
- Workers demonstrating an ability to train for middle management positions as they become available

Enabling

Empowerment is an important step in getting employees involved in the decision-making process. It is not enough by itself; employees must also be enabled to follow through with the decisions that they have made in a timely and efficient manner.

Enabling employees means giving them the tools they need to carry their decisions through. You must enable them to enact the changes they have suggested. To accomplish this, employees may need money for new or better equipment, time and money for specialized training, and above all, commitment from middle and upper management to let them try their ideas without restriction and without criticism.

While it is critical that management and employee decisions be evaluated for effectiveness, this evaluation must be centered on the process or the change and not on the person initiating the changes. Managers and employees both will make decisions that do not ultimately improve processes. These must not be labeled as mistakes that can be embarrassing and self-defeating; rather, they are all attempts to improve understanding from the start that some will work and others will not.

According to Batten, successful managers are not just people following orders or meeting established agendas; they are people who have the ability to see beyond the numbers, the gadgets and the quotas. Successful managers see their workers as their primary responsibility because only through a good relationship with them can work be accomplished.

Values like self-motivation, empathy, personal communication, goal-setting and time management lead the list that will help all managers become successful leaders. Managers who lead with positive example and strong values can direct their employees toward achieving higher personal goals. By building a motivated and goal-oriented work force, production can be increased and quality becomes more predictable.

The health of a company is directly related to the health and well-being of the workers that make up its organization. Once the human factor is considered and protected, then statistical analysis and other quality control techniques can be implemented with more consistency and a better predictability for results.

Building a quality workplace rarely happens by chance. There needs to be a well thought out plan that can be followed and evaluated for efficiency. Learn the dynamic diversities of your workers and be willing to accept them for their strengths and dedication. A quality work culture is one that encourages individuality, makes use of the different strengths of the workers, and finds ways to turn weaknesses into strengths. It takes time to investigate all the idiosyncrasies of the workers, and a deliberate action to support them rather than interfere.

With an organizational system that encourages customer and employee input throughout the production and service processes, managers can have the pulse of their business at their fingertips. Their ability to make quick decisions and implement important changes is directly influenced by this knowledge, and their success is measured by its accuracy.

CHAPTER 11

The Chef Supervisor

OBJECTIVES

When you complete this chapter, you should be able to:

- Define supervision and describe the function of supervising.
- Describe the difference between management and supervision.
- Defend the need for chef managers to have industry-tested technical competence.
- Describe the attributes of role models in professionalism.
- Describe the guidelines for impeccable personal hygiene.
- Describe the means of demonstrating an affinity with quality.
- Define the role of chef as coach.
- Describe the initial steps in building an aggressive and competitive team.

SUPERVISION DEFINED

Supervision is the act of supervising employees in the performance of their duties to assure consistency in quality and constancy of production. It is an act that is usually performed by the person or persons who have the greatest amount of experience and knowledge in a particular job or set of jobs. The word supervision refers to the ability of the supervisor to see beyond the repetitive and mundane aspects of the job, always to focus on company goals and aggressively to seek constant improvement. Effective supervisors need to be technically competent, have leadership potential, good people skills and the ability to motivate others to do a job.

While all supervisors are managers, not all managers meet the definition of supervisor. Managers deal more directly with directing and assessing the process, and supervisors deal with the efficiency of the workers. Workers may manage themselves and their particular stations, yet never supervise a single person.

Chef supervisors must also be role models in professionalism, be drawn toward quality production and service, and have the foresight to position their workers as a competitive and effective team. To meet this end, chef supervisors must be good communicators, efficient planners, careful organizers and strong leaders.

TECHNICAL COMPETENCE

A good supervisor should have a strong foundation in the technical skills and knowledge needed to perform the jobs they are supervising, plus the experience of testing those skills in live situations. At the same time, they must realize that the workers who do those particular jobs day in and day out are the real experts, with keen insights and practical suggestions. A poor supervisor is one who thinks they know everything, doesn't listen when employees give suggestions and uses threats rather than praise and leadership to motivate.

Experience is one of the factors that separates supervisors from managers. Managers may know only the process and the predicted results, while supervisors know how to get those results through people in relaxed as well as in stressful situations.

ROLE MODELS IN PROFESSIONALISM

In order for chefs to be good supervisors, they must demonstrate in their own actions the level of quality and professionalism that they expect from their workers. It is natural for workers to emulate their supervisors, good or bad. Therefore, it is critical that chef supervisors maintain a high level of commitment, impeccable personal hygiene and a positive mental attitude. They must show respect for the work that others perform and be willing to listen to the ideas of others, no matter how different they may be from their own.

Commitment can be demonstrated by the chef supervisor who goes to work every day or night with a positive attitude and is enthusiastic about his or her work. They are always on time and prepared for work. Family and life problems are left at home and work becomes therapeutic. Successful supervisors control their mood swings, have consistent behavior patterns, never scream or make false accusations and always have an encouraging word to say about someone else's quality of work or behavior.

Impeccable personal hygiene includes:

■ Maintaining clean and appropriate uniforms or dress
■ Clean shaven or neatly trimmed beards and mustaches for men

- Hair that is trimmed or well maintained by hair nets and hats
- Polished professional shoes or clogs
- Consistently demonstrated hand-washing routines
- Controlled behavior for those who smoke or chew tobacco products

It is easy to motivate others to follow professional, healthy and safe personal hygiene guidelines when the supervisors consistently follow the same standards. Employees will emulate their supervisors regardless of written policies or industry practice.

Positive mental attitude can be demonstrated by greeting employees at the beginning of their shifts and thanking them at the end. Positive comments and constructive criticisms go a long way toward building up employee morale, cooperation, and teamwork, whereas accusations, threats, and constant belittling of employees and other supervisors set the tone for unproductive stimuli and uncomfortable working environments.

Showing respect toward others will breed a return of respect from employees toward management and other workers. Good listening skills and a willingness to consider new ideas inspires others to try harder and constantly seek improvement.

AFFINITY TOWARD QUALITY

Supervisors can demonstrate an affinity toward quality in production and service by insisting on meeting quality standards at every step of production and service. Supervisors who constantly insist on doing things correctly, not taking shortcuts, will motivate employees to uphold the same high quality standards.

During slow periods and rush times, quality rather than production speed and table turnover has to be the priority. When supervisors take shortcuts in production and service to save time and turn over tables, employees see these as acceptable procedures. They may even look for shortcuts of their own to help speed up production and keep them from doing what they perceive as extra work. Accepting shortcuts to save time can progress to depending on them to get the job done. The cycle continues when supervisors and employees begin to look for shortcuts to the shortcuts, and they lose sight of the quality standards set in the plan.

One example of a shortcut which has a major effect on production and service is often practiced at the receiving door. Does the supervisor or employee take the time to inspect every item received from purveyors to make sure it meets company standards, or do they receive closed boxes to save time? While it may save time in receiving, this practice often leads to the receipt of inferior products that will take more time to process and will end up costing more money for usable portions. It can also cause critical product shortages that affect production, service and, ultimately, customer satisfaction.

Another way chef supervisors can practice their affinity toward production is to insist on tasting soups, sauces, accompanying side dishes and other menu item components before serving them to the customer. The person who always tastes can adjust product flavor and correct problems in texture before it affects the quality of the served item. When employees see supervisors take the time to taste and adjust products, they are more likely to do so themselves. Thus it becomes an encouraged practice rather than an insisted-upon rule or procedure. A consistent practice becomes standard procedure and acceptable behavior.

Plating foods for service also depicts the supervisor's concern for quality. Is food plated, sauced, and garnished properly? Does every plate look appetizing, or does it look rushed? One method to ensure quality in plating is to have photos made of each menu item as it is supposed to look before being served. The cooks, expediter and service personnel can then easily compare the prepared dish to the approved company standard for easy reference, eliminating objectivity and personal preference. Plated foods that do not look like the photos can be re-plated or re-done altogether before committing them to customer scrutiny.

TEAMWORK

To position your staff as a competitive and affective team requires chef supervisors to take an active part in directing and leading them every step of the way. It is not a part-time job that happens late at night or on the weekends, but constantly and consistently.

Teamwork begins with placing employees in positions that capitalize on their strengths. Every person has strengths and weaknesses. A good supervisor tests each team member in each of the team's many positions, and matches workers with the positions in which they can succeed. A good supervisor continues to evaluate each team member's performance and may make several position changes before settling on a final organizational structure. In food service, this translates to having all employees train in a variety of positions, new and existing, from prep cook to line cook to garde manger to pastry cook, and even to purchasing steward, to see for which position the person's individual set of skills is best suited. If after a few weeks the coach feels the person is not working well in the position they settled in, then it is the responsibility of the coach to move the person to another position, and another, until a good match is found. A coach reluctantly dismisses team members because they know that, given the skills, knowledge, and willingness to work, each employee can have a productive and contributory position on the team. Only employees who cannot be motivated to work as a team need to be dismissed in order to preserve the integrity of the team itself.

A good supervisor is also one who is truly interested in the well-being of the team members. They learn each team member's personal goals and ambitions, and strive to help them achieve them. For some it may be to move progressively up the organizational ladder, while for others it may be to maintain a solid job with regular hours and steady responsibilities. Other employees may be looking only for a short-term job to meet short-term goals, such as a summer job for college students or a temporary job for people in transition. Trying to force a career-minded employee into a part-time or split-shift situation will ultimately lead to discontent and employee turnover, whereas forcing a part-time employee to continually accept a full-time workload and heavy responsibilities will lead to similar results. Matching a person's level of motivation to the type of job is as important as matching their skills and knowledge. All good teams need good, solid, full-time players with career-minded commitments as well as part-time and short-term players with simple and easily achievable goals.

The modern chef wears three hats: the toque blanche of professional culinarians, the hat of management, and the hat of supervisor. Even in very large and complex organizations, like the casino and convention hotels that have multiple levels of food service and where the executive chef may spend 90 percent of the day managing the operation, the modern chef still needs to supervise the upper and middle line managers (the executive sous and sous chefs) and must have the technical expertise to guide the planning and quality improvement processes, whereas in smaller operations, like the independent restaurant, the chef may spend equal time managing, supervising, and producing. In both extreme cases, and everything in between, they have become super chefs capable of fulfilling many levels of responsibilities while leading and motivating their teams.

CHAPTER 12

Communication

OBJECTIVES

When you complete this chapter, you should be able to:

- Define communication and discuss the importance of proper communication in business.
- Describe the process of validating that the intended message is sent and received.
- Discuss factors that affect a person's ability to receive information accurately.
- Explain how physical expression affects communication.
- Describe some of the most common forms of written communiqués used in professional food service.
- Describe some of the key elements in verbal communication.
- Describe how physical expression and tone of voice can influence the interpretation of verbal communication.
- Describe some of the benefits of using verbal communication.
- Describe common forms of physical communication, their dangers and their benefits.
- Discuss the elements of good listening skills.

THE PROCESS OF COMMUNICATION

Proper communication is the key to sharing information. It is the mechanism of exchanging ideas, of motivation, and of direction. Without proper communication, information cannot be delivered or processed accurately and workers are left to their own interpretations and perceptions to guide them.

Communication is an exchange of information. It involves the person or persons sending the message, the message itself, and the intended receiver of the message. Communication is effective when the intended messages are received and interpreted accurately.

Effective communication can be achieved with careful planning and proper execution. It involves understanding the processes of communication, determining which form of communication is best suited for the situation and getting a response that affirms that the message has been received as intended.

Communication can be as simple as a nod of a head or as complicated as a doctoral dissertation. It can be oral, written, pictorial or as simple as a physical movement or gesture. No matter what the medium, good communication is achieved when an intended message is given to a specific audience with the intent to inform, instruct or seek information. Whether it is a simple gesture or a 300-page paper with footnotes and an annotated bibliography, communication can be a great tool for sharing information when used properly—or a misleading contrivance when used incorrectly.

The person sending the message has the greatest influence on whether or not the message is sent and received properly. They are the ones who often originate the information, construct the message and determine the method of delivery. These choices set the tone of the message, the clarity of the information itself, and set in motion a means to determine if the communication was received and understood properly.

Often the level of urgency in the message is decided by virtue of the sender's position in the organization. The higher a person's position, the more critical the information becomes. It is critical that owners, supervisors and managers take special care to deliver only intended messages and information. The information they send is interpreted as company policy and should reflect company goals and overall management philosophies.

The message or information must be constructed as concisely and accurately as possible. The shorter the communiqué, the less likely it is that it will be misinterpreted. Long, wordy communiqués are unnecessary and time consuming to read, and the critical parts of the message can be lost in rhetoric or semantics.

To test the accuracy of the communiqué before it is sent, ask yourself these questions:

1. What information do I want to send?
2. Are there specific details that must be followed, such as size, portion, shape, time, or date?
3. Is there room for interpretation?

If there is no room for interpretation, then give the specifics in as much detail as possible. If there is room for interpretation, specify the parameters or protocol that should be used as guidelines. A freely interpretive communiqué has no guarantee of being received properly or of soliciting the desired response.

Verify that the message or information is received by asking the receiver to repeat the critical parts of the communiqué to you. In this interaction, you can verify that the message was received properly, establish that the person the message was intended for received and understood the message, and determine the probability that the message or information will be carried out or remembered.

You must take into consideration the person or persons that the communiqué is intended for when forming the communiqué and deciding on the best delivery. Are they highly skilled and motivated employees who need little direction and supervision, or are they new trainees who need clear and exact guidance? In both cases, there is a preferred method of communication that is best suited to the situation.

Highly skilled and motivated employees need little guidance in performing the daily routines of their jobs. Short notes or quick verbal announcements may be all that is necessary to communicate directions or production amounts to these individuals. They can receive information in small fragments and use their own experience and knowledge to decide their production priorities and timing. Workers with less experience or skills need longer and more complete directions to accomplish their daily jobs. These individuals don't have the experience to help interpret announcements and short-scripted notes. They need more information and in greater detail. They depend on the support given them through carefully written or clearly worded verbal communications from supervisors and managers.

Differences in language and levels of technical sophistication also affect a person's ability to receive and interpret communications correctly. In many food service and hospitality operations, there is more than one spoken language and variations of common language that need clarification before the message can be properly sent.

Variations of Spanish are quickly overtaking French as the dominant second language in professional American kitchens. Mexican, Cuban, Puerto Rican and Haitian workers are finding employment with American restaurants, cruise ship lines, and hotels, all around the country from Texas, New Mexico, California and Florida to Illinois and New York. It is important for food service managers, chefs and general managers to learn key words and phrases from their worker's own languages in order to communicate effectively.

Managers must also communicate at the same level of sophistication as their audience. Supervisors and managers who use large, technical words often find their communications are not understood and their directions are not being followed.

Effective supervisors and managers make it part of their job to learn about each worker's language idiosyncrasies, and fashion communiqués that are at the worker's level of comprehension. Not only does this aid in comprehension, but it helps build morale when management recognizes language differences and tries to overcome them.

FORMS OF COMMUNICATION

There are many forms of communication. This chapter will explore written, verbal, physical expression, pictorial and non-communication. Art, music, and architecture are also forms of communication, but these are intended to express emotion rather than to give information.

Non-communication is a form of communication since ideas and information that are not spoken or written can be interpreted as an affirmation of information. For example, employees who are never told not to eat lobster for their employee meal or not to take leftover food home may feel that it is all right to do so. This is an interpretation of information that was never sent, yet it was received and left to the interpretation of the individual.

For food service and hospitality management, written and verbal communications are the most frequently intended forms of communication. Unfortunately, the one form of communication that is given most is unintended; it takes the form of physical expression. A manager's facial expression, tone of voice and bodily movements can communicate feelings, emotions and assessments of employee performance without uttering a single word.

Often, unconsciously, people show their emotions through their looks, their smiles, and their gestures. When these emotions are pleasant and supportive, related physical expressions can positively affect a person's work habits and motivation. However, when the emotions are based on stress, anger or frustration, the accompanying physical expressions can negatively affect morale and, consequently, productivity and consistency. A good supervisor is consciously aware of their own humor and mood. When necessary, they hide their own feelings to show a positive and supportive attitude to their workers. When angered or stressed, supervisors need to dismiss those negative feelings and constantly promote motivated feelings and expressions.

Written Communication

Chefs use many forms of written communication to convey messages and information to staff and upper management. These take the forms of memorandums (memos), prep lists (see Figure 12–1), recipes, job descriptions, purchase orders, inventory and sales reports and menu descriptions.

Written communications need to be accurate and concise because there may not be a chance for immediate interaction between the sender and the receiver to clarify a statement or a fact. Written communications are often mailed to a person's home, posted on a wall for everyone to see, or filed away in a ledger, recipe file box, or personnel folder.

Memorandums are the most frequently used form of written communication in business. While there is a specified form to use in constructing memorandums, it tends not to be as formal as written letters or as complex as sales and production charts.

Memorandums, like letters, need to be addressed to someone. This is easily accomplished by the notation TO: at the heading, or top, of the memorandum. In this way, everyone who sees the memorandum will immediately be able to identify if the information is meant for them personally, or shared with them to keep them abreast of policy changes and announcements. Examples may include:

- TO: Kitchen Staff
- TO: Night Cooks
- TO: Joe Smith

The more definitive the heading, the greater the chance that the people the information is intended for will read the memorandum. Simply posting announcements or information on bulletin boards in non-addressed memorandums will not solicit the desired result, and may be construed by some workers as non-communication. "I wasn't told" or "I didn't know" may be common reactions to non-addressed memorandums casually placed on walls, bulletin boards, or in hallways. Memorandums sent to one person are not usually posted.

The memorandum is then referenced to a particular event or category of information. The abbreviation RE: denotes the purpose or scope of the information contained in the memorandum. Examples of referenced memorandums may include:

- RE: Sales Forecast
- RE: Health Benefits
- RE: Holiday Schedule

Referencing memorandums to a particular category of information or event can allow employees to identify quickly the relevance of the information to their job or assignments, and to file them into appropriate folders for future reference.

Memorandums have to note a source or author that gives credence to the information or announcements it contains. This is usually noted by the desig-

Food Prep Assignments

Cook/preparer: _____Stacy_____

Day: ___Monday___ Date: ___June 3___

Items Needed	QTY Needed	Name of Party	Time Needed	Instructions
Diced onion	5#	Hot line	11 A.M.	Rotate stock
Sliced wt mush	3# box	Salad line	11 A.M.	Rotate stock
Shrimp salad	2 x recipe	CDC luncheon	12 P.M.	Del to pantry

FIGURE 12–1 Prep Chart for Cooks

nation FR:, which is an abbreviation for FROM. Examples of this notation may include:

- FR: Executive Chef
- FR: Human Resources
- FR: General Manager

Posted memorandums may be addressed to one or many workers, but intended for everyone to see. Personal memorandums are usually not posted, but may have the notation cc: at the bottom of the page or pages to denote who else received a copy. Examples of these may include:

- TO: Joe Smith
  cc: Personnel Folder
- TO: Kitchen Staff
  cc: General Manager

In the first example, Joe Smith knows that the information he received in the memorandum has also been placed in his personnel file for later use by management. In the second example, the kitchen staff knows that the general manager is being informed of critical information that affects the overall operation, for reference or to solicit further comments from upper management and possibly the owners. In both cases, the person or persons the information is intended for is clearly defined, and the routing of the information is noted for future reference or to denote its importance.

Memorandums usually include single pieces of information or related sets of information. They are intended as quick references that should be easily understood and remembered. Multiple pieces of information or complex announcements are better suited to more formalized letters or policy folders. In those forms, the intended audience can review the information at their own leisure and may be more encouraged to write a response or acknowledgment of the information.

Prep lists or assignment sheets, as shown in Figure 12–1, are used to give important written instruction to the food preparation, service and cooking staff regarding the day's production needs. Prep lists are usually posted in an open area easily seen by the appropriate workers, high enough for everyone to see and low enough for people to check off tasks as they are completed. Chalk boards, dry erase boards, or large sheets of paper are all adequate media for posting prep lists.

The order of the items on the prep list may denote order of priority. Items listed first should be started and/or completed first, and items listed last may have less immediate importance and can be started and/or completed at the end of the shift. If order of priority is intended in the prep list, this must be communicated to the workers either through training, verbal announcement or by numerical designation. An example of a prep list may be:

1. Shrimp salad: 5 pounds
2. Blue cheese dressing: 1 × recipe
3. Sliced mushrooms: 10 pounds
4. Chicken cordon bleu: 50 portions

Posting of the prep list allows everyone involved to see the list and work from it at the same time. Employees are instructed to check off the completed items as a reminder to themselves and as an announcement to the other cooks and the chef of the status of completing the list. It is a psychological boost to employees physically to check off items they've completed. It gives them a sense of accomplishment, of contributing to the whole organization and allows them to evaluate their own performance with respect to timing and organization. Allowing employees to meet and exceed short-term goals helps build morale and strengthens the concept of teamwork.

Recipes are another form of written communication. They give specific instructions on the preparation, plating, and serving of standard menu items. Well written and tested recipes can provide invaluable guidance to cooks, food preparation workers and service personnel.

Recipes are plans that need trained workers to interpret and execute. They are written using common industry language and act as standards to assure consistency in production and service. Recipes are also working descriptions of menu items that wait staffs can study in order to accurately communicate the ingredients and procedures to their customers. More on recipe writing and recipe management will be discussed in Chapter 19, Establishing Operational Standards.

Job descriptions communicate job expectations to new employees. They should describe the employee's relationship to the whole organization and the part they play in the kitchen or dining room team that they are joining. Job descriptions should list specific and detailed job responsibilities and performance expectations.

Well written job descriptions can also become evaluation standards for supervisors to use when assessing an employee's abilities, work habits and motivation for advancement. Employees who meet and exceed job responsibilities are prime candidates for advancement, while those who only meet expectations may need more time and training in order to assume more responsibilities at a later date.

Poorly written job descriptions give little, and often ambiguous, information pertaining to the employer's expectations of the job. It is unfair to evaluate an employee's performance without first giving them a detailed description of the job and the company's expectations. This is analogous to evaluating a cook's ability to produce a specific menu item without a recipe. Neither can be expected to meet specific expectations without structured communication.

Purchase orders are written accounts of food and non-food items (sundry items) ordered from specific vendors. They list the items ordered with specific descriptions of ingredient standards, including grade, size, count, and weight, the units the items are sold in (pounds, cases, gallons), the quantity of units ordered, and the cost quoted for each item.

Purchase orders are tools to communicate what has been ordered, from whom, the date of the order, and when to expect delivery. They allow the receiving personnel to match what was ordered against what was received. In this way, shortages or substitutions become known right away and alternative plans can be made before it becomes a crisis situation. Receiving personnel can also check the quoted price against the invoiced price to assure the accuracy of costs, which affects inventory control and menu pricing.

Purchase orders can also be used by accounts payable (the office responsible for paying bills) to match orders against vendor invoices. In this way, they can be assured that they are paying for items actually received. More detailed information on purchase orders and their relationship to the flow of goods will be discussed in Chapter 20, Menu Management.

Inventory and sales reports are two primary types of written records used daily in food service operations and other businesses to control costs. They are used strategically to plan purchases, determine production requirements, and forecast labor needs.

Record keeping is a form of written communication. The sender is the person responsible for collecting and recording the information; the message is the information itself, albeit numbers and percentages; and the message is received when read and analyzed. Accurate information, properly collected and recorded, can help employees in the performance of their jobs and can help managers to assess the health of the business.

Recording numerical information requires customizing standard business ledgers or creating specialized forms with an appropriate number of columns and headings. They can be constructed to suit a variety of needs, depending on the information needed to plan and conduct business. Reports should be constructed so that the important information is easily found and the supporting information, the headings, is clearly defined and labeled. For example, sales reports can be constructed to highlight sales by date, by shift (breakfast, lunch, dinner), or even by the hour, depending on the need for specific or general information. A new operation needs sales by the shift, or even by the hour, for several weeks to determine a sales pattern, whereas managers of established operations may only need sales by the shift to determine sales trends and new marketing strategies. Many computer software programs can be used to create these customized forms.

Menu descriptions are another form of written communication. The sender is the chef or manager, the message is the description itself and the intended receiver is the customer. Properly constructed menu descriptions give the customer a complete picture of the items being offered. They need to be informative, accurate and concise.

For many reasons, written communications are the best means of conferring information to other people. Here are the positives:

- The sender can take time in constructing and wording the communiqué.
- The communiqué can be tested for clarity before being sent out.
- The communiqué allows the receiver to reflect fully upon the intended message before acting or responding.
- The communiqué becomes a permanent, dated record that the message has been sent.

Verbal Communication

Verbal communication is the most common form of communication used in a working environment. It is the quickest way to deliver a message and solicits an immediate response or acknowledgment from the receiver.

Some key elements in verbal communication include:

- Know what to say before you say it.
- Speak directly to the person or persons the message is intended for.
- Use language that the receiver can easily understand.
- Use direct eye contact to see if the message is received and to measure the receiver's reaction to the message.
- Expect an immediate response or action.
- Avoid this form when excited or angered.

Giving directions to employees is the most common use of verbal communication. Directions help get projects started and keep them moving toward company standards. Without clear directions, employees cannot be expected to complete tasks or evaluate their progress. Directions can motivate or frustrate the employee depending on the complexity of the directions, the choice of words and the tone of voice used.

Effective verbal directions should contain only one point or idea at a time. Employees cannot be expected to remember multiple directions and may get confused when confronted with them. A properly trained team member is already committed to several tasks at the same time, as defined by normal production routines. Additional multiple directions may be forgotten or given less priority than is wanted. Multiple directions or ideas should be written down for easy reference.

Give specific directions, avoiding ambiguity and confusion. Use common language, avoid complex phrases, and explain technical words or procedures to assure that the employee knows what they are being asked to do.

Speak clearly and directly to the person or persons you are giving directions to. Speak loudly enough to be heard, but not too loudly, as this may be interpreted as anger or negative feedback.

Always check that the direction has been heard and understood before going on with other directions or leaving the employee to complete an action. You can do this by asking the employee to repeat the directions, demonstrate a procedure, or ask their own questions to verify understanding.

Verbal communication can often relay more information than the message itself. Emotion can also be communicated by the tone of voice that is used when delivering the message. A soft, pleasant tone of voice accompanied by a smile gives a message of caring and respect, whereas a gruff, harsh tone signifies anger or disapproval. The same message can be interpreted entirely differently given the tone of voice and facial expression that is used.

Personal and friendly conversation is a use of verbal communication skills that can motivate employees and bring them together as a team. When used frequently, common greetings and farewells can do more to motivate an employee than any other single factor. Something as simple as saying "Hello, how are you?" or "Thank you" relay much more than the words themselves. They also relay the message that you care about your employees, that you respect them and have compassion for their personal circumstances.

Some of the benefits of using verbal communication include:

- Personalized information
- Immediate reaction or feedback
- Immediate acknowledgment and comprehension
- The ability to express emotion such as caring and respect by combining verbal communication with voice tone and facial expression

Physical Communication

Forms of physical communication include handshaking, waving, clapping and the proverbial pat on the back. These nonverbal, non-written forms of communication still involve the three main parts of communication: the sender, the message itself, and the receiver; however, they are often subliminal components. The sender is the one initiating the gesture, the message is appreciation and respect, and the receiver is the one the gesture is intended for.

Negatively motivated forms of physical communication include pushing, banging on tables, throwing things and grabbing the arms or shoulders of other people. These should never be used in professional settings. They are degrading, threatening and dangerous. They neither motivate nor discipline, and they may be grounds for harassment or assault. They demonstrate disrespect, break apart teams and isolate individuals from the group.

Another way our physical stance influences communication deals with respecting or breaching a person's personal space. Proxemics is the study of the way we structure distance and space. There are direct correlations between the distance we place between ourselves and the people with whom we are talking, the message we send, and the reactions we receive.

Everyone has a certain amount of space surrounding them that is considered their personal space. For many, it is an area of about zero to four feet. Respecting or breaching a person's personal space will determine whether or not the intended message is received and what the reaction may be.

In normal conversation, people need to maintain a proper distance between themselves and the intended receiver in order to communicate effectively. Speaking to someone farther away than ten or twelve feet may require raising your voice and may give an unintended message of anger, frustration, or immediacy. Speaking to someone closer than one and a half feet may be awkward or even threatening, and will also send the wrong message. The perfect speaking distance is between four and eight feet.

The only time that you can breach a person's personal space is when you are invited in. A handshake, for example, breaches a person's personal space but it is the other person's option to extend their hand in acceptance or not. Friendship gestures like hugs and kisses also breach this space, but they must be desired by both persons. There is little need for these gestures in professional settings.

LISTENING SKILLS

In order for communication to succeed, it requires that a person is listening or willing to receive the message. Since communication is a two-way process, both the sender and the receiver alternate the need to listen. The receiver must be listening to the message or the message is lost, and the sender must be ready to listen to the receiver's response to acknowledge acceptance and understanding of the message.

Effective listening skills can be learned. The effort alone can go a long way toward building respect and cooperation from other people. To practice good listening skills, consider the following key points:

1. Make eye contact with the person you are talking or listening to (except in Asian cultures, where eye contact is considered rude and offensive).

2. Stop what you are doing to give your full attention to the message being sent.

3. Nod your head up and down to show acceptance of the message.

4. When seated, lean slightly forward to show a willingness to listen.

5. Allow the other person to finish their message without interruption, then give feedback or make a response.

6. Suppress personal bias and be willing to hear what the other person is saying, even if it appears to go against your own belief or concern.

7. Always respond positively to another person's ideas or beliefs; statements like "That's interesting" or "I haven't considered that" affirm a willingness to listen without making a commitment either way to the message.

Types of Listening Skills

There are at least five different types of listening skills or behaviors that a supervising manager can choose from when wanting to get the most out of their communications with employees, equals and their own supervisors or boss. Each skill can produce great results when applied to the exact situations they describe.

1. **Appreciative listening:** When the purpose is to show appreciation or gratitude for what someone has done and is then reporting to you, pay attention to the context and style of presentation; respond visibly to tone of voice, language and rhythm; look for humor in the message and try to identify with the pleasure in the sender's message.

2. **Empathetic listening:** When the purpose is to support the sender as he or she is telling you some of their concerns, provide them the opportunity to express themselves without interruption, and accept the message without judging. This skill lets the sender know that you care about what they are telling you and lets the sender do most of the talking. You might ask open-ended questions (non-directional) or remain relatively silent and not offer solutions immediately.

3. **Comprehensive listening:** When the purpose is to organize and make sense out of the message being delivered, try relating the message to your own experience to understand the relationships between the various ideas and determine the sender's rationale. Demonstrate this skill by elaborating on what is being said; ask for clarification; bring up related topics; summarize frequently and then try and summarize the message using your own words.

4. **Discerning listening:** When the purpose is to get complete information, determine the main message, sort out the details and decide what is important, or not important, information. Demonstrate this skill by tak-

ing notes; ask for clarification often; concentrate on what is being said; eliminate all distractions and repeat what you have heard to ensure its accuracy.

5. **Evaluative listening:** When the purpose is to make a decision based on the information you are being given, relate what you are hearing to your personal understanding of the situation while questioning the sender's motives for the message, looking for factual support for the purpose of accepting or rejecting the information given. Demonstrate this skill by actively agreeing or disagreeing with the message as it is given; express skepticism if the information seems ambiguous or personally motivated; share your opinions with the sender, putting the sender into the listening mode until a decision is reached.

Chef managers who practice good listening skills encourage their employees to think for themselves and express their own ideas. This is the best way to demonstrate respect for other people and motivate them to improve themselves and their work. Demonstrating good listening skills will, in turn, encourage others to listen more closely to what you say.

Good communication and listening skills are required of the Total Quality Management process. They affect motivation and cooperation, the two most important factors in team building and quality improvement. Communication and listening skills need to be practiced, assessed for efficiency, and made a consistent part of effective management.

CHAPTER 13

Managing Diversity

OBJECTIVES

When you complete this chapter, you should be able to:

- Discuss the complexities of diversity factors and how they relate to motivation and production.
- Describe the influences that define a person's social framework.
- Describe the demographics of American hospitality and food service workers based on gender and ethnicity.
- Describe Blake and Mouton's Impoverished Management and Team Management classifications of managers.
- Describe how some segments of the hospitality industry try to dehumanize production and service tasks.
- Define what Joseph Batten calls a value-led visionary.
- Describe how diversity affects communication.
- Describe how to attract and keep good employees when unemployment is low and skilled workers are hard to find.
- Describe how shared personnel development plans can help bridge diverse social groups.
- Describe how a positive working environment can become a cyclical strategy for staff development.

DEFINING DIVERSITY

People usually refer to ethnicity, race, and gender when defining diversity. On the surface, these may be the obvious factors, but in business, they are by far not the only ones. People are also diverse in social framework, religion, goals and ambition.

   Ethnicity is defined as a person's cultural heritage. Greeks, Italians, Spaniards, the Chinese and Japanese all have customs, beliefs and social structures unique to their cultures' history and practice. Since America is the world's melting pot, these various cultures have migrated into an American culture, holding on to their basic beliefs and philosophies while adapting nonessential ideologies to a new way of life. In many larger cities around the United States, these cultures protect their heritages by living in segregated neighborhoods that house selective churches, schools, stores and restaurants. Industries bring these diverse cultures under the same roof, often for the first time. The hospitality industry, in particular, employs a wide range of culturally diverse people who share similar tasks, work schedules and daily meals in an atmosphere of service and hospitality. Family practices, which are protected in the home, are often abandoned in the workplace.

Race is a broader category used to group people with similar skin color, facial features, and other genetically influenced physical characteristics into distinct geographical groups. African, European, Asian and Mongolian are four of the world's largest racial groups. Each race has its own characteristic physical features that can be distinguished from the others.

Race is used to define large geographical groups of people that contain multiple traditions, histories and philosophies. Unfortunately, similar behavioral traits are also often assumed to be determined by racial designation. Assumptions regarding psychological and ethical similarities within specific races are unfounded generalities that help form stereotypes and are the beginning of discrimination.

Gender refers to a person's sex, male or female. Whereas chefs have typically been male, women are entering the hospitality industry as cooks and chefs in record numbers. This increase in women chefs is partly due to culinary schools that enroll and graduate women students every year, treating them the same way as male students and measuring their abilities with the same expectations and professional standards. Other inspiration comes from national role models, like Julia Childs and Alice Waters, who have proven that women can be just as successful as men in professional kitchens.

While these categories of people define diversity, they are not the key factors in determining a person's willingness and ability to work. A person's social framework and upbringing do more to produce a motivated worker than any of the other factors combined.

People form a social framework out of the environmental influences in their lives. Family structure, the type of house or apartment they live in, the school system they're exposed to and other such factors present a network of stimuli that affect a person's personality, ambition and self-respect. When these factors are positively enforced, they help produce intelligent and motivated individuals who can be productive workers and leaders. When a person's environment is unstable, it is difficult for them to learn positive characteristics or to find the role models that can lead them to success.

Chef managers must look past obvious diversity issues such as ethnicity, race and gender, and concentrate on personality and commitment when hiring and training new employees. With the right kind of influence and guidance, people from all aspects of life can be productive workers.

THE DIVERSE HOSPITALITY INDUSTRY

The American hospitality industry employs a wide range of people for all levels of employment opportunities. People from various ethnic, social, educational and cultural backgrounds are attracted to the hospitality industry because of its flexibility in hiring practices and the great demand for employment opportunities.

The U.S. Department of Labor Bureau of Labor Statistics published reports suggest that growth in the number of minority workers is a huge factor in the overall labor force expansion for still the fastest growing service industry in America. White non-Hispanics accounted for 84 percent of the labor force in 1996, but will drop to 83 percent by 2006. The proportion of Hispanic workers (of all races) in the labor force is projected to grow from the 9.5 percent registered in 1996 to 11.7 percent in 2006. Asians and other non-black minorities should expand their share of the labor force from 4.3 percent to 5.4 percent, while the African American share should only rise from 11.3 percent to 11.6 percent.

Including wait staff, the typical food service worker is female, aged thirty and younger, is a high school graduate, single, either living in a household with family or with other wage earners, a part-time employee, and has a history of short tenure in jobs. Women represent the majority of all workers in the hospitality industry in all categories besides that of cooks. The typical food service manager, on the other hand, is a white male, aged thirty-five or older, and employed in private industry with a good track record of employment. In an organization dependent on people's service skills for success, motivation stimuli become a complex question from the beginning.

The hospitality industry attracts people with varied occupational goals and ambitions. Many are just looking for a job to pay bills while going through college, and others are supplementing a household income with extra work. A large percentage of workers are people who could not get jobs anywhere else. The demand for hospitality workers is projected to reach nearly 12.5 million by 2006, which will make it the largest employer in the United States besides government. Because the demand is outpacing the supply of trained workers from culinary programs around the country, employers feel pressured to hire just about anyone who walks in off the street.

The problem for food service managers, including chefs, is to train and motivate a diverse work force to accomplish similar goals.

Some managers take an aggressive approach to training and motivating employees and are more concerned with the product than with the people they have working for them. Others believe it is through understanding the complexities of their employees' backgrounds and ambitions that they are better able to direct them according to their individual strengths and personality traits to create even greater and more consistent production.

MANAGING DIVERSITY THROUGH LEADERSHIP

The Managerial Grid III, by Robert Blake and Jane Mouton, describes different authority-based leadership styles and their effect on employee morale and production. Using such labels as country club, team, organizational man, impoverished, and authority–obedience, they create a picture outlining the complexities inherent in business organizations that depend on a diverse population of people for a large part of the work. The hospitality industry would clearly be represented.

Using a grid with Concern for People on one axis and Concern for Production on the second axis, the authors describe five different leadership styles aligned to specific points on the grid. The two most opposing styles that are commonly found in the hospitality industry are Team Management and Impoverished Management. Team Management places the emphasis on building a committed work force based on trust and respect, and through which high level production is possible. Impoverished Management places little interest in people and places the greater emphasis on management participation in production and formalized work procedures for all tasks. Impoverished Management would like to dehumanize tasks as much as possible for the sake of consistency.

Ignoring Diversity Doesn't Work

Some managers believe that the complexities of dealing with people in work situations actually take away from effective production. The whole concept behind fast food service is to dehumanize the production and service as much as possible to ensure speed and a consistent product (McDonald's, Wendy's, Burger King, all serve exactly the same product in thousands of stores across the world).

Impoverished Management leadership ignores the diversity issue and tries to have all their workers act the same, talk the same, look the same, and perform the same. They often create training situations where new employees are trained on the job by existing employees. They believe this builds an interdependency between employees which helps bind them together as a team. They'll learn the way the other workers do things and thus keep consistency in product and presentation. Those who can assimilate will be happy, hardworking employees, while those who cannot will be fired or demoralized enough that they quit.

Managers who follow the Impoverished Management style of leadership truly believe that their way is correct and that by dehumanizing tasks and procedures, the "human error" factor can almost be eliminated. Likewise, they can deal with a less skilled work force when production is made as mechanical as possible. This also helps to keep employee costs low and management costs slightly higher. However, this style of management has a detrimental affect on quality improvement since the employee is not expected to participate.

These managers also believe that transitions inherent in areas of high employee turnover become less stressful to manage when training becomes simplified. They foster policies of cross-training as a way of ensuring that positions of importance can be filled at a moment's notice, even if only temporarily, by an existing employee. Management, or the "warm body" scenario, can be used to fill less important positions during transitions.

What this concept protects against, it also creates: a revolving door work force with extremely high turnover, poor morale of remaining employees, stressful management, and lost time and production. The consistency it seeks is disrupted by the constant hiring of new employees, even those that are trained.

Dehumanizing the tasks takes away people's abilities to expend thought and emotion; they themselves become very machine-like and mechanical. Unfortunately, since they are not machines, this tends to lead to complacency, inconsistency and accidents.

Trying to understand the complexities of the people within an organization and making every effort to alleviate dissonance may prove more beneficial to consistent production than dehumanizing the tasks. In the hospitality industry, managers battle with both perceptions of leadership styles.

The Human Equation

Team Management leadership style focuses on the human factor in business organizations. Managers practicing this style place equal importance on production and workers, and believe that production improves as morale and team spirit improves. They further believe that effective management is possible only by involving people and their ideas in determining the strategies of work and achievement.

Joseph Batten, author of *Building a Total Quality Culture*, places the entire emphasis of management on the human equation, that is, the strengths and weaknesses inherent in dealing with people in working environments. Batten professes that it is exactly the complexities of dealing with humans that make organizations strong and enduring. The networking of individual strengths, relying on those strengths and building an organization that recognizes strengths and weaknesses is the foundation for good business.

Batten believes that managers create their own business culture based on their personal philosophies and motivations, and in order to motivate workers properly, they have to begin with themselves. Good leadership is itself a job which needs planning and hard work to accomplish. Few people are born natural leaders, but many can be taught good leadership and guided along, just as with any other task or job. Managers who are themselves directed and motivated can more easily direct and motivate others. Managers who are themselves lazy, disorganized, or simply confused also have these traits reflected by their employees.

Batten preaches that "the total value of an organization is the sum of the values it promotes, teaches, and practices," and that this begins and ends with management. He calls this kind of manager a "value-led visionary."

A value-led visionary is a manager who bases a large part of the decision-making process on human values and ethics, always planning for the future and thriving on quality and customer value. The buzzwords used to describe value-led visionary include vision, creativity, responsiveness, internal entrepreneurism, conceptual thinking, innovation, pro-activity, integrity, mental agility, morals, values and re-orientation.

Paul Hersey and Kenneth Blanchard, authors of *Management of Organizational Behavior*, go even further by claiming that human resources are an organization's greatest resource. The authors preface this by quoting John D. Rockefeller, the famous American entrepreneur who said, "I will pay more for the ability to deal with people than any other ability under the sun." Rockefeller knew that his success was built mainly on his ability to motivate the people who worked for him, and not on actually performing work himself. He was able to accomplish a great deal through the motivation of others.

Hersey and Blanchard investigate strategies for accomplishing high employee motivation, which Rockefeller and other leading business leaders learned through trial and error. Management of organizational behavior becomes the primary responsibility of management; being able to predict results based on an understanding of those behaviors means success or failure.

The human factor, therefore, dealing with the perceptions of people and their ability to grasp information has a direct effect on how well they receive and absorb communications. Both psychological and sociological perspectives influence a person's ability to absorb information. This scenario may be related to other studies on human behavior, such as studies of learning styles, management styles, and teaching styles. The greater the diversity of the information given, the responses desired, and the people the information is intended for, the more important the need for various forms of communications in getting the message across.

Diversity Affects Communication

Another factor of the human behavior question is in the participants' willingness to be involved in the communication process. If the participants want to gain something out of direct communications, then they are more apt to give and receive information. If their priorities are not the same, then they will put up barriers to giving and receiving communication. Talented and savvy people could erect these barriers and not let the giver of the information know. The perception of the communicator could be that they practiced good communication, but in reality, the information exchange was cursory at best.

Even Frederick Taylor addressed the issues of proper communications in his scientific management theories. Taylor spoke about strict communications playing a key role in acceptable task fulfillment by employees. Communications, like everything else in business, should be an organized and planned function of management.

Organizations are a social system which stimulates intangible needs such as perceived value to the company, the ability of key players to work together, clear lines of authority, and clear channels for discussion. All these things influence the more tangible behavior which is production—getting the job done. Most personnel problems occur when organizations forget the human equation in management.

Those who can embrace diversity as a benefit to an organization, and not as a weakness, will be able to achieve more from a well motivated and vibrant work force than they can from an homogeneous crew. Dealing with a diverse population of workers does take time and a committed effort on the part of management, but the results are lasting and rewarding.

THE SOCIAL CHALLENGE

Frederick D. Sturdivant and James E. Stacey, authors of *The Corporate Social Challenge*, have collected a series of case stories on how certain businesses react to employee needs in the workplace. The reading is very complex in giving details about a number of different businesses, but the relevant connections between work and human behavior transgress the various businesses.

With competition for good employees rising for all businesses, the people factor becomes increasingly important. In addition, employees are demanding such considerations as equal rights, time off for family emergencies, smoking bans, etc., and businesses have to be willing to adjust their employment policies and benefits in order to keep a good work force.

Some managers mistakenly believe that when their employees have their material needs well met regarding insurance, pay and vacation time, etc., other factors such as praise for good work and a sympathetic ear for concerns are less important. These managers might make comments like "Be thankful you have a job." But where unemployment is low and skilled workers have a choice of jobs, the monetary factors balance out. The factors that make the difference are respect and gratitude.

Employee morale building is a full-time commitment. In the long run, it will have the most effect on employee retention, motivation and production.

THE PSYCHOLOGY OF WORK

Andrew Dubrin, author of *Effective Business Psychology*, applies basic psychology theories and motivation techniques to the world of business. Dubrin insists that the workplace is an extension of human life. The same motivations, desires and anticipations in life are found and generated through work.

Dubrin's approach to basic management in organizations is to help managers develop their own plans for self-motivation, determination, goal setting, and time management. By building these strong personal qualities in managers, they in turn become better able to direct other people, both by example and by having gone through it themselves.

Personnel development plans should include workshops and seminars presented by professionals trained in organizational psychology. Contacts can be made at local colleges and universities to identify the proper trainers and to commission their services. Topics for the workshops could include:

- Self-motivation
- Goal setting
- Time management
- Organizational development
- Communicating effectively
- Team building

Employees can be grouped together and given similar training, this time using the managers as facilitators and team leaders. Group activities that involve management and all employees will help create common goals and objectives that will continue in the workplace. The strength of the community is based on these common goals; they become the bridges that cross all lines of diversity.

Diversity is not a problem; it is a factor of life that transcends the community and the workplace. Managers who embrace diversity issues and try to find solutions rather than problems can motivate almost anyone to do a proper job. Look beyond the obvious and try to find the positive attitudes and performances in all people. In this way, you show respect for people and their differences.

In an atmosphere of cooperation rather than of domination, workers are self-motivated to work harder and more consistently. In an act of self-preservation, workers are more likely to protect a positive working environment through hard work and commitment. In return for respect and appreciation, production increases and quality is assured. This becomes a cyclical strategy to staff development that promotes teamwork and quality improvement efforts.

Section 4

THE CHEF LEADER

Chapter 14
Defining Leadership
Chapter 15
Team Building
Chapter 16
Personal Development

The role of chef continues to change under the growing complexities of competition and the dynamics of working in a diversified workplace. The chef's role is more complex than it ever was. Today it takes a mastering of technical skills, people skills and leadership skills to maintain excellence in the world's professional kitchens. Chefs must be ready to meet all challenges.

Leadership skills are an elusive set of skills that prescribe practice rather than implementation. Leaders motivate others through example, coach others to obtain the most out of their lives and constantly challenge themselves and others to improve. It is leadership that can make a weak team strong, a strong team great and turn a great team into winners.

Leadership skills can be self-taught. All that is needed is a willing student, a constancy of purpose, and a working environment to test and measure progress. The kitchens and dining rooms of the world make great classrooms, where success can be measured by repeat business, contented staffs and increased profits.

CHAPTER 14

Defining Leadership

OBJECTIVES

When you complete this chapter, you should be able to:

- Define leadership using an analytical and transcendental inference.
- Describe how authority-based leadership is earned and/or awarded.
- Describe how motivational leadership is earned.
- List and describe multiple behavioral traits that help define motivational leadership.
- Describe the concept of impartial leadership.
- Discuss ways of demonstrating the constancy of purpose that helps to define motivational leadership qualities.
- Discuss the importance of developing leadership in others and the ways in which it can be accomplished.

DEFINING LEADERSHIP

There are two ways of defining leaders:

1. Those who have the responsibility and authority to direct other people by virtue of their position in the organization
2. Those who inspire other people regardless of position or authority

While both definitions refer to the act of directing others, one is based on authority and the other on inspiration and guidance. When both occur at the same time, it is a dynamic and productive combination.

The analytical first definition speaks of the people who are at the top of organizational ladders as leaders. Examples are military officers giving orders, employers telling workers what has to be done and musical conductors directing a choir or orchestra. Authority and responsibility often help to define this kind of leadership.

Leadership by the transcendental second definition de-emphasizes authority and places the importance on motivation and guidance. A leader is one who motivates and inspires other people regardless of position or authority. Motivational leadership can occur at all levels of work, in all departments, and can involve a greater number of people. This is the leadership that all managers should strive to achieve.

Authority-driven Leadership

Authority-driven leadership is a part of every organization that has a linear organizational structure. Although there may be many rungs on the organizational ladder, there is only one top. The leader occupies that position.

Organizational leadership can begin with one person or a group of people. Proprietorships have one leader, limited partnerships may have a couple, and corporations have a board of directors who share the role of leader. In all three cases, the role of leader implies giving direction to the company as a whole.

Other leadership roles are awarded to people in the organization with multiple responsibilities. These are the people responsible for whole departments or entire shifts of employees. General managers, food and beverage managers, chefs and some dining room managers have leadership roles in their area of direct responsibility. Their roles imply giving direction to groups of workers with similar responsibilities and being responsible for the performance of the group. These leadership roles are awarded based on the authority and responsibilities delegated to the individual.

Authority does not automatically dictate respect or an ability to motivate. Respect has to be earned and motivation inspired through positive actions. Leaders can abuse their authority by placing production quotas and bottom line profits ahead of their employees' welfare. When employees feel cheated or neglected, they lose respect for authority and ignore direction. Leaders cannot lead if the workers are not willing to follow. Authority-based leadership is not enough to lead the hospitality industry into the future.

Motivational Leadership

Motivational leadership is defined as the act of inspiring other people through example, equity and constancy of purpose. It is based on behavior rather than on authority, and can transcend the organizational ladder. Motivational leaders lead by example and earn the respect of other employees through hard work and dedication.

To become a motivational leader requires commitment and sacrifice. The commitment is to constant improvement and a continuous drive for excellence. Without this commitment, motivation is impossible. Sacrifice comes from the willingness to change. The willingness to listen to other people and try their ideas first may sacrifice one's ego, but the gain in respect can be exponential.

Motivational leaders can exist at all levels of the organizational hierarchy and across all departmental boundaries. A wait person may be a motivational leader to a cook simply by their dedication to pleasing the customer, or a cook to a wait person because of the consistent quality of their food. In a well trained team, there are often many motivational leaders.

Authority-based leadership can often be motivational as well. When the head of the company or manager in charge takes an active part in the success of their employees, they can motivate as well as direct. This becomes a dynamic combination.

Impartial Leadership

Leaders must be constant in purpose and consistent in their delivery in order to turn a diverse work force into a cohesive team. It is an arduous task filled with obstacles that can be overcome by hard work and determination. Impartial leadership is measured by commitment to the leadership guidelines given above and by the demonstration of equity to all workers.

Impartial leadership recognizes and awards the contributions of all workers, regardless of their position in the organization. These leaders look for the positive contributions of all their employees, nurture their strengths and help them overcome their weaknesses. They counsel rather than criticize when mistakes are made, and instruct to correct behavior rather than discipline to punish it.

MOTIVATE THROUGH EXAMPLE

In Chapter 11, The Chef Supervisor, we discussed the need for supervisors to be role models in professionalism; motivational leaders live and breathe professionalism. These leaders demonstrate their personal commitment to professionalism, teamwork and quality improvement by their own actions. Others follow their example.

Professionalism is not defined by the hat or uniform a person wears, but by their behavior on and off the job. The consonant professional practices a set of positive behavioral traits and quickly self-corrects if they stray from them. Professionalism is not only following high standards, but is being willing to admit openly when mistakes have been made. Here is a partial list of behavioral traits that can improve one's self and motivate others to improve:

- Be on time and prepared for work every day.
- Display a friendly and energetic posture throughout the day.
- Develop and follow a plan for work, prioritizing tasks according to the dependency of others on their completion.
- Be technically competent and current with the trends.
- Make quick and proficient decisions.
- Complete each task, meeting or exceeding the standards set by the company.
- Strive for perfection.
- Freely share information and skill with co-workers and subordinates.
- Be courteous and helpful to others.
- Always be honest and freely give advice.
- Listen to others and respect their advice.
- Be respectful of other people's concerns and idiosyncrasies.
- Openly give praise and acknowledge other workers' contributions.
- Be fair and non-prejudicial when giving criticisms; do so in private.
- Show gratitude for the commitments and professionalism of others.

This is by far not an inclusive set of behavioral traits that define professionalism. It is merely the beginning of what should be a lifelong commitment to improvement and cooperation.

CONSTANCY OF PURPOSE

Constancy of purpose can be defined as consistency in behavior. Leaders who consistently demonstrate their commitment to high standards inspire others to do the same. Motivational leaders are constant in their drive for perfection. Their behavior stays consistent through all the stress and pressure of their fast-paced kitchens and dining rooms. Their inspiration to others is their steadfastness and endless energies.

Constancy of purpose does not come easily. It is hard work to establish a professionally driven profile and even harder work to maintain its intangible edifice. Here are eight suggestions that can help you maintain constancy of purpose throughout a hectic day:

1. **Begin each day with a well thought out plan of action.** This ensures a solid beginning to the day and acknowledges a series of goals to be accomplished.

2. **Greet everyone at work with sincere concern and friendliness.** This helps set the tone for the rest of the day and lays the foundation for cooperation and teamwork.

3. **Establish priorities for key employees and construct a plan for them to accomplish their goals.** This builds strong links along the production and service lines that you can depend on to hold things together in busy situations.

4. **Re-establish your own priorities, making adjustments for changes or emergencies you were faced with that morning.** Updating your own priority list often keeps you abreast of the critical changes that occur in time and production needs.

5. **Solve problems rather than put out fires.** When problems occur, you are obligated to fix them quickly and go on with production. However, when production slows down, revisit the problem and try to find its cause. Correct the situation so the problem doesn't return.

6. **Be available for employees when there are questions or concerns.** An active and caring manager is one who is always approachable and ready to assist at any time.

7. **Monitor the progress of all employees, and make an attempt to say something positive to everyone at least once a day.**

8. **Evaluate your own performance at the end of every day.** In this way, you can correct your own mistakes, re-organize your priorities, and set the stage for future improvements.

Leaders who maintain these high standards of leadership throughout their daily routines become the role models of others. Their inspiration is more powerful than authority, and their influence more inducing.

DEVELOP LEADERSHIP IN OTHERS

The definition and explanation of leadership given in this chapter speaks of high goals and quality commitment. We addressed the issues of motivation and direction, examined professional profiles, and reflected upon a series of behavioral traits that help define motivational leadership. We constructed a picture of the consonant professional and measured leadership by the willingness of others to follow. Sharing these attributes with others assures a strong and loyal team.

The greatest measurement of leadership is not in the actions of others, but in the resolutions of the leaders themselves. How willing are the leaders to develop leadership in others?

Good leaders realize the importance of surrounding themselves with dedicated and knowledgeable people. It is through them that leaders achieve their goals and earn their reputations. The best leaders also realize the importance of developing leadership in others. It is the propagation of leadership attributes in others that builds strength of commitment and dedication into every level of the organization.

Leadership qualities can be cultivated in other workers by delegating responsibilities as well as tasks to others. The delegating of tasks is simply telling people what to do, supervising their progress, and measuring the outcomes, while the delegating of responsibilities also gives them the tangent authority to make decisions and to correct problems on their own. In this way, employees are given ownership of the processes they work with and gain personal gratification when targeted expectations are consistently met.

Authority is defined as having the ability to make decisions and correct problems without asking for the advice of supervisors or managers. Tangent authority is the authority attached to single processes and sets of similar tasks. When decisions have to be made at a moment's notice and the manager or supervisor is not always around, delegating tangent authority to key employees allows them to make those decisions in a timely and efficient manner. Delegating tangent authority to key workers makes them feel that they are an integral part of the organization. Higher responsibilities usually breed higher productivity and loyalty.

You can also build leadership in others by allowing your key employees to help conduct training sessions and weekly staff meetings. Not only does this take some of the pressure off of you and senior staff, it helps to build confidence and professionalism in others. Confidence and displayed professionalism are key attributes for leadership.

Building leadership in others makes the whole team stronger, with leaders strategically selected from various positions and levels in the organization. It relieves some pressure from you and senior management to make all of the decisions, it helps ensure that decisions are accepted since they are generated by staff and it begins to cultivate management potential in the key employees chosen for the roles.

Some students may be thinking that if they build leadership in others by delegating tangent authority and allowing employees to lead training and staff meetings, they will be jeopardizing their own jobs. This could not be farther from the truth. Building leadership in others makes people feel important, yes, but important thanks to the confidence you have placed in them. This breeds loyalty that money and schedules cannot buy.

Another tangent benefit to building leadership in others is in cultivating a replacement for your senior staff and even for yourself if and when you decide to make a change in employment or retire at the end of a long career. Cultivating your own replacement will help assure that the same high quality standards you created and supported will be continued after you have gone. There is no other single issue that defines leadership or gives professional satisfaction as clearly as when your own ideas and strategies for success are continued by your prodigies long after you have left.

CHAPTER 15

Team Building

OBJECTIVES

When you complete this chapter, you should be able to:

- Describe the team concept as it can be applied to the hospitality and food service industry.
- Describe the role of chef as coach.
- Apply the analogy of sports coaching to food service management.
- Describe two techniques prescribed by Dale Carnegie that can influence other people to do the things you want.
- Describe some key attributes of coaching that the modern chef must emulate.
- Discuss a strategy of selection to make sure new employees can successfully join and contribute to the team.
- Apply team training strategies to the development of kitchen and dining room staffs.
- Describe, in hospitality terms, the coaching staff of modern food service and its role in leadership.
- Describe the importance of managing the team rather than production quotas and quality controls.
- Discuss management strategies that can help shape kitchen and dining room staffs into cohesive and directed teams.

THE TEAM CONCEPT

The best leaders realize that their success is based on the hard work and dedication of others. While they may assume the credit for motivating and directing the team, they realize that it is the efforts of the team itself that protect quality and improve production and service.

Workers pulled together to accomplish quality goals in timely and efficient measure are a reflection of good leadership. They share common goals, are coached aggressively and take responsibility for their own work. Together, good leaders leading motivated workers make an assertive team.

The team concept is still relatively new to the world of business, and particularly to the hospitality industry. At first glance, it seems incompatible with the hierarchical structure put in place by Escoffier, but in reality, the concept of team includes its own linear authority: the coach at the top, specialized coaches at various levels of responsibilities, the starting lineup, and the bench full of supporting players and relief players. When combined with the theories and practices of Total Quality Management, the team concept becomes the most logical progression for food service management, from a militaristic approach to supervision and leadership to one of setting common goals and motivating everyone on the team to succeed.

The team concept in business is analogous to the many team sports that depend on a group of people performing well together to accomplish a single goal: to win games. Sports teams have a head coach, specialty coaches, a starting lineup of players, and a bench of reserve players waiting their turn on the field. There's usually a minor league or amateur status training camp in sports, and in all cases, the best achievers, the most dedicated and hard working players, make the team.

Applying the team concept to business, the head coach is the boss, the specialty coaches are the line supervisors, the starting lineup is made up of the production workers or sales people, and the bench comprises support workers and apprentices. The minor leagues in business are the small businesses or startup businesses where first-time workers learn and practice the craft that will eventually catapult them into the big league.

Winning games in business is analogous to meeting quality production and service standards, beating the competition, and winning new customers. As in sports, the workers who make the team are the most productive, the most dedicated, and the most consistent performers. The champions in business are the ones that supply a product or service that keeps pace with the changing demands of the customers, and expand their offerings to meet new challenges. The spectators are the customers and the fans are the customers who keep coming back time and time again.

THE CHEF AS COACH

In the world of sports, the coach is the one who selects, trains and motivates the players. The coach is the one who develops playing strategies, supervises players during training and games, places players in the positions that they are best suited for and gives inspiration and motivational guidance before each match and continuously, play by play. The coach also determines which players play in each game, which ones stand on the sidelines waiting for their turn and which ones need to be cut from the roster.

Every decision the coach makes is for the betterment of the team. Coaches depend on the team to win games and take them to the championships. The ability of the players to work well together as a team is critical to their success, and the ability of the coach to lead and inspire the team is essential.

Kitchen staffs are not unlike sports teams. The best cooks are the ones who work the line, the prep cooks and apprentices support the cooks and are in training themselves for cook positions and the workers who do not contribute or do not work well with others are let go. Although each worker has his or her own responsibilities and sets of tasks to complete, each is dependent on the other to get the job done. The game, to expand the analogy, is each meal period, catered event, or special function that the team has to perform.

It should be an easy assimilation labeling the chef as coach following the same comparisons. However, for many chefs it would mean a complete change of philosophy and a putting aside of traditional management practices. Most chefs are used to being the sole boss, giving orders with the expectation that they will be followed without hesitation or question. In the competitive business of hospitality and food service, just as in the competitive world of sports, authoritarian leadership is not enough to get the most production and loyalty from staffs.

The modern chef has to be motivational and inspiring as well as competent. Being a successful chef today requires more than just personal hard work and dedication; it also requires getting other people to work hard, to increase production, and to improve quality. The chef cannot do it alone, but is dependent on the success of others to place the team in the forefront of the industry.

The chef who accepts the role of coach rather than boss concentrates first and foremost on developing a winning team. A strong and committed team will in turn produce high quality, consistent results and become the winners that will lead the restaurant to the top of the field. Leading restaurants are the ones with full reservation books and long waiting lines.

To do this requires the chef first to select the players, train them to succeed and then share the benefits of winning. The championship medals in business can be measured by increased salaries, better working schedules and competitive benefits. When employees share in the success of the business through personal growth and security, then they are more likely to continue to strive for improvement and remain loyal to your company.

ATTRIBUTES OF A GOOD COACH

A good coach is one who makes the team a personal priority. Coaches are not so much interested in their own success as they are in the success of each team member and the team as a whole. They believe that the strength of the team determines their own strength, and their own weakness is displayed through the poor attitudes and weak performances of non-committed team members.

Good coaching requires good communication and leadership skills, as outlined in Chapters 12 and 14. It also requires an ability to influence others and motivate workers.

One of the twentieth century's leaders in the art of influencing and motivating other people was Dale Carnegie, the founder of the Dale Carnegie courses in Effective Speaking and Human Relations. His number one bestseller, *How to Win Friends and Influence People*, has been sold to over 15 million people who wanted to gain success at home and in business. The popularity of the book is testimony to its effectiveness in developing personal and business relationships, and to the timeliness of the message.

Carnegie's book is a comprehensive study of human behavior and the driving forces that influence and motivate people. In it are various axioms of the human psyche that Carnegie suggest are tantamount to the personal drive for acceptance and perseverance. Implementing these axioms in daily interaction with friends, family and workers will guarantee better success in dealing with people and influencing them to do the things you want.

One of these axioms deals with the human need to feel important. "There is only one way under high heaven to get anybody to do anything," wrote Carnegie, "and that is by making the other person want to do it." For Carnegie, this is manifested in the human desire for recognition and sincere appreciation. According to Carnegie, "The desire for a feeling of importance is one of the chief distinguishing differences between mankind and the animals." Carnegie explained that this human need to feel important was the one factor that influenced such great people as Abraham Lincoln, Charles Dickens, and J. D. Rockefeller to become the men that they were. He goes on to suggest that by recognizing this need in the people you come in contact with and contributing to its manifestation, you can influence behavior and predict positive and contributory consequences.

To accomplish this, follow another one of Carnegie's axioms: "Give honest, sincere appreciation." By giving honest and sincere appreciation to other people, you make them feel important, which is what they want most of all. Make them feel wanted and they will do anything you ask.

Carnegie went further to suggest that one way to motivate and inspire other people is to "have a genuine interest" in them and their well being. "People are only truly interested in one thing," wrote Carnegie, "they are interested in themselves—morning, noon, and after dinner." By demonstrating a genuine interest in other people, you will be feeding into their own psyche, giving them a feeling of importance and self-worth. That self-worth will motivate them to do what you ask and to follow your example. There is no other single motivating factor as influential as the one that puts the spotlight on a person and their achievements.

Accomplish this by taking the time to greet your employees by name. "If you want to make friends, let's greet people with animation and enthusiasm." Demonstrate an interest in their family lives, their goals, and their own ambitions. Show respect for their opinions by taking the time to listen, and be willing to implement their suggestions first. Be genuinely interested in others, compliment their contributions, and they will be more willing to do what you ask.

Here are some attributes of a good coach for the aspiring chef manager to emulate:

- Have a genuine interest in the well-being of other people.
- Give honest and sincere appreciation for the efforts of others.
- Place your priorities on the betterment of the team.
- Respect other people and their opinions.
- Demonstrate a dependence on other people for their contributions.
- Openly give due approbation and praise.

By donning a coach's jacket in addition to a toque blanche, chef managers can achieve championship results through a motivated and loyal team. It is through the success of their teams that coaches achieve renown, prestige and reward.

SELECTING TEAM PLAYERS

Chapter 10, Personnel Management, dealt with recruiting and training new employees, but there the concentration was on selection of qualified applicants for new and replacement jobs. Here we will also consider selecting new employees who can become team players. It is not enough to have knowledge and technical skills; the critical issues deal with an ability to work well with others and share the spotlight as well as the criticisms.

When reviewing applications and résumés for new employees, look for skills that are lacking or insufficient in your current team members and try to find those applicants who can supply them. It is not always enough to hire someone with versatile skills if their primary skills are duplicated in present employees. If you already have qualified broiler cooks and sauté cooks on your staff, don't hire others who may compete with those skills. Instead, hire workers with expediting skills, garde manager skills, or sauce-making skills. Hiring workers with skills similar to current employees' skills may make your team members feel threatened or unnecessarily challenged. Look for the weaknesses in your staff and hire to fill those missing skills, not to duplicate existing ones.

Look for longevity in new applicants' résumés. How long did they stay at the last job? The last two jobs? It is not your business to help people build a dynamic résumé for the benefit of others; your sole purpose is to hire people who will continue to contribute to your team year after year. Longevity in past jobs is a sign of company loyalty—someone who will make a good team player.

When you first meet new applicants, offer them your hand. A firm handshake is a confident handshake that reflects a person's commitment and self-determination. A soft handshake may be a sign of insecurity and reflect a person's apprehension about their ability to do the job they are interviewing for.

Looking in a person's eyes while talking to them can sometimes tell you whether the person can be an aggressive team player or will be satisfied with sitting on the sidelines. Someone who looks back is confident in themselves, and those who look away are insecure or unduly nervous.

The next test would be to walk the applicant around the operation before you've offered them the job. Observe their reaction when they meet your other team members. Are they outgoing and friendly, or held back and reserved? Do they offer to shake their hands or are they standoffish? Friendliness and open-mindedness may be the most important skills new employees need to have to become solid team members. Technical skills can be learned or refined, but how can you teach someone teamwork if they are self-centered?

Test applicants in the position that is being offered before hiring them. It is important to match people's skills to a particular position and not hire someone simply because they are looking for a job and you need someone. Employees need jobs they can be successful in rather than positions that are too difficult or too easy. The position should be challenging to new employees, for challenge breeds excitement and builds a sense of dependency on others to get the job done. Jobs that are too easy are quickly mastered, allowing new employees to show off, which immediately builds resentment in veteran employees. Employees who are challenged by the new job are forced to seek the help and advice of the seasoned workers. This dependency, together with friendliness and open-mindedness, builds teamwork and camaraderie.

Team Training

Team training is no different than any other type of skill training. The best way to accomplish it is through practice, practice and more practice. It needs to be deliberate and timely, and must involve all members of the team.

The first step in accomplishing team training is to establish firm schedules for employees that repeat themselves week after week. While some employees may ask to rotate from shift to shift, and some managers feel it necessary to have flexibility in scheduling for the purpose of team training, it is first necessary to identify and preserve the team of players responsible for each shift of the operation. This means identifying the key workers, the dedicated line workers and key servers for each shift, the main support workers, the prep cooks, bus persons and back waiters, as well as the janitorial and ware washing staffs. One team comes on duty as another goes off. Cross-utilizing staff workers in multiple teams should be avoided except in emergency situations.

Having the same workers work the same positions every day builds an interdependency and camaraderie between shift workers that becomes invaluable to team building. Workers learn about each other's strengths and weaknesses. They learn when they can depend on others for support and where their extra effort may be needed to carry the team through busy times. They share the good and the bad, the stress and the relaxation, that is unique to their shift. Together they learn that they can be successful at making work fun and exciting by the efforts of the team, and that everyone's position on the team is equally important to the overall operation.

These shift teams should hold meetings separate from the other shift teams to discuss operational and quality control issues that affect their particular shifts. They should have brainstorming sessions where everyone on their team can share their opinions and ideas. These meetings should be regular, have set agendas with some room for new input, and should be kept to a minimum amount of time so as not to interfere with production or service.

Brief shift meetings should be held at the beginning and end of each shift. In this way, production and service projections can be discussed to give everyone the same picture and the same expectations. At the end of the shift, brief meetings can be used as assessments on production and quality, and motivational tools for the group's collective effort. Planning and rewards shared with the team as a whole will also build the team spirit. These need to be high energy and positive meetings that will carry the energy of the team on to the next day.

Collective meetings, where all team shifts are invited to attend, should also be held in order to address issues and share news that affects the whole operation. These joint meetings help to bridge the shift teams into one cohesive company team with common agendas and common goals.

Each shift team should be assigned work that carries over into the other team's realm of production or service. In this way, dependency between teams is encouraged, breaking down barriers that might otherwise impede overall team development. Having one team leave notes or messages to the following team, or crossing over the shift by a few minutes to allow employees who share stations to share important information, will also help make the whole team a more cohesive workforce.

Consistency is controlled through the use of the coaching staff. In hospitality and food service operations, these are the shift managers and the sous chefs. The coaching staff's main concern should be the motivation and direction of the team members, not the tasks themselves. With the focus on developing the team, tasks are accomplished and production is done at a higher level of quality and consistency.

The coaching staff should be scheduled to overlap shifts by at least an hour or more to facilitate communication and planning. This helps to bridge the two shifts and allows work started by one shift to be completed properly by the other. It also helps to unite all workers into one collective team with shared goals that utilize similar strategies in production and service.

TEAM MANAGEMENT

Managing the team requires the chef manager and the coaching staff to step back from the day to day production and service routines to evaluate the effectiveness of the team itself. Does the team function well together? Is there congeniality or strife among team members? Are there team members that want to hog the spotlight, or does everyone work together toward common goals? Investigating these questions and finding solutions to inadequacies can do more for meeting production standards and assuring quality control than any other single form of personnel training or motivation techniques.

Once the team has been identified and training has begun, it is necessary to place members in the positions that they can be most successful in, and in positions that contribute the most to the team as a whole. The employees placed in the lead line positions should have the most experience, but should also be the ones who demonstrate good leadership skills. The support staff should be ambitious achievers with strong skills, speed and accuracy. When employees are placed in respective positions because of skill and level of motivation, their contributions can be powerful and their loyalty secure.

Unfortunately, many workers are placed in positions that they are not prepared for or willing to fill. Many operators adopt an arbitrary wage designation based on position; this forces employees to accept other positions in the organization in order to get a wage increase. For example, many organizations put a limit on the amount of money they are willing to pay dishwashers or prep cooks. They might say to these workers that in order to get a raise, they need to become prep cooks or line cooks, respectively. While they may have been excellent dishwashers and prep cooks, well worth any wage they would be given, they are forced to accept a position they are not able or willing to fill in order to advance. The new position may be too challenging, and ultimately degrading, to their self-confidence and pride in their work. This practice often forces good employees to leave organizations in order to find positions that they are comfortable with and at which they can earn a decent living. The organization is then left with another vacancy and has lost a good employee and team player to save a few dollars.

Sometimes the chef manager may feel that a worker is not making significant contributions to the organization. The first instinct is to fire them and look for someone else, but this may not be necessary. Change the person to another position, and another, until you find the position they are suited to. By doing this, you will be saving an otherwise good employee and will demonstrate to the rest of the staff your commitment to the team. Everyone with a positive attitude can contribute to the success of the organization. By placing the needs of your employees over the assumed needs of the organization, you are earning the respect of your workers, who will be dedicated and loyal in return.

Cross-training your staff is still important. You need to be able to depend on the flexibility of your employees to step in when needed as business fluctuates, and to have people prepared for upward organizational mobility when changes in staff do occur. Cross-training employees is also a team management technique, since everyone on the staff gets to see and feel the jobs of others. This sensitivity to the work pressures and difficulties inherent in all positions makes people respect each other and their contributions to the team as a whole.

The team concept, underscored with strategies of TQM, sets the stage for the professional success of the organization and the personal success of the workers. The dynamic complexities of the hospitality and food service industry can be overpowering even to the staunchest of individuals, yet can be mastered by a team of aspiring individuals led by a dedicated coaching staff. For a well trained team and its chef manager, the challenges of the industry are what make it exciting and the rewards lasting.

CHAPTER 16

Personal Development

When you complete this chapter, you should be able to:

- Describe the need for change in business practices and personal development.
- Conduct your own self-assessment of skills and knowledge.
- Determine a national standard for skill competencies by conducting professional research.
- Establish your personal career goal.
- Design a plan to reach your ultimate goal based on a series of short-term goals.
- List and describe the five steps to take toward professional success.
- Describe the need to change your career plans based on changes in your career goal.
- Discuss some of the issues dealing with the management of time in both personal and professional lives.

A LIFE OF LEARNING

When you made the commitment to a career in hospitality and food service management, you also made a commitment to continued education and constant self-improvement. As the hospitality industry grows and expands with the evolving market, so too must chefs and other managers increase their skills and knowledge and expand their portfolios in order to stay competitive and guarantee continued success.

Competition and a discriminating customer have forced the business of hospitality to change. Past success is no longer a prediction of future success, nor is tradition any longer a salable commodity. Restaurants and hotels have to keep current with customer demands and trends, and it takes an aggressive management team to keep up the pace.

The same competition forces hospitality managers to change their way of thinking, their way of doing things, and their own perceptions of quality of product and value of services. In order to keep pace with the growing demands of the industry, a lifelong commitment to learning and skill development is required. If you want to be a leader in your field, you must be willing to be on the cutting edge of new ideas. Become the innovator and you will secure for yourself a long and profitable career.

SELF-ASSESSMENT

Self-assessment is the hardest thing a person can be asked to do. It is much easier to criticize others, or ask others to evaluate you, than it is to identify your own weaknesses. Especially for those who have proven themselves to be flexible and strong at work, deficiencies in skill and knowledge are easily hidden under the pressures of daily routines. However, before you can progress, you must first know from where you started, have goals to reach for, and a plan of action to achieve them.

Since the purpose of conducting your own self-assessment is for your personal edification, you need to be as critical and honest as possible. The more exact you are in identifying your strengths and weaknesses, the greater the improvement can be. Weaknesses, after all, are merely deficiencies that need to be remedied. Beginning with an honest appraisal of your skills and knowledge, you can construct a realistic plan to improve upon your weaknesses and build upon your strengths.

You need a formal process for your self-assessment. Consider it a part of your job and give it the same dedication and commitment you give to your other daily tasks and responsibilities. A journal is a good way to record your starting assessment and keep track of your progress. By writing it down, you are making a conscious effort to see the project through, and can mentally reward yourself when you fill the pages with documentation of new skills and knowledge.

Begin by listing your strengths. This will motivate you to conduct the rest of the assessment and give you a solid foundation from which to build. You can identify your strengths by examining your own work routine and listing the tasks you do on a regular basis with speed and accuracy. Meat cutting, sauce-making, inventive soup-making or recipe development may be tasks that you complete every day, feel comfortable doing and feel you can do better than anyone else in your operation. These may be the skill strengths that you depend on every day—ones that are well practiced and proven. Then list areas of knowledge that you feel you have expertise in. This may include technical culinary knowledge such as the history of food, food origins and various world cuisines. It may also include academic knowledge learned in school, college, or on your own time, such as mathematics, science or problem solving. Your strengths are what make you special and what give you a feeling of importance in your life and your career.

Weaknesses are harder to identify and even harder to acknowledge. We tend not to look at our weaknesses and depend on our strengths to carry us through the day. Yet weaknesses don't need to carry a negative connotation. Look at them as areas that need improvement instead.

You can identify weaknesses in skills by comparing your work routine to that of others. Have an open mind to different ideas. Read other menus as though you were reading a book; put aside your own food prejudices for the sake of adventure and learning. See what works professionally for others and then decide if it is something you want to emulate or not. If more than one chef is doing the same thing—fusion cooking, for example, or dotting sauces around a plate—then perhaps it is something you should consider learning to do.

Read trade magazines to see what other chefs are doing. Talk to other chefs at trade shows or professional association meetings to assess their skill levels and compare them to yours. Go out to dinner at other restaurants and hotels; this is perhaps the best way to see what other professionals are doing and to test your competition at the same time. You will not always agree with other chefs' ideas on food construction and presentation, but it is a starting point for comparison. Use these comparisons ultimately to identify areas that you do want to improve in. They may also convince you that your methods are more professional and present a higher quality product; put these discoveries into your strengths column and go on from there.

Weaknesses in knowledge may be even harder to identify than weaknesses in skills. To do this may require assessing the behavior of others, which can be an awkward and complicated study. Is there someone you look up to? Someone who seems to be better rewarded for their work, or just more happy doing it? What makes these people succeed? If you can identify communication skills as a person's special trait, then perhaps you need to work on your own. If someone you respect has the respect and admiration of others, then perhaps it is their leadership skills that make them who they are; perhaps you need to work on those traits yourself.

Perhaps you'll discover that a lot of what you used to consider as fact is really fiction; that searing meat holds in juices, for example, or that salting meat keeps it from browning. You may decide that you need to study more food science and conduct your own series of experiments to determine predictable results. Begin by not saying anything that you cannot prove, and try to prove everything that you believe to be true. By doing these things, you are on your way to identifying areas of knowledge that need improvement, other areas that need refinement, and perhaps some that need to be changed altogether.

You have already made the first step toward personal development. By identifying strengths and acknowledging weaknesses, you are now ready to construct a deliberate plan for improvement. What you do with that information is based on where you want to end up in your career.

GOAL SETTING

Where do you see yourself two years from now? Five years? Ten? Do you have a picture of what your ideal job might be? Perhaps you want to own your own place, change from private to corporate enterprise, go into research and development, culinary education, or consulting. Do you have a personal career goal?

Setting a personal career goal is essential to professional success. Without a goal, how do you know when you've reached the success you want? You need to have a destination in order to know if you get there or not. A goal is like a destination. It is a type of job, a level of income and responsibility that you strive to achieve.

Work, by itself, is not a goal. Some may say, "My goal is to work hard every day, and soon I will be successful." However, the only thing they will be successful at is working hard every day. Goals need to be specific to a type of position, a place with a great reputation that you may want to work in, or a salary range that will give you the physical pleasures in life that you desire. The way to achieve those goals is the hard work, dedication and continuing education that you must commit yourself to every day and every night.

Others may say, "My goal is one day to be successful," but what defines success? Success is different for each of us and needs to be personally defined given our own idiosyncrasies, dreams and ambitions. Words like success, wealthy and comfortable living are too general to be good goals. Without specific information on what defines your personal goals, you may never realize when you've achieved them, and you may go through your whole professional career without personal gratification or a sense of accomplishment.

Goals are different for everyone. Some may place financial wealth as a priority; others may be more interested in raising a family; still others may want a little of both. Some may want to be the head chef of the largest and most prestigious hotel in the largest city in the world, and for others being a chef-owner of a small restaurant in the country is the goal. Is one goal better than the other? Goals need to be achievable and realistic given your personal dreams and desires.

What is it that you want? Write it down. Look it over. Sometimes what you write down first is not what you really want, but what you think you want. Do you want the wealth and prestige that comes with managing a large international hotel, casino hotel or convention center complex? Then you must also want to work fifteen to twenty years to obtain those positions, work every holiday, every weekend, 60, 70, 80 hours a week, and carry a beeper so that you can be called into work at a moment's notice. To obtain those positions, you probably don't want a leisurely family life, don't see yourself going fishing or camping on the weekends and you definitely don't like going on long vacations. Or do you?

Every professional decision you make has an effect on your personal life. When deciding your professional goals, you must also take into consideration the consequences of your decision.

PLAN TO SUCCEED

Now that you've completed your self-assessment and determined your goals, you need to construct a plan to make them happen. Goals are rarely achieved by accident or through luck; they require careful planning and a concentrated effort to succeed.

There are five steps to building your personal career ladder. Develop a set of short-term goals that will help you achieve each step and you will be on your way to professional success. Five steps to professional success are:

- Continuing education
- Professional posturing
- Expanding portfolios
- Progressive research
- Cultivating business and social contacts

Continuing education is a major part of your professional goal. For many, formalized education is itself a short-term goal that will lay the foundation for a lifetime of education. For others, participating in a formal apprenticeship program linking education and work experience is more appealing and easier to fit into a professionally oriented career track. In both cases, structured educational programs help form a series of short-term goals that can lead to advancement and success.

For restaurant chefs, hotel chefs and catering chefs, a two-year associate degree or three-year apprenticeship program helps gain upward mobility. Corporate chefs, research and development chefs and chef educators may need to pursue a four-year baccalaureate degree or higher. Culinary educators may also need special vocational education training, depending on the state in which they work. Teacher certification is almost always required in secondary education, and highly recommended in post-secondary education.

Many post-secondary educational facilities also offer continuing education courses. These allow working professionals to improve their technical skills and gain new knowledge without committing themselves to full-time degree granting programs. They may last a few hours, a few days or weeks at a time, and are usually single subject oriented. Continuing education workshops are often sponsored by employers to help develop the skills and loyalties of their employees.

Another major step in reaching your professional goal is to obtain a progressive position in the area of the industry that you are interested in. If you are interested in hotels, then work in a hotel, but if your interest is in free-standing restaurants, then that is where you need to be. This is the only way to learn first hand the intricacies that make up the dynamics of a particular workplace. Hotels are significantly different in their operating procedures, the services they offer and their management structure from restaurants, and restaurants are significantly different from country clubs. Before committing yourself to a lifelong search for the perfect position, make sure it is in an area that you particularly like working in. If not, then change your position until you find the one that fascinates and excites you.

Position posturing can be described as the act of seeking progressively more challenging positions in the area of the industry in which you want to work. As you climb from position to position, you gain experience and knowledge that will be invaluable when you reach the top of your career.

You should begin the process with an entry level job in a small-scale version of your dream job, one that offers high quality experiences and allows you the flexibility of moving around from position to position. In this way, you can learn a great deal about the particulars of your job environment in a relatively short period of time. Money should not be the motivating factor in accepting your first job. Instead, consider how much you can learn and how flexible management is in allowing you to accomplish your short-term goals. One to three years is recommended for this first step up the career ladder. Less than a year in more than one location may mark you as a person who is never satisfied, cannot make up your mind or who lacks company loyalty.

Set a time frame for this first of many short-term goals. If it is two years, then after eighteen months or so, begin looking to make your next move. Always give proper notice to your current employer and allow yourself enough time to seek out your next position. Every step you take has a significant effect on obtaining your goal and should only be taken by deliberate action, after careful study.

Keep your decision to move on after completing the years you determined were adequate for the position. Otherwise, you may stall in your quest for the ultimate position. Your next position should be at a larger and more challenging operation. It should be one that benefits from your skills and education, and can teach you more, give you more responsibilities, challenge your strengths and help you to overcome your weaknesses. Stay with this position two to five years before moving on. With each subsequent job, plan to stay for an incrementally longer period of time. This is good for training and for promoting yourself as a dependable and loyal employee.

Continue to set time frames on these short-term goals and keep to your schedule. With each progressive move, you are building a stronger foundation of skills, knowledge and experience that you will depend on in later years.

Progressively challenging positions give you a comprehensive portfolio of job experience. More than just a résumé of work, a portfolio is a collection of skills, tested knowledge and demonstrated experience that highlights your strengths and abilities.

The term portfolio normally refers to a carrying case that workers use to organize and transport their work achievements to job interviews. It allows artists to carry some of their work with them, photographers some pictures, and architects a few drawings. The professional chef can also collect a series of documents, photos and drawings that best represent their experiences and abilities.

A culinary portfolio could include photographs of finished buffet presentations or finished plated meals that the chef helped to create. It is a good idea to have a camera at your disposal so that you can take pictures when appropriate and decide later which ones to use in your portfolio.

Always include copies of menus that you worked with in your portfolio, especially ones that you wrote yourself. This shows the depth of your technical skills and your knowledge of menu design and costing.

Your culinary portfolio could also include kitchen designs that you consulted on or drew up yourself. This would show your knowledge of the complexities of kitchen design and how it affects menu planning. Even drawing existing kitchens to show the complexity of the work environments that you are accustomed to working in can be an impressive addition to your portfolio.

Letters of reference should also be included in your culinary portfolio. Collect these wherever you go and show them proudly. You should not wait until you decide to leave a particular place to ask for letters of reference. Often people you would like to get letters from have departed before you and are hard to track down. At other times, you are too busy looking for another job and training someone to take your place that you forget to get these important documents. You should seek out letters of reference after your first successful year in a new place. A year is sufficient time for your supervisors to gain an opinion of your abilities and is short enough not to indicate to your employer that you intend to leave. Be sure to discuss your strategies with your current employer. They will be more likely to write you a positive letter of reference when they understand your plans to improve your portfolio and know they can still count on your staying with them for years to come.

Another step on your professional career ladder is committing yourself to constant and progressive research. The consummate professional keeps abreast of all new technologies and information related to their field of expertise. This is a never ending process as technologies improve, information is discovered and achievements are made.

There are many ways to seek current information and keep up to date with new professional strategies and innovative techniques. Take advantage of several methods to ensure proper and timely coverage of current information.

- **Trade magazines and newspapers:** Periodicals are some of the best sources of current information. Since they are published frequently, their editors must always search for what's new and exciting in the industry. Some are available free to professionals, others require a yearly subscription fee and others are available through professional association memberships.

- **Trade shows and exhibitions:** Professional associations and large commercial vendors sponsor local, regional and national trade shows. These allow for the open exchange of current information in the form of seminars, lectures, and vendor exhibitions.

- **Professional conventions:** Conventions are sponsored by professional associations to keep their members abreast of association activities and plans. They also are meeting grounds for professionals from around the country to share information and exchange ideas.

- **The Internet:** The Internet now offers a new source of information research available to anyone with a computer and a modem. You can subscribe to various Web networks that give you access to published books and articles, research data and to other professionals in your field. Many use the Internet as a form of communication, giving and asking information from colleagues around the world.

Choose a variety of research methods to give you a cross-section of the most currently available information. There is enough new information, and changes in professional strategies and techniques, to keep even master chefs busy studying and practicing.

Develop as many professional contacts as you can to help catapult yourself into the professional spotlight. The more people you meet and get to know who are themselves the leaders and motivators in the industry, the more chances you will have for upward mobility.

People are more likely to recommend someone for a new job or and advancement if they already have a professional relationship with them. Recommendations are endorsements of a person's abilities and personality. Few people would recommend another person for a job unless they were sure they could handle the work and the responsibilities. They would not want a person's poor performance to be a reflection of themselves.

Professional relationships can be fostered through participation in professional associations and enrollment in continuing education programs with other professionals. Attendance and participation at trade shows and conventions are also great ways to meet and develop relationships with other professionals. Professional relationships with some will, in turn, help you develop relationships with others as they introduce you to the people they associate with. This can be an exponentially expanding network of professional contacts that will benefit you in your career goals for years to come.

As you obtain new knowledge and new skills, your goals may change. New opportunities may open that you were not previously aware of, or personal circumstances might take an unexpected turn. As your goal changes, so too must your plan change. Write, review and re-evaluate your plan constantly to make sure it stays fixed on the goals you have chosen. By developing strategies that concentrate on your professional career growth, you are bound to reach the success that you imagine.

TIME MANAGEMENT

Lack of time is perhaps the most often used excuse for not doing some projects, and for doing others quickly without regard for quality. How often have you said or heard statements like "If we only had more time," or "I'm way too busy to be careful"? Time is often mentioned as the main reason for not doing certain things, while it is the management of time that truly affects progress.

Time management means organizing yourself to be able to accomplish all the important tasks given to you, at the level of quality they have been prescribed with and in the amount of time given you to do so. Its aim is not to fill up your life or work day with activities, or to be able to solve all problems facing you and your organization; it is to help you identify what you need most, what has the greatest effect overall and to plan how to go about doing it efficiently.

When work time is managed efficiently, time can be prioritized so as to organize all the elements which are crucial to quality management. The fact is, most people waste time, but productive employees waste less of it.

The first step in improving your use of time is to study the time you are already applying to certain projects to determine when you are being effective and when you are wasting time. The goal is to free up time wasted on unimportant or redundant projects and spend it on getting more important things done better.

WASTING TIME

Time is easily wasted by working habits and practices which eat up time unproductively.

Here are some common causes of wasting time:

- Spending too much time on problems brought to you by others.
- Over-supervising; watching someone doing something when it is not necessary to do so.
- Under-supervision which can allow problems to occur which then have to be addressed (time spent on fixing problems that should not occur).
- Scheduling less important work before more important work.
- Starting a job before thinking it through.
- Leaving jobs before completing them; every time you have to start over wastes time.
- Doing things that can be delegated to others just because you like to or want to.
- Doing things that can be delegated to modern equipment like food processors, electric mixers, etc.
- Doing things that actually aren't part of your real job.
- Spending too much time on your previous area of interest or competence.
- Keeping to many, too complicated or overlapping records.
- Pursuing projects you probably can't achieve.
- Failing to anticipate crises.
- Handling too wide a variety of duties.
- Allowing a discussion to continue after its purpose has been achieved.

- Conducting unnecessary meetings, visits and phone calls.
- Chasing trivial data after the main facts are in.

Controlling Time

There is always enough time to accomplish what items are important, and what can be postponed or ignored. It is a simple matter of prioritizing tasks, delegating others and postponing those which have less impact on overall quality productivity. It is that analysis which determines whether or not time is being used wisely.

Some managers use the following as an excuse for poor time management practices: "Other people make too many demands on my time." If they are not your boss, supervisor or owner of the company, then you have more control over this than you might think. Learning to say no can be one of the most effective time savers in these types of situations. However, when saying no, even to subordinates, be courteous, give a brief explanation of why you cannot comply with a request and avoid being dragged into a prolonged discussion about the reasons, which is another waste of time.

Busy schedules are used as reasons for not being able to prioritize work. To control your time and your life however, it is not only possible to prioritize, it is essential. It may seem like a daunting task at first, but by spending the time to prioritize tasks you can save a lot of time later which would have been wasted on doing unimportant tasks. Set priorities and stick to them. Learn to delegate the less important tasks to others; this frees up time to tackle more creative projects that require attention.

The busier the manager or worker, the more important it is to take time out to plan your work activities. Planning is key to effective time management. Without a plan, people are unlikely to be in control of their work day. They will react to events as they happen, consuming most of their time, leaving little or no time to do things properly. These types of workers also tend to work longer and harder than others. Working long and hard hours does not always equate to working smart.

Procrastination is probably the one thing that wastes more time than anything else. Procrastination is the putting off of doing something until it is absolutely necessary to do so. Sometimes procrastination kicks in as a way to avoid tasks that are unpleasant or uninteresting, resulting in quick fixes or fast production where quality suffers. Deal with tasks head on, one at a time; steady progress is a way to accomplish even the most complex assignments. It is also a great motivator, because you can begin to check off the tasks you have completed from your list showing you and others the progress you have made.

"Never put off until tomorrow what you can do today." This familiar adage was written by the Earl of Chesterfield in 1749 and is clearly a warning against procrastination; but just because you can do something now does not necessarily mean that you should do it now.

Obviously, all tasks and projects are not of the same importance. Managers often feel as if they are under pressure to respond to situations or to persons exerting the greatest pressure. This causes some managers to solve problems in the order in which they arise, and not the most important ones first. Dealing with matters in the order in which they occur at times is fine in some circumstances, for example expediting table orders, but in most situations it is an unproductive use of time. Important does not necessarily mean urgent, nor does urgent necessarily mean important.

Compare what you want to do with what you are already doing or planning to do. The results will be a priority list that tells you what to do first, what to do next, and what to do last. Keep a time log of a typical week. Disorganized priorities are common causes of procrastination.

Here are some time management skills that you should incorporate into your personal and professional lives:

- Reserve blocks of time to get the job done and develop the habit of planning effective time.

- Make daily and weekly to-do-lists in order or priority. Check off each task as it is completed. This will provide a feeling of accomplishment at the end of the day.

- Plan what you are going to do at least one day in advance. If you know what tasks await you tomorrow, organize tomorrow's to-do list today.

- Plan telephone calls in advance. By doing this, you will know what you want to cover and can reduce time spent on the phone.

- Plan meeting (one on one or with the entire team) in advance. If you call the meeting, take control of the agenda and stay on the subject.

- Evaluate your time management several times during the day. Take a look at how you're doing about one-third of the way through the work day and again two-thirds of the way through. Will you meet your objectives for the day? If not, what got in the way?

- Learn to handle common distractions. Controlling the time taken by drop-in visitors requires both courtesy and good judgment. Limit the number of people you invite to your area. If you need to be with someone, go to his or her work area. It is much more difficult to get people to leave your work area than it is for you to leave theirs.

- Unsolicited business mail, often referred to as junk mail, often arrives daily in an unending flood and makes demands on your time. If you have someone sort through your mail, give that person guidelines on what you want to see, what should be routed to other employees or simply thrown away.

- Communicate efficiently; keep memos and phone conversations short.

- Complete one job at a time. Important tasks need plenty of uninterrupted time and cannot be completed between other activities. This wastes time; each time you re-start you need to get familiar with the project again.

- Meetings should be planned with objectives in mind. Some of the reasons why people consider meetings time wasters are that they can take too much time to cover too little material or they don't start or finish on time.

- Learn to say no. In some cases, the demands placed on your time will exceed your ability to accommodate all of them.

- Delegate tasks to other employees. To delegate (not dump tasks) is a key time management skill.

- Anticipate the unexpected before it occurs.

- Organize your work area. The area should be organized so it is easy to complete your normal tasks.

- Avoid diversions and interruptions to the extent that you can.

Being busy has nothing to do with productivity. Maximizing how you use your time means a great deal more. It will open up more free time, more time for new ideas.

Section 5

STRATEGIC MANAGEMENT FOR THE PROFESSIONAL CHEF

Chef managers who adopt the philosophy of Total Quality Management in their operations have already admitted to themselves that the traditional ways of managing business are no longer effective. Modern food service managers are encumbered with myriad obstacles, ranging from issues of diversity, prejudice and discrimination to the fluctuation of prices, the perishable nature of food and the demands of finicky customers. No wonder chefs are hungry for a better way of doing things.

The underlying tenet of TQM can be summed up in one short statement: TQM prescribes a practice of continual assessment of the processes that can lead to quality improvement. In this section we will learn how to assess the processes. More than just collecting data such as food cost, labor cost and sales volume, we will discuss ways of displaying the data so that it tells us a story. We will take a step back from the records and the journals to look for patterns and trends and the influences that created them. In this way, we will be able to keep sight of our ultimate goal, quality improvement. We will not get caught up in counting pennies or shaving standards for the sake of controlling costs. We will applaud progress no matter how slight, and take ownership of the results of our hard work.

CHAPTER 17

Managing
the Modern Workplace

When you complete this chapter you will be able to:

- Discuss the improvements in organizational structure that Peter Drucker attempted to apply to GM's operational strategies.
- Describe the processes that make up Drucker's Management by Objectives (MBO) theory of quality production management.
- Discuss what Tom Peters says is the main goal of management in regard to employee motivation.
- Discuss Peters' eight principles of quality management that he says all companies could apply to ensure their success.
- Describe what Peters says are attributes of successful managers.
- Discuss Michael Hammer and James Champy's main tenet of their book *Reengineering the Corporation*, which has set the stage for reengineering management.
- Describe with whom you start when beginning the process of reengineering management
- Discuss the four issues facing managers today which Champy says are the catalyst for re-engineering management: issues of purpose, issues of culture, issues of process and performance and issues of people.

PETER DRUCKER AND MBO

Peter F. Drucker was born in Vienna, Austria in November 1909. After receiving his doctorate in Public and International Law from Frankfurt University in Frankfurt, Germany, he worked as an economist and journalist in London. He moved to the United States in 1937, escaping the clutches of the Nazi party in his home country and the ensuing world war that soon engulfed the whole continent.

Drucker published his first book, *The End of Economic Man*, in 1939 and quickly earned a reputation as a modern and creative thinker and manager. His new found reputation garnered him his first big consulting job with the General Motors Corporation and launched his career as an innovator in modern management theory.

His assignment with GMC was to write a comprehensive narrative of the efficiency of their organizational structure. What he ended up doing was to identify a flaw in their corporate management structure that he felt was based on too many outdated theories and policies. The hard job was to try and convince those people in charge of that structure that he was right.

GM, like many American corporations, had implemented a hierarchical structure depicting a clear and definite vertical approach to authority, responsibilities and reporting. GM considered this practice a corporate plus, but Drucker had something else to say.

Every act of planning, quality control and production was in the hands of upper and middle management, while the role of the employee was simply as a worker performing an expected job. Drucker—who studied the strategies of Shewhart, Deming and many other quality management innovators—insisted on the importance of the role of the employee in overall corporate success, rather than focusing on the management of corporate America. GM was willing to concede.

The resulting report later became a second landmark book entitled *Concept of the Corporation* (1943), where Drucker identified decentralization of authority as a key element to corporate improvement. GM officials were not happy with this commissioned work, for it went against their belief that employees were merely tools to getting work accomplished. Drucker insisted that the role of management was to encourage employee involvement in every aspect of planning, quality design and company performance.

Undaunted by GM's refusal to admit the accuracy of his analysis of management roles and responsibilities first to the employee and second to production and efficiency, Drucker continued to research and write more books to promote further his insistence on the importance of employee contributions to the success and failure of businesses. In 1950, he joined the faculty of New York University's Graduate Business School as Professor of Management, where he enjoyed teaching and learning everything he could.

In 1954 Drucker's third book *The Practice of Management*, went further to instill the importance of improving the social climate of employees in the workplace in order to ensure consistent quality production. Drucker insisted that the quality and performance of the workers was the only advantage one corporation could have over another in a competitive market.

Management by objectives (MBO) was one of Peter Drucker's new management philosophies. MBO is a means of measuring the effectiveness of employees by analyzing their ability to meet certain objectives. First, objectives have to be constructed using strategic planning and thorough consultation between managers and supervisors. Objectives have to be obtainable and workers must be given the tools to complete them. Once established, obtaining the goals of each objective becomes a measurement tool of employee production and efficiency.

While MBO may appear to dehumanize work expectations and create unrealistic goals, it actually gives both the employee and the employer a tool to measure one's efficiency. If workers are given a set of objectives to meet and a certain amount of time to accomplish them, then they can judge for themselves their own ability to achieve success. MBO can be analogous to giving each employee a series of obtainable goals that help build efficiency and self-confidence.

Since 1971, Drucker has been Clarke Professor of Social Science and Management at the Claremont Graduate University in Claremont, California. He has written thirty-five books in all: fifteen deal with management, including the best sellers *The Practice of Management* and *The Effective Executive*; sixteen books cover topics on society, economics and politics; two are novels; and one is a collection of autobiographical essays. His most recent book, *Managing in the Next Society*, was published in 2002.

Drucker also served as a regular columnist for *The Wall Street Journal* from 1975 to 1995, and has contributed essays and articles to numerous publications, including the *Harvard Business Review*, *The Atlantic Monthly*, and *The Economist*. Throughout his career, he has consulted with dozens of organizations, ranging from the world's largest corporations to entrepreneurial startups and various government and nonprofit agencies.

Peter Drucker died on November 11, 2005 ten days before his 96th birthday.

TOM PETERS: ATTRIBUTES OF THE MODERN MANAGER

Tom Peters is another contemporary management writer and commentator who is committed to improving the structure of corporations that will allow them constant achievements and positive growth in competitive markets, particularly those relying on technically skilled employees asked to perform complex jobs.

Born in Baltimore in 1942 and residing in Northern California from 1974 to 2000, Peters now lives on a farm in Vermont with his wife, Susan Sargent. Peters is a civil engineering graduate of Cornell (B.C.E., M.C.E.) and business graduate of Stanford (M.B.A., Ph.D.); he holds honorary doctorates from several institutions, including the State University of Management in Moscow (2004).

In the U.S. Navy from 1966 to 1970, Peters made two deployments to Vietnam (as a Navy Seabee) and a tour in the Pentagon. He was a senior White House drug-abuse advisor in 1973–1974, and then worked at McKinsey & Company from 1974 to 1981, becoming a partner and Organization Effectiveness practice leader in 1979. He is now a Fellow of the International Academy of Management, the World Productivity Association, the International Customer Service Association, and the Society for Quality and Participation.

For Peters, the whole concept of improving corporate posture is likened to the motivational strategies used by sport coaches to excite and inspire players (workers in the corporate world) to try constantly to do their best. Management's role is to concentrate on improving the morale of its employees and managers and by doing so improve the whole social structure of the organization. When there is a shared sense of value and contribution among managers and employees, then the company can succeed even in tight markets with shrinking employee pools to draw from.

Tom Peters' first book was co-authored by Robert Waterman, Jr., and entitled *In Search of Excellence* (1982). In it Peters and Waterman communicate to corporate America that great achievements can only occur when motivation of the workers becomes the primary concern of management. If management could only rally behind workers and credit them with the success of the business, then the whole team of workers, managers and owners would be working together to achieve the same high goals and quality standards.

Peters' second book, co-authored by Nancy Austin—*A Passion for Excellence* (1985)—further promoted the concept of positive emotion in improving production and efficiency in corporations. *Thriving on Chaos* (1987), *Liberation Management* (1992) and *The Circle of Innovation: You Can't Shrink Your Way to Greatness* (1997) were landmark books detailing the need for and critical importance of improving production by motivating and inspiring greatness for all managers and employees. Encouraging employees to succeed is the key to corporate success.

Peters identified eight principles of management that he predicted would work in all types of organizations. They are:

1. Create an attitude toward action; nothing that was true is necessarily true today; look for and expect change.

2. Businesses must try to operate using as lean a work force as possible; too many workers create inefficiency.

3. You must have constant and deliberate contact with the customer, and constantly strive to give them what they want.

4. Improvements in efficiency and productivity must start with the people doing the work; there is never enough training.

5. Create a system that allows employees to assume responsibilities; do not segregate workers and managers into two distinct groups—one depends on the other.

6. Adopt a singular concept of value in product and services; preach it to employees and market it to customers.

7. Enable employees to use their own judgment when making decisions about work or products; since you pay good money to have experts working for you, allow them to demonstrate their expertise.

8. Establish policies and procedures, but have a mechanism to allow employees to make exceptions based on customer input and need.

Peters sums it up by saying in his book *Thriving on Chaos,* "New survivors will welcome change rather than resist it, and realize that people power, not robot power is our only choice" (p. 357).

Modern high-impact managers share the same set of attributes and management tendencies. It is a competitive business world that we must work in, not only competition for customers but competition for employees. Here are some of the attributes of successful managers:

- Have a high level of self-awareness; if you are confident of your own skills and abilities then you can better direct others to build their own confidence levels and therefore efficiency.

- You must have a good working knowledge of human behavior, particularly of motivation.

- Managers must be able to use control when allocating resources; every step you take must have a meaning and a purpose.

- There must be a high standard of personal values; you can not instill in others what you do not possess.

- There must be a balance between having a commitment to production and demonstrating a commitment to the worker.

If you want to be a high impact supervising manager, be committed, build a base of practical knowledge, analyze everything you do, and be prepared to act fast when called upon to make a decision. Always take an assertive posture when deciding strategies and planning for the future.

RE-ENGINEERING MANAGEMENT: JAMES CHAMPY

In 1993, when Michael Hammer and James Champy first published their best selling book *Reengineering the Corporation* (Harper Business), they helped to revolutionize the way corporate owners and managers began to think about the way they did business every day. It was no longer a matter of improving their operating and management systems, but deciding first if the systems should be revised or thrown out to start all over again.

Together Hammer and Champy detail examples of how huge American corporations like Ford Motor Company, Dell Computers and Kodak re-engineered their processes and operating systems to reduce cost, control production and create better efficiencies overall for the corporations and their customers. Miller and Champy's basic tenet is not to fix problems but to throw them out and start all over again; re-engineering them depending on what is needed today and not what has always been done.

Champy continued in his quest to help re-engineer American and then global companies through his consulting practices and two additional books of related subjects: *Reengineering Management, The Mandate for New Leadership*, published by Harper Collins in 1995 and *X-Engineering the Corporation, Reinventing Your Business in the Digital Age*, published by Warner Business Books in 2002. For our discussion we will concentrate on his second book, *Reengineering Management*.

Born and raised in Lawrence, Massachusetts, James Champy entered Massachusetts Institute of Technology (MIT) in 1959 with the idea of becoming an architect, but then switched to civil engineering. He earned his B.S. in 1963 and his M.S. in Civil Engineering in 1965. Anxious to broaden his education, he attended Boston College Law School, where he served on *The Law Review* as a writer and as an editor of *The Annual Review of Massachusetts Law*. He received his J.D. in 1968 and quickly passed the bar exam.

After school, Champy returned to Lawrence to help in the family enterprise, a construction and lumber company, where he soon realized how little he knew about running a business. In that same year, 1969, Tom Gerrity, Champy's roommate from MIT, had an opportunity to start a company based on the work he was doing toward his Ph.D. His first project was to build an automated investment portfolio management system, and he asked Champy and two other MIT classmates, Fred Luconi and Richard Carpenter, to join him as partners. They started with an initial investment of $370 each and named the company Index Systems.

Champy planned to run the new firm, but the death of his father took him back to Lawrence to wind down the family businesses. In 1974, MIT asked Champy to come back to lecture in civil engineering and architecture, to run its Alumni Fund and Alumni Association, and to be publisher of its magazine,

The Technology Review. Eager for some fresh experience, Champy accepted the position and the mandate to revise and improve alumni operations.

Meanwhile, *Index* was growing and changing its emphasis from information technology management to management consulting. In 1978, Tom Gerrity asked Champy to rejoin the firm as vice president in charge of managing and building staff and as general counsel. By 1988, *Index* saw the need to become part of a large company and was acquired by CSC. Soon after the acquisition, Gerrity left to become dean of Wharton and Champy became chairman, leading the firm to international prominence and its growth to $200 million.

In *Reengineering Management*, Champy discusses both the need to re-engineer and the processes that have worked to help major corporations already adopt his tenets and inspiration for better management practices.

Re-Engineering Ourselves

Champy begins his treatise on improvement management with this profound statement:

> The results are in: Reengineering works—up to a point. The obstacle is management. The only way we're going to deliver on the full promise of reengineering is to start reengineering management—by reengineering ourselves.

When Champy and Hammer embarked on their quest to help American corporations improve efficiencies, production and service through re-engineering, they captured the spirit of the quality management movement and insisted that the employee had a great role to play in the transformation. According to Hammer and Champy, not only did the employees play a role in quality control by becoming in-line inspectors controlling quality through the production line, but they had to also become their own managers, able to make decisions and correct situations as they presented themselves before moving the process on to other workers or service personnel.

However, the whole concept of enabling workers as mini-managers ended up threatening middle and upper managers, who had always enjoyed being the boss. Until *Reengineering Management* was published it was considered okay and practical to enable employees to make decisions, but only if those decisions mirrored decisions that their supervisors would support. Managers, therefore, only enabled employees as long as they followed their implied directions.

True enabling, according to Champy, is not just getting the workers mobilized, energized and willing to take on more ownership of the processes, but to give them the tools and the wherewithal to do so. It requires "redesigning work so that people can exercise their skills and capabilities to the fullest extent possible—then stepping back and letting it happen" (p. 115).

Some managers may interpret this as giving up control, but in fact it is sharing control with those workers who are in a better position to affect quality production and service. Control, Champy warns, is the only thing that some managers can hold on to as their authority is challenged day in and day out, but by giving up some of the control inspired managers are actually gaining more control through the work of others than they could ever muster themselves.

To be effective in the complex and competitive marketplace that managers work in today, where loyalty to businesses and services is challenged every day, they must re-evaluate themselves and the workplace they manage. Managers must face at least four critical issues: issue of purpose, issue of culture, issue of process and performance and issue of people.

Here is how Champy defines them:

> *Issue of purpose:* Insistently, persistently, relentlessly, the new manager must ask, "What for?" What is it that we're in business for? What is this process for? This product? This task? This team? This job? What are we doing, anyway?

Issue of purpose is an ongoing analysis of everything that is done in the workplace. First determine if the processes and tasks being implemented are still necessary and if not, abandon them; if they are still critical to the efficient operation of the company, then find the best way of doing them given the current state of affairs. Don't keep doing things a certain way just because they have always been done that way; find out the best way of doing them now, and always try to improve them again tomorrow.

> *Issue of culture:* If successful re-engineering requires a change in a company's whole culture, as seems to be the case in many instances, how is it to be accomplished by the same management that did so well in the old culture? If it is true (and it is) that re-engineering is unlikely to succeed where the corporate atmosphere is charged with fear (and its twin, mistrust), how do we generate another, better environment—one, say, of willingness and mutual confidence?

Issue of culture is the acceptance that power, or authority, no longer directs or motivates as a isolated dictate. The importance of hiring the right people based on experience, training and education also requires managers to expect, not assume, higher levels of quality production and service. However, with those higher skills and knowledge come a personality that can not be pushed around, threatened or coerced into doing a job. Management that continues to use the old tactics of stick and punishment or autocratic authority will only continue to face ever-revolving employee turnover and demoralized motivation and loyalty. Hire better trained and experienced employees, and then take advantage of those higher skills and knowledge by giving them more autonomy in making decisions (enabling) without fear of reprisal when decisions are made contrary to management's own.

> *Issues of process and performance:* How do we get the kind of processes we want? How do we get the performances we need from our people? How do we set norms and standards, or measure results—for worker performance, management performance and the performance of the whole enterprise? Reengineering usually demands radical objectives, leadership and political skills to realize. But how do we know whether we have the stuff? What does it take to be a good manager today?

Issues of process and performance are an extension of the Shewhart cycle, or amended Juran cycle, to include all tasks and processes including management styles and techniques. It is the first time management theory is being challenged on a daily basis to determine the best methods to use for the greatest amount of productive supervision. It carries quality control beyond the mechanics of production and into the hearts and minds of the people doing the work, the human factor and those doing the management and supervision. Reengineering is the holistic approach to quality management.

> *Issues of people:* Who do we want to work with? How can we find them from both inside and outside the company? How do we get them to want to work with us? How do we know whether they're the kind of people we want?

The issue of people explores the dynamics of recruitment, promotion and retention of motivated and skilled employees. Champy immortalizes the team building concept through a series of analytical concepts for identifying and hiring the right people for the right job. There can be no accidental or emergency hires that work out well for the corporation. Every decision to hire a new team member has a great effect on the overall stability and improvement of the team. Never hire just to replace, but hire to improve; just as is done on everything else that has to do with the operation of the business.

"Abandon thoughts of corporate discipline," says Champy, "and focus on corporate spirit by embracing human will. The only way to gain control is to give some of it up and share the challenges, success and failure of the business at hand. In the long run, successes will supercede all else (p. 29)."

Champy is currently the Chairman of Perot Systems' consulting practice, and now heads the firm's Cambridge, Massachusetts office. He lives in Boston with his wife, Lois.

Concept Engineering

When you complete this chapter, you should be able to:

- Identify the components needed to clarify a restaurant concept.
- Define concept engineering.
- Describe the five factors used in concept engineering.
- Describe several ways of researching consumer demand.
- Describe the business factors used to design restaurant concepts defined by location.
- Describe the importance of area demographics for restaurant concept design.
- Describe the difference between demographics and psychographics.
- Describe the role consumer traffic plays in concept engineering.
- Describe a strategy used to investigate area competition.
- Describe ways of creating a unique identity while staying compatible with location and demographic information.

MARKETING 101

The first rule of marketing is to know what you intend to sell. To say that you want to sell food is not enough; there are too many variables to be defined before you can sell food successfully. To clarify your concept, you need to answer, What type of food, in what market, with what style of service, and at what price do you intend to sell food and beverages? You need to create a unique identify in a specific marketplace that will attract a targeted segment of the industry with a high volume of potential customers, and then, by offering quality and value, keep them coming back.

Concept engineering is a practice of researching the variables that help define food service styles and values, and using the information to build a concept meeting environmental and demographic parameters. A successful concept is one that caters to a specified market with the flexibility to grow and change.

In existing and new businesses, successful restaurant owners refine or build their concepts around a series of factors, including:

1. Consumer demand
2. Location
3. Consumer demographics
4. Psychographics
5. Consumer traffic
6. Competition

These six factors are used to create the concept, design the dining room and kitchen, plan the menu, and determine the style of service, menu prices, and menu flexibility. This is the process of concept engineering. The collected data becomes the foundation for ideas and the fuel for inspiration. Personal preference plays a role only when everything else has been satisfied.

CONSUMER DEMAND

Often, the owner or chef uses their own personal preference and ego to shape their restaurant's image. They want their restaurants and dining rooms to be a reflection of their own personality, desires and wants. Unfortunately, many fail because they have not taken into consideration the most important factor in restaurant success: customer demand.

Modern consumers of the food and lodging industries span multiple social and economic groups. The average man or woman chooses to eat away from home in increasing numbers every year due to busy lifestyles and double income households. Dining out can still be a luxury, but it can also be a necessity for many modern families.

The modern consumer is also more demanding of particular foods and services than in the past. Television, movies and a more globally traveled public has made people more aware of world cuisine than ever before. This technological sophistication has helped raise their expectations of the fine foods and services offered at local restaurants, hotels and country clubs. Competition has made them more demanding.

The ability to analyze consumer demand is a skill that can be learned. While not everyone is born with an ability to be intuitive or innovative, anyone can gain valuable insights through directed study and a concentrated effort. Managers and chefs who do so successfully will guarantee for themselves success wherever they go.

To gain a complete picture of consumer demands, begin collecting and studying data from a variety of sources. The depth and breadth of your research will determine the clarity of your insights.

- Trade magazines and industry newspapers run articles on the popular establishments as well as on those having problems staying in business. Study these to find out which concepts are popular and which ones are not. Food service trends, marketing strategies and food technology are also subjects covered in various issues.

- National research polls sponsored by various professional associations can help forecast future customer demand. For example, the National Restaurant Association publishes an annual report on dining-out trends. This information can be used to determine the locations and styles of service for new restaurants.

- The success or failure of other restaurants can be a valuable sign of consumer preference. You can find information on these in trade magazines and on the very streets where you live and work.

- The competition can be investigated. What makes them successful? What makes them close down?

- Written surveys can be solicited from existing customers and potential customers near your restaurant. You can ask direct questions about the types of foods they desire and styles of service they prefer. You can also ask for recommended hours of operation and during what meal periods they would be most likely to frequent your restaurant.

- For existing restaurants, you can record and track the most popular menu items and the ones which are not selling. This can be the most important piece of information for determining customer demand.

These are the tools that can help you understand consumer demand and begin to design a concept to meet it.

LOCATION

The location of the restaurant plays a crucial role in determining the factors that should be used to engineer the restaurant's concept. Concepts cannot be created in a vacuum; they need substance and an identity that is in balance with their environment and the people that make up their customer pool.

These are the business factors determined by location:

- Area competition
- Area demographics
- Consumer psychographics
- Customer traffic

Area competition has already set the standard of quality and prices for food service at your location. Their success is a direct reflection of consumer demand for their product. Find out what their product is and fashion your concept within similar parameters.

An example could be an area dominated by steak houses, barbecue shops, and diners. This suggests consumer demand for traditional food service and basic foods; the guest check averages under $15 per person. Your restaurant should reflect a similar style of menus and pricing. Do not reproduce the competition's concept, but mirror their strengths and their consumer appeal. A concept that involves exotic foods in a gourmet atmosphere with high-end pricing may struggle to survive in this particular location. If that is the type of restaurant you want, then find another location.

While similar in menu and pricing to area competitors, your concept could promote other consumer interests not marketed by the other restaurants. Quality of food, friendly and efficient service and versatility of menu may set you apart from the competition, while still offering menu selection and pricing all ready proven in the area.

AREA DEMOGRAPHICS

Demography is the study of the physical characteristics of populations, including size, age, growth, density, diversity and financial stability. When concentrated on a particular area, an analysis of this information can give entrepreneurs and managers valuable insight into the lifestyles of the people living or working near their establishments. These area demographics are the collection of measurable physical data and vital statistics for specific consumer markets.

Demographic data is generated partially through the government census taken every ten years, and is a part of public record. This information can be obtained easily through local departments of commerce. Information about a group of people's ages, level of education, financial stability, number of family members, and number of employed workers can be vital in determining the type and scope of food service operations that could be successful in that area.

Zoning commissions and license issuing agencies can also give valuable demographic information. These agencies can offer information on the number of start-up companies in a particular area, the number of restaurants already established, and the percentage of residential versus commercial real estate. This information could help you determine the best location for your restaurant or the type of restaurant service to provide: delivery versus sit down, or cafeteria versus table and booth service.

There is a wide range of valuable information available to those seeking to identify or expand a particular market. Information on the average income of families and workers in the area can be obtained, and dominant ethnic groups can be identified. Religious practices can also be determined by the number of churches and synagogues in the area.

The general ages of the people in a neighborhood can also be examined. This information can be used to determine what types of food service should be designed for young families, young professionals, or near retirees. Each classification of citizens helps determine the type of menu, pricing and service required for restaurants and other small businesses to be successful.

Here's an example of using this information. Consider that you want to open a casual, Mexican theme restaurant at a particular location which has just come up for sale or lease. Along the same street are two competing Italian restaurants, a steak and lobster house, one diner, and one café. The place you want for your restaurant used to be a family owned and operated American theme restaurant which had been successful for many years until the family retired and put the place up for sale. Your research also finds that the predominance of people in the area are of Irish, English, and German descent, with 35 to 40 percent of them retired or near retirement age.

After careful study and investigation of the competition in the area and the demographics of the people, you determine that the local consumer may not be adventurous with their food choices. The information also suggests that the consumer in the area prefers a middle of the road Continental or American cuisine restaurant with leisurely but value-minded menu and service. In light of this information, you may want to change your concept to meet the identifiable demands of the local consumer, or change your location for the Mexican restaurant that you wanted to build.

A good location for the Mexican restaurant might be in another area with a population of either young professionals or young families. If area competition offers an eclectic choice of restaurants like Chinese, Italian, American, and brand-name restaurants (such as Bennigan's, TGI Friday's, and Chili's), then Mexican may be a welcome addition.

Local real estate is another source for demographic information. In a residential neighborhood, the cost of single homes and the average rent of apartments and townhouses is a direct reflection of average family income. This is turn influences the menu prices people are willing to pay. In metropolitan areas, the types of office buildings within walking distance of your restaurant also help determine menu selection and costing.

The demographics within the area of your restaurant may not be permanent residents at all; instead, it may comprise primarily commuters who come into your area only for work. For inner city restaurants, the majority of customers are the people who work in nearby offices, banks and other retail stores. Restaurant locations near government office buildings and courthouses may be frequented by judges and lawyers; if near hospitals, they may be visited by doctors and nurses. Although only a minority of these people may actually live near their work, their demographic profile is still a major influence on area restaurant menus and pricing.

PSYCHOGRAPHICS

Consumer psychographics also play a critical role in defining restaurant concept and design. Whereas demographics refers to the physical and financial aspects of a group of people, psychographics refers to their wishes, wants and desires.

A group's psychographics is a compilation of their constituent's psychological profiles. These psychological profiles are harder to determine and more loosely defined than demographics, but of equal importance. Psychological data is not easily looked up in record books or on charts, and require careful analysis and speculation to help define them. The best way to obtain this information is through written and verbal surveys of actual or potential customers, such as the survey shown in Figure 18–1. Surveys can be customized to obtain information pertinent to restaurants, retail food shops, bakeries, hotels and any other hospitality service operation.

A psychological profile portrays a person's wishes and desires. In the restaurant and hospitality industry, that translates into the demands potential customers will place on product and services. Here is some of the information that can be obtained through psychographic research and review:

- The times people choose to eat away from home
- The reasons why people need overnight accommodations
- Whether people are likely to frequent a free-standing restaurant, a hotel restaurant, a retail food store or a fast food restaurant
- How often people eat out during the week and on weekends
- Whether customers prefer cyclical, standard (unchanging) or daily restaurant menus
- If there is need for hotel, grand ballroom style catering
- How often customers will choose specials versus standard menu items
- How concerned customers are about nutrition, health and safety

AAA Restaurant Survey

Please help us serve you better by taking a few minutes to complete this survey. Your answers are confidential and your candor is appreciated.
Please check all that apply:

1. Which meal periods are you more likely to spend away from home?
   _____ breakfast _____ lunch _____ dinner
2. Which menu items are you more likely to order from a restaurant?
   _____ chicken _____ beef _____ seafood _____ vegetarian
   _____ low fat _____ international
3. What kind of music do you usually listen to?
   _____ rock and roll _____ jazz _____ rap _____ classical
   _____ country & western _____ pop
4. For what reasons do you decide to patronize a restaurant?
   _____ celebrations _____ convenience _____ family gatherings
   _____ business _____ entertaining
5. Which restaurant(s) are you more likely to visit?
   _____ family-style _____ theme-based _____ independent
   _____ ethnic-based _____ fast food
6. What type of service do you prefer in restaurants?
   _____ table service _____ self-service _____ French service
   _____ white glove _____ carry-out
7. Which are your favorite cuisines?
   _____ Italian _____ French _____ Greek _____ African American
   _____ traditional American _____ Asian _____ Spanish
   _____ Mexican _____ Indian _____ Fusion (ethnic mix) _____ Cajun
8. How often do you order dessert when dining out?
   _____ often _____ not often _____ never
9. When choosing desserts, which are your favorites?
   _____ frosted cakes _____ ice cream _____ pies _____ puddings
   _____ cheesecakes _____ éclairs

FIGURE 18–1 Sample Restaurant Survey

- Whether hotel guests will appreciate and use an exercise room or swimming pool
- If there is any interest in vegetarian items on restaurant and catering menus
- The relationships between speed of service, friendliness of service, quality of product and value

Psychographic profiling is a method of research that places like attributes to people who share psychological preferences. For example, people who like classical music have a high probability of also liking instrumentals and musicals, and people who like jazz probably also like rhythm and blues. Restaurateurs and hoteliers can also use like comparisons when developing new menu items and new hotel services. For example, in hotels where a large percentage of the rooms booked are singles, a large and inviting lounge may be appropriate for those single guests to mingle in after their day's work is accomplished. If most of the rooms booked are doubles shared with children, then a game room or video arcade may have a greater perceived value.

Psychographic profiling also suggests that people make buying decisions based on past performance. Studying the purchase history of a group of people will help determine the sale of future products. For example, if the people in a general geographic area frequently choose to eat in theme-based restaurants, then other theme-based restaurants would do well in the same market. If they regularly patronize ethnic restaurants, then starting a new ethnic restaurant or adding ethnic-based menu items to your regular fare would help increase sales.

These are a few of the pieces of information that help to define a customer's dining and lodging habits. This information, combined with demographic data, can help fashion a need for additional food outlets, hotels and country clubs for specific geographic regions.

CONSUMER TRAFFIC

Customer traffic patterns play important roles in restaurant concept engineering. Do your customers walk, as in shopping malls or inner city locations? Or do they drive to your suburban or high-class restaurant? The ease of traveling to your location in part defines the type of customer you will attract.

The easier it is to attract people to your restaurant, the greater is your potential market. Do all your customers drive, as in suburban areas? Then your concept can be more leisurely and your menu selections more filling. Customers will generally have more time to allow for dining and want fuller and more complete meals. Pricing may be higher, depending on nearby competition, because these customers are more likely dining out as much for entertainment as they are for substance. They are often willing to pay a little more for the service that good restaurants offer.

Is there a mixture of walking traffic and drivers? This would likely be in cases of neighborhood restaurants in large residential areas. Because of its proximity to residents with easy access to a range of customers, the restaurant is more likely to be frequented by families with children or by an older population who doesn't like to drive far for meals. Your concept should offer a variety of standard and easily recognizable menu items, a friendly, comfortable atmosphere, moderate pricing and have children and senior citizen specials. These restaurants are likely to be just as busy for breakfast and lunch as they are for early weekday dinners and weekends.

While location is not an absolute barometer that helps owners design profitable restaurants, it is a major factor that needs consideration. High-class restaurants can be successful in residential areas, and Mexican restaurants can be successful in Greek or Italian neighborhoods, but they would be risky businesses to run, given their locations. Running restaurants is risky enough. Design a concept that matches your location and the demographics/psychographics of the potential customers it will serve and you have a better chance for success and profit.

COMPETITION

Competition needs to be studied in order to engineer the right concept for the right location. The success or failure of others gives valuable information to those willing to learn.

The proximity of other restaurants to your location determines their competitiveness for your potential customers. Restaurants within a three mile radius should be studied thoroughly, while those farther away may not affect your sales at all.

First, take a look at the successful restaurants in your area. Success is measured by longevity; any restaurant that has been in business three years or longer can be considered successful. Newer restaurants are not yet proven and should not be your only inspiration to open a similar or compatible concept. Restaurants that have been around ten years or longer have already captured a large share of the consumer market. Study these carefully to find out their strengths and customer appeal.

Next, look at the restaurants that have not been successful in your area. You can find out this information by contacting commercial real estate agencies in the area. They can give you a list of restaurants that are for sale and can tell which ones have already closed up. While it is true that restaurants close for many other reasons other than poor concepts, concept engineering can not be ignored.

You can also tell successful restaurants by the waiting lines or reservation-preferred policies. Struggling restaurants seldom have waiting lines and promote reservation policies only for holidays and special events.

The best way to judge the strengths and weaknesses of competing restaurants is to scrutinize them from a customer's prospective. Patronize them. Visit their dining rooms and bars. Visit them on different days of the week and at different times of the day, and ask a lot of questions. Waiters and waitresses can be very talkative when approached in a friendly manner. With a list of direct questions, you can gather a lot of information in a short period of time. Here is a sample list of questions you might begin with:

1. Is it always this busy (quiet) in here?
2. Is the owner or manager around?
3. Can you tell me what's good?
4. Can I have _____ instead?
5. What are the specials?
6. What's your most popular dessert?

This type of questioning can solicit valuable information about the health and integrity of your competition without being offensive or intrusive. They are questions that are asked by customers every day, and the wait staff would be used to answering them. To a potential competitor, the information can help customize a concept to the natural influences of the location and the customers who frequent the area.

CORPORATE IDENTITY

Once you've studied the demographics and psychographics and investigated the competition, you are ready to begin to engineer your concept. The final result of your efforts will be a unique concept that fulfills the demands of the customers, creates a service format suitable to the type of consumer traffic used to get there and satisfies the business strategies and personal ambitions of the owners.

Another rule of successful marketing is to create a unique identity, compatible with the competition, yet improved or different in a significant way. While being compatible with the influences of location, demographics and psychographics, you can create a unique identity that helps your operation stand out among the competition.

Do this by studying the competition and building your concept around their strengths. Innovation and creativity do not always mean originality; sometimes the difference can be better quality or greater consistency. Strategic management of your concept gives you the information needed to help you fill a vacancy in the market or improve the quality of product or service, or both. Research alone can give you the foundation from which to build a successful concept.

Concepts compatible to the area can still present themselves in a unique light that customers will appreciate. Uniqueness can be as simple as the hours of operation or as complex as menu flexibility. In either case, you can build a unique concept that varies enough from the competition to set it apart, yet is compatible enough to attract the same customer pool.

Here are some areas in which you can become unique in your market:

1. Hours of operation, including days open or closed
2. Variety of meal periods served
3. Flexibility of menu
4. Friendly and hospitable service
5. Varied menu that includes traditional and current food trends
6. Nutritional and vegetarian menu items
7. Portion sizes and choices of accompaniments
8. Plate presentation
9. Seasonal specials

There are many other ways to build a unique yet compatible concept. Only a thorough study of the information can give you the insights to create your own identity in a competitive market. While each market is different, the strategy is the same: Study a variety of factors, select the strengths of the competition to emulate, and make a difference by improving quality of product, service and consistency.

CHAPTER 19

Establishing Operational Standards

When you complete this chapter, you should be able to:

- Describe the important needs of setting standards for production and service.
- Define standardization.
- Describe methods of increasing the predictability of success in production and service.
- Define specifications.
- Describe commonly used specifications related to food production and service.
- Describe the components needed to adequately define operational tasks.
- Describe a method of grouping tasks together to form operational procedures.
- Define standards of operation.
- Describe methods of documenting operational standards for workers.
- Describe the four steps needed to assess operational standards.

THE VALUE IN STANDARDIZATION

The importance of standardization is to ensure consistency of product and predictability of results. Standardized recipes allow various cooks to produce the same menu item at the same level of quality and in the correct portions time and time again. Standardizing operational procedures will allow various employees to perform the same tasks or activities at a consistent level of efficiency and accuracy.

Standardization is the creation of a process or procedure that is so well defined and described that it can be reproduced by people of the same skill level with little or no variation. Standardizing operational procedures gives managers a basis for measuring and assessing their effectiveness, and provides grounds for re-evaluation or change. Procedures are effective when they allow for the consistent production or service of quality products, and can be measured by the predictability of success. Variations in procedures can allow for inconsistencies which can influence the delivery of a consistent quality product.

Predictability of Success

When procedures are performed by various individuals, you expect the results to be the same. Following a standardized recipe, for example, produces the same menu item each time it is ordered. This ensures that the customer receives the same item, seasoned the same, with the same recipe components, and presented in the same way each time they order it. It also allows the restaurant to collect an appropriate amount of money based on ingredient usage and portioning. The predictability of success is very high for standardized recipes tested over a period of time. The same predictability of success can be applied to other operational procedures to test their efficiency.

Predictability of success comes from the ability to predict results. This is critical to the efficient running of complex operations so that planning, control and accurate assessments can occur. Procedures and operations that are well defined with measurable criteria and properly assigned and communicated are likely to be performed properly and to deliver expected results. Since many operations are dependent on others—vegetable prep for vegetable cookery, for example—the greater the number of standardized procedures, the more smoothly production and service can occur.

Establishing Specifications

In order to maintain any standard, you must have a method to measure the product or procedure against an established goal. Establishing exact and measurable criteria for procedures, products and services is to specify the information and procedures required to reach the desired results. These criteria are commonly called specifications and can be applied to all aspects of the food service and hospitality industry.

In food service, you need to decide on specifications such as size, weight, volume, trim, portion and amount. Each designation gives specific information based on a planned and approved standard to assure consistent results.

Size of product can affect purchasing as well as production and service. Do you use 90, 80, 70, or 60 count (the number of potatoes it takes to weigh 50 pounds) baking potatoes on your menu? The higher the number, the smaller the potatoes, since it takes more of a smaller potato to fill the same size box.

Size is also a measurement of many fruits such as lemons, oranges, apples, cantaloupes and honeydews. If one time you order 88 count lemons (88 lemons to 50 pounds) and the next time you order 115 count lemons, your results will be different. Not only will the presentation be different, but the cost will be different. The predictability of success can lessen each time an item is ordered without an exact and measurable specification.

Weight and size are often interchangeable in food specifications. Shrimp, for example, are sold by weight. Yet their size is predictable according to the purchasing specification. Do you need U12 shrimp for shrimp cocktail (under twelve to a pound) or 21/25s (twenty-one to twenty-five shrimp per pound)? Shrimp is sized according to the average number of shrimp in one pound. Specific needs must be communicated to vendors or inconsistencies in size will lead to inconsistent cost, customer satisfaction, and restaurant profits.

Weight is based on either a purchasing specification or a preparatory specification. Does the menu call for 8-ounce, 10-ounce, or 12-ounce filet mignons? Does the veal portion specify 4 ounces or 6 ounces of veal? Exact specifications can assure the proper preparation of menu items with predictable customer appeal and profits. Varying the weight by as little as half an ounce per portion can significantly affect the results. For example, if you are selling 10-ounce filet mignons and each one sold actually weighs 10½ ounces, after just twenty steaks you will be giving one away free. The customer won't even notice the extra ½ ounce, but your profit margin will reflect the loss.

Some operators use recipes that count meat portions rather than using weights; these give ambiguous instructions and can create great inconsistencies. For example, the recipe may specify three pieces of pounded veal cutlet, or two flounder filets, neither giving exact measurable specifications. One cook might use 6, 7 or even 8 ounces of veal depending on the size of the cutlets, or 7, 8 or 10 ounces of flounder depending on the thickness of the filets. The specifications should read 4 ounces of veal cutlets pounded thin, or 6 ounces of flounder filet cut into a minimum of two pieces. Using exact and measurable specifications assures a consistent product that the customer can expect to receive every time it is ordered, and the owners can expect the same amount of cost, and therefore profits, from each sale.

Volume is a liquid measurement and does not accurately measure dry ingredients. Specifications for liquids should be given in volume measures such as cups, pints, gallons, teaspoons, tablespoons, etc., while dry ingredients should be given in weight measurements like pounds and ounces. Some dry ingredients are measured using teaspoons and tablespoons, which are volume measurements, but the amounts are generally too small to weigh on American scales. The European metric system, which utilizes grams as a unit of measure, is much more accurate for small amounts of dry ingredients.

The amount of trimming given to meats is another specification that can give exacting measurements. A recipe may call for 12-ounce ribeye steaks, which appears to be very specific, but compare it to a more complete list of specifications: 12-ounce ribeye steak, cut from Choice meat with ¼-inch fat trim. The second set of specifications is obviously more exact and can produce a more consistent product each time.

Portion and amount are critical specifications for the assurance of consistency in product, cost, and profits. They are also one of the greatest areas of contention for customers who receive an item stated in portions on the menu that is not received. For example, if a recipe for stuffed shrimp says "six jumbo shrimp stuffed with a generous amount of crab imperial," the ambiguous words are jumbo, stuffed, and generous, but there had better be six shrimp.

Portion and amount are often a reflection of weight and size measurements. If the recipe calls for two 4-ounce chicken breasts, each filled with ½ ounce of boiled ham and ½ ounce of Swiss cheese (for chicken cordon bleu), you must follow these instructions explicitly. Imagine one cook using 5-ounce chicken breasts and 1 ounce each of the ham and cheese. The end results will be significantly different in appearance and cost. One day a customer gets the proper portion and amount and the next a greater portion and amount. What will be their impression? That they got a good deal the second time? Or that they were cheated the first time?

Suppose the recipe for grilled shrimp Caesar calls for eight grilled 21/25 count shrimp and the cook uses 31/36 count shrimp instead. One day the customer gets the salad with these eight large grilled shrimp and recommends the dish to their friends. Their friends come in the next day and get the salad with eight smaller grilled shrimp. Won't they be disappointed in the portion? Portioning and amounts are critical to assuring proper costs and profits. This is necessary to properly run the business, pay all the bills, and also for the consistent satisfaction of the customer.

The wait staff's procedures also need exact specifications to assure good customer service and satisfaction. What garnish goes with what plates? What are the proper salad or dessert garnishes? How long must a customer wait before being greeted or served by the wait staff? These are all important questions that need definition in order to assure consistent quality service.

Many operating procedures also need specifications in order to measure their efficiency and improve their effectiveness. The receiving function, for example, needs the same size and weight specifications as defined by the recipe specifications to assure the proper foods have been ordered and received. Receiving also needs timing specifications to state how long it should take to receive and store goods taken from various vendors, and to assure stock rotation procedures.

Food storage needs a set of timing specifications based on the perishable quality of the product and product usage. Dry goods can be held for six months or longer (based on need and storage space), frozen foods three months or less, and refrigerated foods one week or less. Fresh seafood, being the most perishable, needs to be used within two or three days of receipt. Without specific measurements of time and stock rotation procedures to assure meeting those time restraints, foods may be kept beyond optimum quality specifications and inferior products may be cooked and served.

Specifications are measurements applied to the ingredients in foods, operating procedures, and timing issues related to food preparation and service. The more specific the instructions and the better they are communicated to the staff responsible for their completion, the greater the probability of success. As the probability of success continues to climb in multiple aspects of food service, your operation can move closer toward meeting Philip Crosby's Zero Defects concept in quality control and management, as discussed in Chapter 7, Discovering Philip Crosby's Zero Defects.

IDENTIFYING SEPARATE TASKS

Identifying the tasks performed in food service operations on a daily, weekly and monthly basis is the first step in establishing operational standards. Many of the dozens of tasks performed each day can be examined microscopically to assure that proper standards are set at each stage of their performance, and the information organized, preserved and communicated to the people involved in their delivery. Once this is accomplished, the tasks can be grouped into related sets of tasks, which then become standardized procedures. This process of assessment and planning becomes the foundation for quality control.

Tasks are individual assignments or procedures that should be evaluated on a one-to-one basis. While identifying all the tasks performed in a modern kitchen may seem to be insurmountable, many are common assignments like chopping and dicing that already have specific parameters and descriptions. Other tasks, like receiving, storage and stock rotation, need more immediate attention. An hour or two a day may be all that is necessary to begin the process of systematically identifying tasks. No matter how large the assignment may seem, it is finite in scope and can be accomplished with patience and dedication.

Either by computer or in handwritten form, write one task at the top of a single page and identify its components below. The components should include who is responsible for completing the task, a step-by-step description of the activities it takes to complete the task, and other tasks that are affected by its performance. Here is an example:

Task 1 Checking in goods ordered from vendors

People involved: Receiving clerk

Activities:

1. Collect purchase orders from which orders were placed.
2. Greet delivery person and identify who will check the delivery.
3. Clear an area around the receiving door where items can be brought into the establishment from the truck and checked against predetermined specifications.
4. Check invoice against purchase order to assure items that were ordered are received.
5. Check all goods against the following list of specifications:

brand ordered	quality of packaging	safe temperatures
unit purchased	quality of product	size/trim specs
unit received	dry goods dry	costs

6. Identify on invoice items that are missing or returned for not meeting specifications.
7. Sign invoice when receipt has been accepted.
8. Dismiss delivery person and secure receiving area door.

People affected: Storeroom manager

Here is a beginning list of tasks that need defining specifications. Begin with these and expand the list until all individual tasks have been properly identified and specific instructions have been given:

1. Checking in goods ordered from vendors
2. Placing goods in proper storage areas
3. Issuing goods using a first-in/first-out strategy
4. Maintaining a par stock of goods
5. Performing food preparation tasks (list all food preparation tasks, such as slicing mushrooms and dicing vegetables)
6. Setting up production line stations
7. Preparing mise en place for stations
8. Recipes
9. Ordering food to be produced
10. Plate garnishes
11. Wait staff pick-up

12. Ware washing
13. Trash removal
14. Inventory checks
15. Equipment maintenance (list all equipment maintenance tasks, such as refrigeration coils cleaned and knives sharpened)
16. Cleaning assignments

Either the chef manager or the employee can create these task descriptions. Following the guidelines of TQM, it would be beneficial to involve as many people as possible in the construction of task descriptions to assure their accuracy and ultimate implementation.

GROUPING TASKS INTO PROCEDURES

Once all of the tasks have been identified and given specific instructions, they need to be grouped together into sets of tasks which become standard operating procedures. For example, from the starter list given above, the receiving and storage procedures include this set of individual tasks:

- Checking in goods ordered from vendors
- Placing goods in proper storage areas
- Issuing goods using a first-in/first-out strategy
- Maintaining a par stock of goods

Group tasks are then assigned to stations or departments that are responsible for their follow-through. Training must occur to assure that everyone involved in completing the tasks knows the specifications of each assignment and its relationship to the overall operation. In this way, consistency of production and service can be guaranteed.

Here is a list of group tasks or procedures relevant to many food service operations:

- Receiving and storing
- Issuing by requisition
- Butchering
- Vegetable preparation
- Salad preparation
- Stocks and sauce preparation
- Broiler cook station

- Sauté cook station
- Fry cook station
- Bakery station
- Expediter/service station
- Wait staff station
- Dessert station
- Dish/ware wash station

Each group of tasks can be described by a series of operational procedures and/or a collection of standardized recipes. These become operating manuals for each department or station within the operation. They also become the foundation for establishing standards of operation, assessing the effectiveness of the procedures and assuring the efficiency of each department.

CREATING STANDARD OPERATIONAL PROCEDURES

Well defined operational procedures and standardized recipes become the foundation for consistent quality production and service. Together they guide workers toward common goals with measurable and predictable results. But what determines those goals? How do workers know when they've reached their objectives?

Production and service objectives are often called standards of operation. These act as guides to measure the efficiency of processes and the consistency of results. When created with input from management and staff, operational standards represent achievable goals that everyone in the organization can focus on.

The quality teams discussed in Chapter 4, Foundations in Quality, suggest that a combination of players from management, production and service staffs should have input into establishing operational standards. Gathering input from various levels of workers helps to build a commitment from everyone to strive to achieve the established standards. Obtainable standards become guides for production and service and should never be used to criticize or complain about a worker's performance. Problems that arise in meeting the standards are reflections of the process, which can be re-evaluated and re-designed to create greater consistency.

National trade magazines can also give evidence of operational standards set by other companies around the country and the world. Standards in food cost percents, labor cost percents, sanitation practices and nutritional cooking philosophies can be borrowed from national averages and current practices.

These should be investigated and comparisons made to reflect what is possible in your own establishment.

Customers should also have input into establishing operational standards in food production, presentation, and service. Their input can be gathered through written surveys, contact with the service staff and managers, and by keeping and analyzing an item sales journal. Item sales journals list the quantity of each item sold in relationship to overall sales. This is a true picture of what customers prefer and which items should be re-evaluated, changed or dropped from the menu. Customer satisfaction can also be measured by repeat business and is affected by the quality of foods, service times and the helpfulness of the service staff.

The simplest way to depict an operational standard is in a photograph. This is especially true of recipes, where photos of the finished product can be taken and displayed for production staff and servers to see. Matching the products produced with these pre-approved photos can assure consistency. Photos can also be taken of areas of the kitchen and dining rooms to show proper setup of rooms and maintenance of sanitation and organization standards. For example, a photo of a properly set up, organized and clean storeroom can be a guide for all people accessing the storeroom to maintain the standard, and a photo of a wait station in the dining room can depict the emphasis on cleanliness and readiness of service utensils. Photos are clear reminders of standards that have been set and guide workers toward accomplishing consistent goals.

Other operational standards cannot be photographed. The timeliness of receiving goods and storing them, for example, can have a standard time set—should be completed in less than an hour—but time cannot be photographed. Journal entries are a way of documenting time standards. Keeping a journal of all goods received and listing the vendors, the time the truck arrived, and the time the order was received and stored can help establish timing standards and assure adherence to them.

Charting information is yet another method of displaying operational standards. For example, keeping a charted record of refrigeration temperatures taken at six hour intervals allows workers to see that safe and standard refrigeration temperatures are maintained at all times. When there is significant variance in temperature maintenance, then repair people are called in to correct the problem before loss of product or interruption of production can occur.

Posters can also be used to promote operational standards. The Department of Health and Safety requires a posting of hand-washing signs in food preparation areas and in bathrooms used by food production and service staffs to remind workers to wash their hands before returning to work. Motivational posters can be used to tell wait staffs to smile and be friendly, kitchen staffs to work as a team and help each other out, or ware washers to keep dish machine and pot wash areas clean and safe. Motivational posters can be purchased or created in house and can communicate operational standards dealing with employee behavior.

Operational standards are not quotas to measure a worker's performance or targets to measure a company's ability to operate; rather, they are guides to keep all workers and companies on track to perform the best they can given the circumstances of the organization and the procedures that have been put in place. Variance in meeting standards are a sign that operational procedures must be investigated and changed to allow for more consistent and efficient performance.

ASSESSING OPERATIONAL STANDARDS

Once operational standards have been set and communicated to the staff, they need to be assessed as a regular part of doing business. Constant evaluation of operational standards keeps the organization growing and improving standards to meet changing customer perception and expectations.

Shewart's cycle, discussed in Chapter 4, can be the mechanism used to assess operational standards. Recall that it is a cycle of observing, recording, comparing, and analyzing data. Standards too can be measured using this method of discovery and assessment. The four steps needed to assess operational standards are:

1. Observe production and service.
2. Record data.
3. Compare to previous standards.
4. Analyze results.

Observing standards needs to be a deliberate task, checking products and services against predetermined standards to assure consistency. This is not the same as an inspection process, which looks for flaws or errors; it is a maintenance system that keeps the operation working.

Record your observations in a journal or log. After a period of time—a week, month, or quarter—records can give you information to show consistency or inefficiencies in processes.

Compare observations against predetermined standards. In this way, you can determine the efficiency of the procedures that led to their production. You may also determine levels of acceptable variance from standards. For example, a picture of a plated dinner, recorded to show a standard of production, may take several minutes to arrange on the plate to assure the final picture represents the proper standard. In some cases, two or more photos may be taken before getting the picture exactly right. During production and busy service times, workers will not have the same amount of time to produce and present each dish. In this case, the photo represents the absolute standard and the goal of production is to get as close to that standard as possible.

When standards cannot be reached consistently in slow and busy times, then the processes themselves need to be analyzed. What in the process is keeping the standard from being met? Go back to the specific set of tasks that lead to the product in question and analyze each in light of the findings. Are there tasks that are missing or not clearly written? Are there too many tasks for a single person to complete in a given period of time? It is critical to involve everyone on the quality team responsible for the particular standard to analyze the processes. A prep cook may have some insight on improving one of their tasks that will allow the line cook to produce a better product. The receiving clerk may have some ideas on improving receiving standards to get fresher products and keep them rotated properly. Collectively, ideas can be shared and solutions suggested that will ultimately improve the processes, improve the final product, increase morale and improve teamwork. Companies that can consistently achieve these goals are targeted for success.

Operational standards do not need to stifle creativity, for there is room for creativity in the creation of the standards themselves. The use of menu specials may also leave the door open for more frequent uses of creative talent, but even creativity needs standards to follow. Specials must still represent the overall concept of the restaurant style and be a reflection of consumer preferences.

Creating and assessing standards is a long and complicated process. For existing restaurants, it may take months to complete the first round of standards, while operators of startup operations may devote full-time study to the task. In both cases, it is a necessary assignment that will help guarantee quality production and service.

CHAPTER 20

Menu Management

OBJECTIVES

When you complete this chapter, you should be able to:

- Describe six important criteria that need to be fulfilled in effective menu management.
- Describe the information that customers can get from reading a restaurant's menu.
- Explain the relationship of kitchen design to menu management.
- Create a chart matching the appropriate piece of kitchen equipment to the production of a specific menu item or preparation.
- Explain the relationship of dining room design to menu management.
- Discuss ways of ensuring legibility in menu item descriptions.
- Describe three different strategies for determining menu pricing.
- Explain the significance of having signature items on the menu.
- Explain the importance of tracking menu item sales.
- Describe the inferences that can be derived by studying a menu item sales chart.

WRITING THE MENU

The menu is the most important tool for marketing the food service operation, directing food production and service, projecting food and beverage sales and controlling costs. Whether it is a standardized menu, a cyclical menu or one that changes every day, it is critical that the menu be well prepared and presented in the manner consistent with the restaurant's concept and mission.

Menu design deals with the physical layout and construction of the menu itself. This is too complicated a task for this text. Information on menu design is available in other texts that fully address the relationship of menu design to marketing and promotion. Menu management deals with assessing the information written in menus, resulting menu sales, costs of menu items, and the revenues needed to assure an efficient and profitable operation.

The first step in menu management is to write a menu that meets these six important criteria:

1. Meets consumer demand
2. Compatibility with kitchen and dining room design
3. Legibility and accuracy of menu descriptions
4. Use of standard kitchen and service procedures to produce menu
5. Strategic menu pricing
6. Proportionate sales

These criteria need to be met in order consistently to produce menu items that satisfy a discriminating consumer at a high level of quality and provide an expected level of revenue for the operation. Each criterion is subject to ongoing analysis to assure the efficient running and competitiveness of the operation.

MEETING CONSUMER DEMANDS

Chapter 18, Concept Engineering, described the process of concept engineering and the importance of identifying consumer demand. The collected information and follow-up assessment give the guidance necessary to write a menu that meets those demands. Here are some of the questions you will need to answer using the menu as your primary communication tool:

- What meal periods do you serve?
- What meal periods do you write individual menus for, or do you have one menu to cover the whole day?
- How often do you plan to change your menu?
- What style of cooking/cuisine do you offer?
- How many menu categories do you offer on each menu?
- How many different cooking techniques are represented on the menu?
- Are there considerations for vegetarian diners?
- Are nutritional cooking techniques applied throughout the menu, in a category of menu items, or not at all?

- How flexible is the menu? Does it allow customers to change accompaniments, sauces, ingredients or cooking techniques?
- What is the range of menu pricing?

Answer these questions before writing a new menu or changing an existing menu. Make sure the answers are represented in the embodiment of the menus themselves and taught exhaustively to the wait staff. Teach the kitchen staff how to accommodate special requests and deliver a product consistent with the menu descriptions. Your operation will be measured by how well you accomplish these tasks.

Assess consumer perception before it affects the bottom line. Simply asking for a person's opinion can often solidify their appreciation and loyalty. Wait staffs should be asked to record customer questions and concerns so that corrective action can be taken quickly. Short surveys can be used to collect customer feedback for long-term planning such as upcoming menu changes or offered specials. Soliciting continuous feedback from patrons involves them in the planning process of the organization and assures that you are meeting their expectations for the quality of food and service.

COMPATABILITY OF KITCHEN AND DINING ROOM DESIGN

In writing the menu, it is essential that the menu items and styles of service offered are compatible with the kitchen layout and dining room design. When there is a perfect match of equipment, work space, design, and menu item production and service, there is a greater chance of success.

Successful menu planners know the strengths and limitations of their kitchens and dining rooms. They learn to create menus that complement the type and amount of equipment, the amount of storage, production and service space, the layout of the equipment and service areas and the traffic flow of goods to consumers. They exploit strengths and are cautious when dealing with weak areas.

The type and amount of large equipment has a direct effect on the versatility of the menu. In existing kitchens, the equipment is already in place. For new operations, space, utilities and startup investments all influence the type and amount of equipment that is purchased. In both cases, having the proper equipment to reproduce the menu is critical to the restaurant's success.

If the concept of your menu is to provide a variety of cooking styles, then you will need a variety of cooking equipment: broilers, fryers, ovens, rotisseries, open burners or flat-top ovens, grills and even a salamander (small broiler that is used to melt cheese or brown sauces as a finishing process to some menu items like French onion soup and crab Imperial). If your menu requires a lot of deep frying, as in a Mexican restaurant that fries its own tortilla chips, then multiple fryers will be necessary to keep up with production. A restaurant with an emphasis on healthy cooking would benefit by having a grill or broiler for no-fat cooking, a rotisserie for healthy roasting of fowl, fish and beef, a steamer for vegetable cookery and a large salad prep station with a lot of refrigeration space and prep area for multiple salad preparations and accompanying chutneys and salsas.

It is helpful to contact manufacturers of kitchen equipment who can give you specific information related to the amount of food that can be cooked on a particular piece of equipment, recovery times for deep fat fryers, and versatility of single pieces of equipment. This information can be helpful in writing the menu that best incorporates the strengths of the equipment that is in place.

Once you know the equipment that is in place or that will be purchased and their production specifications, you can build a chart to make sure your menu items can be produced successfully. On one side of the chart, list the equipment; on the other side, list the menu items that require the particular piece of equipment. This will graphically demonstrate the pieces of equipment over-utilized, under-utilized, and perfectly matched to menu expectations. See Figure 20–1.

When you've completed the chart, you'll have to decide if any particular piece of equipment is used too often or not enough. If used too often, then decide whether or not to add another piece of equipment if space, utilities and costs allow, or to change some of the menu items. If a piece of equipment is not used enough, then add more menu items that require its use. This give and take will ultimately result in a menu which is perfectly balanced with the kitchen equipment.

Equipment	Production Specs	Menu Items
Broiler: 30 × 24, 3 temp controls	720 square inches of cooking surface, holds approximately 50 steaks, chops or burgers	Burgers, pork chops, filet mignon, ribeyes, grilled vegetables
2- basket deep fat fryer, single well, 18w × 14h × 24d; 5 gal. capacity	Two 5-pound baskets, recovery time 8 minutes per batch	French fries, jalapeño poppers, potato skins
6-burner stove and oven; conduction; oven compartment 30w x 18d	8 inch burners, 2000 BTU each; oven compartment holds full sheet pans	Shrimp scampi, veal piccatta, tenderloin tips, omelets, seafood Alfredo, flounder almondine

FIGURE 20–1 Charting Equipment for Optimum Utilization

Kitchen design also plays a role in menu management. Does your menu have a lot of grilled sandwiches requiring multiple accompaniments and dressings? If it does, then you'll need a sandwich station designed to give the cook easy access to the grill, toaster, storage space for various breads and rolls, refrigeration space for cheeses, toppings, and condiments, refrigerated bins for garnishes, and cutting board space for cutting finished sandwiches. The sandwich station could also be placed near the deep-fry station so that the sandwich cook can cook French fries, onion rings and other fried accompaniments for sandwiches.

Does your menu place an emphasis on designer vegetable accompaniments for each entrée? If so, you'll need extra refrigerated space near the sauté and steamer station to keep all the various prepped vegetables and sauces or condiments on the line during production. Think through the steps required for the production of group tasks and design the stations to accommodate the projected levels of production needed for each meal period. In existing operations, again it is advisable to solicit input from the people already working the station before adding or changing menu items.

The design of the dining room also plays a role in the production and service of some menu items. Salad preparation, garnishing and service is often the sole responsibility of the wait staff. If that is the case, they need easy access to a well designed work station where multiple workers can work side by side during busy production times. The station will have to hold ample amounts of prepped lettuces, vegetable accompaniments, garnishes and dressings and have space for holding cracker baskets, pepper mills, grated cheeses and any other salad accompaniments. Perhaps the restaurant manager wants desserts presented on a dessert cart; make sure there is ample aisle space to allow the easy movement of the cart during busy times. Instead of a cart, you may have to bring desserts to the table on a silver tray for the presentation of the daily selections. In either case, the design of the dining room must be taken into consideration before implementing many menu suggestions and service styles.

LEGIBILITY AND ACCURACY OF MENUS

The legibility and accuracy of menu descriptions assures that the customer receives what has been purchased. It is the first step in assuring customer satisfaction. Incomplete or inaccurate menu descriptions can lead to customers getting something they didn't want or expect, potentially with food ingredients they don't like or may be allergic to. Poorly written menu descriptions increase the possibility that even properly prepared and presented foods can lead to unsatisfactory sales.

Legibility in menu writing refers to the controlled use of technical language or descriptions in writing menus. Menus should be written so that the average customer can decipher the information without asking a lot of potentially embarrassing questions of their dining guests or the wait staff. Accuracy refers to an exact description of the menu item, including a description of the cooking technique used, the level of spiciness, and food ingredients that people may choose to avoid or may be allergic to. Follow these guidelines to assure your customers can read and interpret your menus the way they are intended:

- Foreign words should rarely be used except in restaurants that promote international cuisine.
- Avoid non-descriptive or flowery words and phrases, like cooked to perfection or deliciously prepared.
- Make nutrition claims only when you can document that the claims are true.
- List all key ingredients, e.g., onion, garlic and hot peppers.
- List ingredients that people may be allergic to, such as nuts and wheat.
- Describe the dish as it is prepared, for example, "Jumbo shrimp sautéed in whole butter with lemon, chives, and cracked black peppercorns served over angel hair pasta."
- Acknowledge the level of spice in hot, seasoned foods.
- Always state when alcohol is used in the cooking or baking preparation.
- Always tell the truth. Lump crabmeat should be lump, not back fin or special; Stilton cheese is a specific type of bleu cheese; milk-fed veal has never been placed in pasture; and Dover sole is not a type of flounder.

TRUTH IN MENUS

Many states have legislated that written menu descriptions must depict accurate information regarding ingredients and procedures. This is commonly called "Truth in menu legislation." Whether legislated or not, it is the ethical responsibility of chefs and operators accurately to name ingredients and menu items that portray the actual ingredients used.

Unscrupulous operators and chefs sometimes use the names of expensive ingredients in menu descriptions where, in fact, less expensive ingredients are used. They do this to raise sales of a particular menu item without the added expense associated with using the expensive or exotic ingredient. Some commonly misused ingredient names are: Dover sole, lump crabmeat, milk-fed veal, Chesapeake oysters, and prime beef. Other common falsehoods would be to use smaller shrimp than the size quoted, 16/20s for U12s, for example; inferior wild mushrooms for expensive morels; or farm-raised salmon for wild salmon. These deceitful practices have been at the expense of unsuspecting guests and of a proud profession.

False nutritional labeling is another tactic that some operators, chefs and food manufacturers use to promote menu items as healthy choices when they are not. When this became an abused practice, the Department of Agriculture and the Food and Drug Administration passed the Nutrition Labeling Act of 1990 to protect the American consumer. This piece of legislation has forced food manufacturers to place nutrition labels on their products to substantiate any nutritional claims. In 1996 this ruling was expanded to include foods produced in restaurants. Restaurant menu items that now claim to be low fat, low cholesterol, or low calorie must be backed up with standardized recipes to prove the claims. When writing menu descriptions, do not use phrases like heart healthy, light fare, or nutritionally balanced unless you can prove the claim.

STRATEGIC MENU PRICING

Strategic menu pricing is a method of pricing menu items to assure customer satisfaction, area competitiveness and company profit margins. When these conditions are not met, restaurants struggle for success.

Menu pricing can be determined by using three different strategies: standard menu pricing, signature item pricing and sales volume pricing. Utilizing all three of these strategies can contribute toward a consistently profitable operation.

Standard menu pricing is the calculation of menu price based on a targeted overall food cost percent. Partially based on national averages and confirmed by the individual company's history of costs and profits, a targeted food cost percent becomes an integral part of profit and loss statements (P&Ls). Along with beverage cost percent and labor cost percent, food cost percent is a predictor used to assess a company's financial health and a guide for determining menu pricing. A detailed discussion of restaurant costs and cost control strategies can be found in comprehensive texts on the subject.

Food cost percent is the relationship of food cost to total sales. Once the cost of food is calculated for each menu item from a standardized recipe, a sales price can be determined using this simple formula:

Sales price = Cost of food ÷ Food cost percent

For example, if the cost of a particular menu item is $5.00 and the targeted food cost percent is 35 percent, the applied formula looks like this:

$$\text{Sales price} = \$5.00 \div .35, \text{ or } \$14.28$$

Many operators round this number up to the nearest $0.50 for a menu price of $14.50. Rounding prices up makes it easier manually to calculate guest checks.

Calculating menu prices based on a standard food cost percent is only part of the overall menu management strategy. Offering signature dishes at lower than average prices can do as much for promotion and marketing as it can for the bottom line of profits.

Signature dishes are specialty items or specially priced items not available from area competitors. They can be so unique that your place is the only one that offers them, or priced so low that buying them seems like a bargain for consumers. They are designed to attract large populations of customers and keep them coming back.

Signature dishes are often well recognized preparations that have large consumer appeal but are generally priced too high for the average customer to purchase on a regular basis. Stuffed lobster tails, steamed jumbo shrimp, jumbo lump crab cakes and prime rib of beef are examples of items that could become your restaurant's signature dishes.

By applying the normal food cost percent to high cost items, you may be pricing the menu item too high for the average consumer to purchase. A stuffed lobster tail, for example, that costs $12 to $15 to prepare and serve would have to be listed at $36 to $45 on the menu, too high to sell on the same menu that offers entrees averaging $15 to $20 each. Operators who still want to offer stuffed lobster tails because of their general popularity may price them using a higher food cost percent, perhaps as high as 45 to 50 percent of the selling price. The resulting price, between $26 and $30, is high enough to signify the complexity of the preparation and the cost of the ingredients, but low enough to attract new customers.

The operations that practice signature menu item pricing accomplish two things with this menu pricing strategy. First, they promote their operation as accommodating, value-oriented and consumer friendly. This alone can be a significant reason for customers to try new operations and become loyal patrons. Second, the dollar return on each sale made is often higher or the same as other menu items, contributing significantly to the company's bottom line. Using the lobster tail example, a normally high 50 percent food cost would list the bargain price at only $24 to $30. Still, however, each order sold would return $12 to $15 in gross revenue. Other menu items with significantly lower food cost and priced between $15 and $20 utilizing the standard pricing strategy of 35 percent food cost would return a slightly lower gross revenue at $10 to $13. The lobster tail returns more money to the bottom line than the other menu items, and isn't any more complicated or time consuming to prepare and serve. In these cases, the operator and the customer both benefit.

The third strategy used to price menu items is based on the volume of sales of particular items in relationship to the total sales. Volume of sales, by itself, can generate enough money to the bottom line to make having a popular menu item at a lower than normal price a good business strategy. Fast food restaurants base a large part of their pricing strategy on their volume of sales. Even though they may only generate a few dollars for each sale, the total number of sales they make each day contributes significantly to their operating budgets and consequent profits.

Other restaurant operators may choose to offer a few of their menu items below the standard pricing guidelines to try to generate a large number of sales. It is analogous to other companies offering reduced price sales for the purpose of attracting a lot of customers. For example, a stuffed chicken breast that cost $3.50 to produce would normally be sold for $10.00 (at 35 percent food cost), but if listed for $8.95 (39 percent food cost) would generate a greater volume in sales and encourage add-on sales like appetizers, salads and desserts. An item that enjoys a high volume of sales also adds to the overall efficiency of the operation. Repeating the same tasks frequently helps reduce the possibility of mistakes and moves inventory more quickly, reducing waste and spoilage.

Other menu items may be priced below the standard food cost percent. For example, a grilled 4-ounce chicken breast sandwich may cost only $1.15 to make ($0.50 for the chicken, $0.35 for the roll and condiments and $0.20 for fries and catsup). Normal pricing would place it on the menu at $3.30, but every other sandwich on the menu is priced at $3.95 or higher. Most operators would price the chicken breast sandwich also at the competitive price of $3.95 and realize a food cost percent of only 29 percent. The combination of items priced below the standard 35 percent and those priced higher than 35 percent will ultimately allow the restaurant to obtain its overall strategic food cost percent and realize its projected profits.

TRACKING MENU ITEM SALES

Another menu management tool is the tracking of menu item sales. The information gathered by a simple accounting of menu sales by item and category can give an operator valuable information for the planning and control of the whole operation. A good tracking system allows operators efficiently to plan food and beverage purchases, production amounts and schedules, as well as the labor needed for production and service.

POS (point of sale) computer systems and other computerized wait station terminals keep track of food and beverage sales each time a wait person places an order through them. Managers can then check periodically to monitor the sales for various meal periods, for each wait person, and the total at the end of the day. Standard wait station reports contain an item by item sales journal, dollar sales by category, total dollar sales, and tax information. In lieu of computers, a manual system can be developed utilizing information right from the guest checks.

Most operators keep a menu item sales journal that allows them to track the sales of individual items by the meal period and day of the week. Patterns soon emerge, allowing operators to plan a greater level of production for busy periods and lower levels for slow periods. An example of a sales journal sheet that can be customized to track your menu sales is given in Figure 20–2.

Although it takes time to keep records like the Menu Item Sales Journal, the investment of time is well worth the effort. Some POS systems can be linked directly to a PC (personal computer) through an integrated software package to make it easier to collect the information and produce charts and graphs depicting the trends. Whether computerized or done manually, this is one of the most important strategic pieces of information you will need in planning and controlling your menu.

Collecting the data is not enough. You must take the time to analyze the data, look for trends and share the information with the people involved in

Menu Item Sales Journal
Entrees
Week of: 6/10–6/16/05

Dates:	Mo 6/10	Tu 6/11	Wd 6/12	Th 6/13	Fr 6/14	Sa 6/15	Su 6/16	Total	% Sales
Prime rib	23	19	17	32	48	54	36	229	17
Ribeye	10	8	9	14	22	23	19	105	8
Large filet	14	12	11	24	31	35	35	162	12
Stuffed chicken	16	14	18	28	36	41	38	191	14
London broil	6	4	4	6	8	10	5	43	3
Chicken Marsala	5	5	7	6	10	9	9	51	4
Rotisserie chicken	10	12	11	17	22	38	41	151	11
Shrimp scampi	8	10	9	19	27	22	29	124	9
Stuffed rockfish	11	13	10	21	39	37	40	171	13
Seafood fettuccini	9	11	9	12	21	19	15	96	7
TOTALS:	112	108	105	179	264	288	267	1323	92

FIGURE 20–2   Menu Item Sales Journal

production and service. Always include other workers in the analysis process. This will give you insights from their perspectives that will help form the final decisions and increase the predictability of success for future menus.

One week's worth of numbers is not enough to make a sound judgment. Only when patterns evolve over several weeks can you make credible decisions about making changes. Assuming that the chart in Figure 20–2 repeats a pattern over a period of several weeks; here are some inferences that can be derived:

- Saturday is the busiest day of the week, with Friday and Sunday running close behind.
- Monday and Tuesday are the slowest days and require less labor.
- London broil (3 percent sales) and Chicken Marsala (4 percent sales) should be reconsidered; either change the recipes, or remove them completely.
- Stuffed rockfish runs 37 to 40 percent of sales on the weekends; you may want to run other combination seafood specials on the same days.
- Prime rib is the most popular steak; perhaps run two different portion sizes, large and small, to appeal to more customers
- Ninety-two percent of all customers order entrées. By offering smaller portion steaks or more combination seafood dishes, you may increase this to 95 to 96 percent of total sales.

By keeping records on menu item sales, you can determine the popularity of menu items, the days and times items are most popular, items that should be removed from the menu and categories of menu items that should be expanded. Together with customer comments, this information can help customize your menu for maximum efficiency and profits.

Successful restaurant operators manage their menus just as they manage all other operational components, with a commitment for quality and efficiency. A well thought out and properly executed menu can help a restaurant succeed even in a highly competitive market. It is the foundation on which all other procedures and services stand.

CHAPTER 21

Production Management

When you complete this chapter, you should be able to:

- Define the concepts behind production management.
- Explain why recipes are at the crux of production management.
- Describe some of the concerns related to adding or changing recipes on an already existing menu.
- Describe some of the problems inherent in designing recipes calling for ingredients specific to that recipe alone.
- Design a menu that can be successfully reproduced using a minimum amount of equipment.
- Explain the relationship of menu sophistication to the level of technical skill in kitchen and dining room workers.
- Define mise en place and explain its importance in production management.
- Describe the strategy of cross-utilization of ingredients in production management.
- Explain how recipe development can also promote waste control and reduce unusable trim.
- Describe a strategy of planning for leftovers and its effect on production management and cost control.

PLANNING FOR QUALITY PRODUCTION

Quality production can be achieved in every food service and hospitality operation in America. It will not happen by accident, but with good planning, commitment and hard work, consistent quality production can be the standard way of doing business in the twenty-first century. Success in maintaining consistently high standards of production will be measured with increased business, customer loyalty, high employee morale and predictable profits. Inconsistent production is the enemy of success and must be combated at every stage.

It takes a concerted effort to make quality production an achievable goal. Every job performed and task completed contributes to the overall success or failure of the operation. Production management is a system of processes and strategies ensuring that workers and managers have the tools necessary to perform their responsibilities effectively. A good system maintains control while encouraging input and creative thinking. Both efficiency and strong motivation can be the result of a well thought out plan. Good training and forward thinking help make quality production a standard that can be met.

DEVELOPING RECIPES

Recipes are at the crux of production management. They give us a list of ingredients that have to be specified and purchased, they tell us how to set up our production lines, and they are representative of the skill level of the staff that needs to produce them for sale and service. Recipes, and the strategies used to develop them, are at the foundation of quality production.

When developing recipes, consider the bank of ingredients already being specified and purchased by the operation. Whenever possible, use existing inventory items to create new recipes or change existing ones. This helps to control purchases, capitalize on cost, rotate stocks, and streamline production.

For example, if you want to add another seafood item on your Friday night menu, consider using the seafood items already being specified and purchased for other menu items first. If you use 21/25 count shrimp for scampi and shrimp with linguini, then use the same size shrimp for stuffed shrimp, grilled shrimp, or any other new recipe calling for whole shrimp. By doing this, you can purchase larger amounts of single products, bargain for the best possible prices, and contribute to consistent production. Imagine if you used a 21/25 count shrimp for scampi, a 36/40 count shrimp for shrimp po-boys, and a 51/60 count peeled shrimp for shrimp salad. You'd have to buy and store three different sizes of shrimp; storage and preparation issues would become more complicated; and mistakes by cooks and prep cooks could increase. What happens when a cook uses the 21/25 count shrimp for the po-boys, or 51/60 count shrimp for the scampi? Cost becomes unpredictable and customer satisfaction can fluctuate when one size shrimp is designed to be used and another is substituted.

Do not specify any single ingredient for any one preparation. This will decrease purchasing power and increase the possibility of mistakes. For example, if you want to add a shrimp cocktail to your menu and decide arbitrarily that U12s will be used (fewer than twelve shrimp to one pound), then instead of buying a large amount of a single size shrimp, you will have to purchase smaller amounts of different sized shrimp and hope the prep cooks and line cooks can keep the two separated during production and service. What happens when shrimp cocktail doesn't sell well? What do you do with all those U12 shrimp you purchased? You can cut them up for shrimp salad, but that would be expensive. What happens when shrimp cocktail sells well? Where do you get backup supplies of U12s during peak production? You can't use the 21/25s because they are too small and customers will notice the difference. Rather than purchase a specific ingredient for only one preparation, consider modifying the recipe to call for an ingredient already being purchased. This begins the cycle of cost control measures that will help make your operation successful and keep customers satisfied with the consistent quality.

Production lines are set up based on the recipes being produced. Using like ingredients in multiple preparations reduces the space needed for preparation and final cooking. Using similar cooking techniques also reduces the amount of space needed for equipment, the equipment itself and the workers needed to perform the tasks.

You can reproduce a full service menu with as few as three main pieces of cooking equipment: a grill or broiler, an oven with burners on top and a deep fat fryer. With these three pieces of equipment, dozens of items can be consistently produced in a relatively small space. By developing recipes to maximize equipment usage, you will save money on equipment and labor. Construction costs for new operations will also be less when equipment and space is designed for peak efficiency, which is all controlled by the recipes needing to be reproduced.

For example, American diners can consistently reproduce breakfast specialties, lunch sandwiches and dinner entrées using only two main pieces of cooking equipment: a griddle and a deep fat fryer. All manners of egg cookery, from scrambled to omelets, can be cooked on a griddle. Poaching can also be accomplished by placing a pan of water in one corner of the griddle for easy access when needed. Home fried potatoes, hash browns, bacon, sausage, ham, pancakes, and French toast, grilled Ruebens and Monte Cristo sandwiches can also be cooked on one large griddle. The fryer can be used for French fries, breaded fish sandwiches and entrées, breaded shrimp, batter dipped vegetables, fritters, and a host of other diner-style fried foods. A third piece of equipment, an oven with burner tops, allows for freshly made soups and sauces, and the oven for roasts.

Recipes must also reflect the level of expertise expected from the preparation workers, line cooks and servers. A sophisticated menu incorporating multiple step preparations, the use of exotic and fragile ingredients, and requiring special service techniques such as French table service (finish cooking or plating in the dining room), can only be consistently reproduced when the level of cooking and service skills match the level of recipe sophistication. A problem usually occurs when a standard family-style restaurant, which normally produces basic foods, begins to offer classic Continental, French, or Asian-style cuisine on the menu without properly training the cooking and service staffs. The results will be substandard foods, a frustrated staff and confused customers. It is always better to develop recipes that comfortably match the skill level of the staff and the common expectations of the customer. The danger comes from trying to be all restaurants to all customers.

EVERYTHING IN ITS PLACE

A commonly used kitchen phrase, mise en place, is a French phrase meaning everything in its place. It usually describes the preparation and organization of ingredients for food production lines. In a broader interpretation, mise en place could reflect a strategy of management and organization that maintains appropriate levels of all products for the preparation and service of foods and beverages. This expanded definition would include maintaining proper inventories of food, beverages and sundries (non-food items like paper and cleaning supplies), an organized system of food preparation and a proper inventory of kitchen equipment and tableware.

Properly maintained inventories are based on par levels determined by historical usage. Par level refers to an average amount used given how often deliveries can be made and how perishable the products are. For example, mayonnaise has a relatively long shelf life (holds well in dry storage until open) and is received through any general food vendor who can deliver to an establishment every day if necessary. Mayonnaise is used in composite salads like shrimp, chicken, and tuna salads, for sandwich making, and in salad dressings. Your inventory records can tell you how much mayonnaise you used in the past and projected sales can help determine the future need for the product. Let's say you used four gallons per week. Coincidentally, mayonnaise is purchased four gallons to one case, so your usage is one case per week. You may set your par level at one and a half cases or six gallons, allowing for unexpected large increases in sales. Another item—like fresh flounder filets, which have a very short shelf life (perishes quickly)—may have a two- or three-day par level based on how often you can order fresh seafood and how much you use.

Preparation cooks, line cooks, waiters and waitresses depend on properly maintained inventories for the products they need when they need them. This is a form of mise en place with everything needed for food production and service stored properly in the storeroom or refrigerators and freezers.

An organized system of food preparation can assure line cooks that products they need partially prepped before final cooking are available in the quantities and freshness that they need. Mise en place of prepped ingredients also entails that the line cooks know where in storage the prepped items are, including backups. For example, suppose your sauté cook depends on getting partially prepared vegetables from the preparation cooks for their line production. Proper organization would allow the sauté cook to easily identify the products needed in the refrigerator, use the oldest prepped items first and notify prep cooks when they've taken the last of a particular item. Having the needed items in place (refrigeration, freezer, dry storage, or line storage) when needed and in proper quantities is proper mise en place.

A proper inventory of kitchen equipment and a plan to keep hand equipment clean and circulated through production is also a critical aspect of this overriding mise en place. Having everything in its place when needed includes pots, pans, knives, cutting boards, ladles, spoons, whisks and small appliances like food processors and mixers. An organized operation has just enough equipment for immediate use, and a well maintained system of ware washing so that used equipment can be quickly washed and returned to service for continuous needs.

Buying the right amount of equipment is the first step in maintaining equipment mise en place. The second step is maintaining proper equipment inventories by replacing lost or broken pieces. The cleaning and easy access of equipment completes the cycle that ensures needed equipment is in place and ready for use at all times. The worst that can happen is not having enough equipment because of improper buying or improper cleaning. Whenever a preparation or line cook has to wait for a piece of equipment to do a job, the company is losing money and jeopardizing consistent quality.

CROSS-UTILIZATION

Production management is partially controlled by designing a menu that utilizes a small inventory of food ingredients to produce a large variety of menu items. This is achieved by choosing items that can be cross-utilized, i.e., items that can have various cooking applications applied to them, that take well to various seasonings, and that have a wide customer appeal.

The tender cuts of meat, seafood and poultry are the most versatile when it comes to applicable cooking techniques. They can all be broiled, grilled, fried, sautéed, roasted or poached for a variety of menu item preparations. Tougher cuts of meat can only be braised or stewed, which limits the number of menu items that can be made from them. These should be reserved for specials such as soup production, buffets in the form of casseroles and employee meals that are planned for one night only.

Most tender cuts of meat, seafood, and poultry can be cooked using a variety of spices and herbs. This also adds to their versatility on the menu. It is better to build a menu dependent on a variety of spices than on a variety of meats.

Cross-utilization can be further applied by designing various menu items using the same or similar cuts of meat, seafood or poultry parts. The previous example of using one size shrimp for a variety of menu items is a good example. Another example is in the size of the filet mignon chosen for the menu. If the menu calls for a large and small cut of filet, then design the one to be half the size of the other. For a large filet, an 8- or 10-ounce portion is ample; the smaller cut should then be 4 or 5 ounces respectively. In this way, the meat cutter only needs to produce one size, the larger one, and the line cook can simply cut them in half when a smaller portion is sold. This is better than cutting a variety of large and small steaks. If one size doesn't sell, you run the risk of spoilage and waste. Another example could be in the use of chicken breasts for lunch and dinner portions. Use one size chicken breast—a 4-ounce breast, for example—for appetizers and lunch preparations, including lunch entrées and sandwiches. The same size breast can be used for dinner preparations by using two instead of one. In this way, food supplies and the rotation of supplies is not dependent on any one menu item. Preparation can be limited and yet menu variety can be great.

WASTE CONTROL

Controlling waste in food production and service is another factor of proper production management. Poor planning and inefficient preparation and service procedures can create large amounts of waste that dramatically affect company profits by increasing food, labor and trash removal costs. Proper planning and execution of procedures reduces waste and increases the efficiency of procedures.

Planning for waste control begins with the development of recipes and the food specifications needed to produce them. Every buying decision should be based on the following factors:

- Amount of trim needed to obtain proper ingredient preparation
- Possible use of the usable trim from foods
- Amount of expertise needed to obtain properly trimmed foods
- Cost of buying fully or partially trimmed and pre-portioned foods

When purchased food supplies require a large amount of preparation time in order to turn them into usable portions, the possibility for waste of product and waste of labor costs is prevalent. For example, if your menu calls for a large number of trimmed, boneless and skinless chicken breasts, do you purchase whole chickens or pre-trimmed and pre-portioned chicken breasts from a purveyor? The decision to buy whole chickens requires extra storage space and a certain amount of expertise to bone-out whole chickens. It also creates a large amount of chicken bones, fat and skin as well as an abundance of chicken wings, legs and thighs that have to be utilized in some other fashion. Buying pre-trimmed and/or pre-portioned boneless and skinless chicken breasts saves on storage and preparation space, eliminates the time and expertise needed for trimming, and reduces the amount of unwanted byproducts.

Many purchased foods require some trimming. Broccoli, for example, has as much as 50 percent trim when purchased whole and only the flowerettes are needed. You can purchase precut flowerettes (flower clusters only) from produce vendors, but the cost is significantly higher. The decision to buy whole broccoli can be validated if the usable trim can be incorporated into other menu items with little extra labor or cost. Cream of broccoli soup, vegetable stir-fries, vegetable terrines, quiche, and casseroles can incorporate peeled broccoli stems with a few florets for garnish. If some of these ancillary menu items can be fitted into your concept, then buying whole broccoli can be a cost-effective decision.

Meat cutting is perhaps the hardest food preparation issue to tackle. Do you buy whole cuts of meat that need to be trimmed into proper specifications and portions, or do you buy pre-trimmed and pre-portioned meats? Pre-trimmed and pre-portioned meats cost significantly more than full loins of beef or whole legs of veal or lamb, but could be a savings considering the amount of expertise required to trim meats properly and the possible use of trimmed byproducts like meat scraps, bones and fat.

Meat cutting and fish filleting requires special training and experience to master. The cost of that training, or the salaries of workers already trained in those skills, may be far greater than the cost of buying portion cut meats and fish filets from vendors. In addition to the cost of training or higher salaries is the cost of time it takes properly to trim and cut meat, poultry and seafood. These costs add up to a lot of money that many operators would rather pay to a meat, poultry, or fish supplier where they already have the expertise and can more fully utilize the trim and other fabrication byproducts. Small and large operators are increasing their demand for portion cut meats, poultry and fish as a means of controlling costs, consistency of product and waste.

PLANNING FOR LEFTOVERS

Operators plan to produce exactly as much food as they know they are going to sell. No one wants to worry about what to do with the leftovers. Unfortunately, no one has been able to master this strategy 100 percent of the time with 100 percent accuracy. Therefore, everyone in food service worries about what to do with the leftovers.

The big culprits are the prime ribs of beef that have to be cooked in large amounts in anticipation of Friday and Saturday night sales, or the baked potatoes that follow. Other culprits include fresh baked bread and pre-prepared salad bar items. If you can't predict sales volume 100 percent, then it is better to have a plan for the leftovers before you have any.

Placing leftovers in the freezer is not an answer. Freezers are frequently used as the harbor for thousands of dollars worth of cooked or partially prepared foods just waiting to be used up as specials, buffet items or employee meals. Without a plan to deal with the leftovers, freezers soon are filled with foods that represent hundreds of dollars of inventory and possible sales.

Planning for leftovers includes a definitive effort to design menu items or specials that depend on the byproducts of other menu items. Whenever possible in planning to place an item on the menu that you know will generate leftovers, like the prime rib that you don't want to run out of on busy or slow nights, plan alternative menu items or categories of quality specials that are designed to use what is left at the end of service.

For example, let's examine the issue of dealing with leftover prime rib. This is a problem many restaurant owners and chefs have to deal with because of the popularity of beef rib loins and the long time it takes to cook them properly. With prime rib taking over three hours to cook in conventional ovens and even longer in slow cook ovens, it is difficult to cook it in batches or quickly to adjust amounts based on sales. The dilemma is to cook enough prime rib without running out and without having too much left over.

For restaurants with a never-run-out policy for menu items and specials, leftover prime rib becomes a natural consequence of offering it on the menu. What then do you plan to do with the leftovers? One thing you could do is offer prime rib sandwich specials the next day for lunch. Take the left over, cold prime rib and cut it into 5- or 6-ounce portions and grill it as a sandwich meat served on a crusty roll with lettuce, tomato, and dressing. You could trim the prime rib even further and cut it into half-inch cubed pieces that could be used in various special preparations. You can reheat these in brown sauce with sliced mushrooms and red wine to serve over noodles, pasta, or rice, or grill them with small diced potatoes, diced onions, seasonings, and a little brown sauce to serve as an alternative side meat on breakfast and brunch menus. In all three cases, there is a plan to utilize the leftover prime rib in quality menu presentations that increase menu variety, customer appeal, sales and profits.

Likewise, leftover baked potatoes can be used to make home fried potatoes for the same Sunday brunch, leftover bread (not served) for seasoned croutons, and salad bar fixings for soups, casseroles and vegetable medleys on the hot line. Properly planned leftovers can become profitable menu items in their own right while increasing the versatility of the menu.

Production management is a series of plans, strategies and assessments that helps ensure an efficiently run operation. Along with diligent effort and dedication, quality production can be achieved consistently.

CHAPTER 22

A Place
for Creativity

When you complete this chapter, you should be able to:

- Describe ways to build creativity into the daily menu while maintaining standardized recipes and procedures.
- Explain why creativity in food service must be built from the tested and proven foundational cooking methods.
- Explain parameters of concept control in the use of controlled creativity in food service.
- Describe a testing procedure to assure that created new specials meet the needs of the consumer and the operation.
- Describe ways of marketing creativity to your customers.
- Describe the use of specials to promote creativity on menus.
- Explain how allowing a limited and controlled use of creativity can motivate employees and customers.

FOUNDATIONAL BASIS

Even in the most strict and disciplined food service operations, there are opportunities for the controlled use of creativity. Daily specials, soups and vegetables du jour are some common areas of production where creativity is encouraged.

Creativity is an outlet where many chefs can imprint their own personality and style on the design of new menu items and specials. It allows chefs to stretch their abilities and exercise their knowledge of fine food preparations. However, creativity is not a free-for-all of ideas, food styles, and flavors. Like all strategies of production, creativity must be properly planned, tested and assessed for efficiency and quality.

Creativity needs to be based on the foundational standards of quality food production, presentation and service. These are the tested and proven components of food production and service that are part of every successful operation. Creativity does not abandon tradition, but builds upon it to create new dimensions in food production and service.

Originality comes in the pairing of foods, seasonings and cooking styles in an innovative way. Fusion cuisine, the intelligent pairing of different international cuisines in a single plate, is a practical application of creativity in quality food service. Creative presentations can be made by changing the placement of food on the plates, the design put into the sauces and by using garnish, color and textural contrast to excite appetites and please palates. Creativity guided by experience can be a refreshing change of pace for employees and customers alike.

CONCEPT CONTROL

While controlled creativity can be allowed and even encouraged in many food service operations, it should be used to enhance rather than change the restaurant's concept. Restaurants that focus on family-style dining, for example, would not offer the same types of specials normally found on haute cuisine or fine dining menus. Although the new menu items may be very creative, they might also be too adventurous for the average working parent who takes the children out for dinner. Instead, specials should mirror other menu items in flavor, style and presentation to encourage sales by increasing menu variety.

The use of creativity in designing specials does not give the cook or chef total freedom; creativity must be channeled to meet the expectations of the current customer base. A restaurant dependent on repeat business must always consider their customers' expectations of food and not create dishes that go too far beyond those expectations. Restaurants are not classrooms where chefs can educate customers in the finer points of dining out. Rather, they are businesses that supply a specific product to a particular pool of customers. Being so creative that customers don't understand the makeup of a particular dish, or can't appreciate the flavors of complex preparations, will more likely confuse people than encourage or manipulate sales.

INTERNAL TESTING

There should be a standardized process of internal testing before placing new items or specials on the menu. This will guarantee that the cooks and wait staff learn the intricacies of their production and service and that the proposed items meet the same level of quality as other menu items. Without proper testing and internal promotion, consistency of production and enthusiastic sales can be hard to predict, no matter how innovative or creative a special may be.

The person initiating the design of the special, whether it is the line cook or chef, should first explain the concept of the dish to all those involved in its production and service: cooks, prep cooks, wait staff, and managers. In this way, they can receive advice and refine the idea before the food is committed to the plate. Then the item should be prepared following a step-by-step procedure to assure consistency of production.

Everyone involved should then evaluate the actual plated item based on appearance, color, texture and flavor. If necessary, final adjustments can be made to assure that the item meets quality standards.

A final test would be to offer samples to customers to get their immediate feed-back. This assures that the item meets your customers' high expectations and involves them in the decision-making process. This alone can go a long way toward building customer loyalty and improving quality and consistency.

Once an item has passed this internal test, it can be added to the menu or promoted as a daily special. Popular daily specials are often repeated and can give the chef insight into producing other specials related in theme or composition. Specials that remain popular week after week may ultimately be added to the standard menu.

MARKETING CREATIVITY

Marketing creativity is a way of telling customers that they can expect new and innovative menu ideas as well as consistently high menu item production. In a business dependent on repeat customers, there must always be something new offered to keep customers coming back. Since it is so difficult to change the entire menu every day, daily creative specials can make the difference between mediocrity and ardor.

When marketing specials, the word itself should denote something innovative and unique. Many operators make the mistake of offering slow-selling items as daily specials in an effort to move an item at a lower price or in combination with other foods rather than losing it to spoilage and waste. This is not a way to promote innovation, creativity or quality. Customers will soon realize that the daily specials are made from old food or food that does not sell well. For example, a daily special of broiled salmon steak with a small salad and glass of wine says to a customer that the salmon must not be selling well so they're giving you a small salad and a glass of wine to entice you into buying it. This is probably not the message you want to send.

Specials should be special. They should be unique creations, available only at your establishment. Specials are not always made up from existing menu items, but often are a reflection of popular items. For example, if broiled salmon is a regular menu item, a successful special might be broiled Arctic char. Buying new food ingredients assures the freshness of the product and promotes the special as a unique and innovative dish. In many cases, specials demand a higher price rather than a bargain deal, but when properly designed and promoted, they become attractive to new and repeat customers.

Du jour categories on the menu are also a way of promoting creativity. Du jour means of the day and implies creativity and innovation. Soup du jour, fresh fish du jour, and vegetables du jour are all possible standard menu items that allow the cooks and chefs to apply their creative talents on a daily basis. When done properly, these menu items can also increase customer appreciation and add to their dining excitement.

Other ways of promoting specials are by using table tents, menu inserts, chalkboards in the front of the dining room or by wait staff suggestions. Incorporating a variety of methods will assure that your customers are aware of the specials being offered before they make their dining choices.

Table tents are good tools in casual atmosphere restaurants, since people usually have a few minutes to wait before the waiter or waitress is ready to take their order. Customers can take those minutes to read through the table tent suggestions before ordering their food.

Menu inserts can appear either as a whole page of specials placed in the fold of the menu or as a clip-on attached to an adhesive clip inside the menu cover. The benefit of using menu inserts is that the information is constantly in view of customers while they are making their meal decisions. Menu inserts are also very versatile and can be replaced easily for different meal periods or as specials change.

Some restaurants write specials on chalkboards placed at the front of their dining rooms to get customers' attention as they come into the establishment. This is also a good tool to use if your restaurant usually has a waiting period before guests are seated. Giving customers something to read as they wait at the front door helps make the time pass quickly and encourages customer decisions at a point in which they are most vulnerable, i.e., while they are most anxious about their forthcoming meal.

Whatever method is used to promote specials in a written format, it is critical that the presentation be of similar class and style as the printed menu itself. As a marketing tool, anything that is presented to the customer is a presentation of the whole restaurant's commitment to quality and service. Sloppy, messy or otherwise unkempt written special tents, boards or inserts give an impression of poor overall quality.

The wait staff is an excellent tool to use in promoting specials. Guests usually expect the wait staff to know about specials and to be able to make personal recommendations regarding them. This is also an opportunity for the wait staff to talk to the customers and make them feel at home in your establishment. Make sure your wait staff is versed in the specials of the day, their ingredients, methods of preparation and level of spiciness. Wait staffs should always be given the chance to sample the specials themselves in order honestly and accurately to promote their sale.

CYCLICAL SPECIALS

Chefs and restaurant managers can be easily prompted to create special menu items by taking advantage of the seasonality of foods and capitalizing on the cyclical nature of holiday promotions. In some cases, customers may choose to visit a particular restaurant or hotel based on their past experiences at special times of the year.

While most foods are available year round thanks to a global marketplace, many are still subject to seasonal availability, especially for the freshest and tastiest of flavors. Knowing and taking advantage of these seasonal foods can give chefs and managers a keen advantage when planning cyclical menu specials.

Information about seasonal foods is readily available from vendors. It is equally important to them to promote seasonal items because they also benefit from the lower prices and longer shelf life associated with fresh seasonal items. Produce vendors can give specific dates on the availability of fruits and vegetables, meat vendors can give information on the best times of the year to purchase certain types and cuts of meat, and seafood vendors can give the best dates and times for specialty seafood items. Using vendors as an information resource is a practical and productive way to stay in tune with the availability of foods in a particular region, and from around the world.

The holidays are a natural way to promote specials and entice customers to purchase food or services from your establishment. People are already in the mood to go out to eat or to stay someplace special to make their holidays memorable. Holiday, birthday and anniversary celebrations are among the largest percentages of reasons why people eat out or stay in nice hotels. Holiday packages are among the most lucrative for hotels and restaurants because not only are people already excited about going out, but they are willing to pay more than usual for an exciting experience. With a little ingenuity and good planning, hotel rooms and dining rooms can be filled with people wanting to have a good time. Give them that good time along with good value and happy memories, and you will have loyal customers for a long time.

While standardization is critical to the success of restaurants and other food service establishments, creative menu applications and specials can be used to extend menu variety and increase customer appeal. This controlled use of creativity helps to keep the standard menu an exciting and evolving marketing tool.

A NEW AGE FOR QUALITY FOODSERVICE

Chapter 23
The Business of Quality Food Service
Chapter 24
The Future of Information Technologies

Over a hundred years ago, in the foreword to his book *Le Guide Culinaire,* Escoffier observed that as "progress marches on and each day brings forth new recipes and methods," so too must the operation and management of the establishment that prepares and serves food change. Quality management, Fishbone diagrams and MBO ask all managers, including chef managers, to re-evaluate the way things used to be done for the sake of a better way.

Chef managers who share an appetite for precision operations and strict authority with a passion for quality food must wrestle with the notion that people on both sides of the sales equation, employees and customers, are the operation's greatest concerns. The chef has the expertise and the formal authority, but the cooks and wait staff are the in-line mechanics of flavor and presentation, and it is the customer who approves or disapproves. Building positive business relationships with all of them encourages quality cuisine.

Technology is helping chef managers and other hospitality managers gather more and clearer information on trends, business patterns, sales histories and even customer comments that then allow them to effect more consistent levels of quality foodservice. Learning how to use and manipulate these instruments becomes as valuable to the modern manager as other tools of the trade. Computers, faxes, cell phones and palm-held organizers are no longer toys for the young and the affluent, but critical tools in the satchels of all business professionals.

CHAPTER 23

The Business of Quality Food Service

When you complete this chapter, you should be able to:

- Describe the importance of balancing art with business in food service operations.
- Discuss ways of raising the level of predictability of success in quality food service operations.
- Describe ways of determining the customers' perception of quality.
- Describe some of the factors that might be used to measure quality in food service operations.
- Explain the difference in quality measurements for fine dining, family-style, and fast food restaurants.
- Explain how measures of value are different than measures of quality in food service.
- Describe the marketing strategy that there is value in being first.
- Explain Hertzberg's theory of job enrichment.
- Explain how TQM complements traditional food service management practices.
- Explain why chefs may already be using statistical assessments in their operations without fully understanding the concept.

BALANCING ART AND BUSINESS

The business of food service is a complicated science of balancing art and dining pleasure with margins and profits. Although the business of hospitality supplies lodgings and food to its customers, it cannot succeed without also supplying a profit to the bottom line. The diligent chef, now manager, uses the traditions of food service as the foundation, takes inspiration from the customer, and uses his or her own skills and knowledge as weapons against mediocrity and tools for his or her art while being diligent in business and management.

The foundations of food service, with its primal beginnings, its heraldic hospitality influences, and its renaissance with the arts, are now being tested in a global financial market with shrinking budgets, diverse workplaces and bottom line accounting. The quality of food service, however, can be protected through this tight financial metamorphosis.

Incorporating a vigorous training program for chefs in customer relations, personnel management and the philosophies of TQM can help assure quality of food and services for the consumer and profitability for the owners. When the quality of product and services, value for the consumer and profits for the owner become planned and controlled aspects of the business, then the achievement of success can be more certain.

THE CUSTOMER DEFINES QUALITY

A fundamental tenet of TQM is that the customer is always right. While some chefs struggle with this concept, fierce competition has forced them to listen more and command less in the kitchens and dining rooms.

Other operators and chefs champion the consumer's cause. Penny Mc-Connell, for example, director of Food and Nutrition Services for Fairfax County Public Schools and past president of American School Food Service Association, is determined to have her student customers help define quality. McConnell is so sure of the power of building customer satisfaction that she has created a report card to measure customer values. In the school dining halls that McConnell supervises, she has her managers use these report cards to solicit student comments on the foods and services provided. McConnell says, "Each manager is required to go through the dining room each month and interview a minimum of ten different students to complete this report card. It forces them into the cafeteria. And once they've done it, they love the interaction with students."

This interaction leads to better communication between customers and suppliers. Better communication then leads to greater confidence for the supplier that they are meeting the needs of the customers, and for the customers that their values are being met. It takes a committed leader like McConnell to convince managers that customer criticisms are fuel for smooth operations, not barriers. The status quo had always been the standard in the past, but change for the sake of the customer needs to be the new standard.

A similar approach can be customized for restaurants, hotel dining rooms and banquet rooms, catering halls, and all other food service and hospitality operations. With direct customer feedback, operators can keep their customers satisfied by making changes to meet their evolving standards, usually with little change in procedures or recipes. Customers see this as having their wants catered to while suppliers see this as good public relations.

DEFINING QUALITY FOODSERVICE

"The consumer is the most important part of the production line," according to Edwards Deming. He says that the first step in producing a quality product is to decide who your customers are and then find out what their definition of quality is.

In food service, a definition of quality may include variations of speed of service, fast or leisurely; size of the portions, grandiose or petite; and seasoning of the food, mild or spicy. Depending on the market a particular establishment is trying to attract, owners must first determine the customers' definition of quality and then give them the best products and services possible for the money that they are willing to spend.

Deming laid the foundation for a new definition of quality by focusing it on the diverse attitudes of the everyday consumer rather than on traditional standards or quotas. In the food service industry, that new definition of quality has proven itself through the many varieties of successful food service operations and services. When planned and executed properly, all levels of food service, from white tablecloth restaurants and private city clubs to fast food conglomerates, can capture significant segments of the dining-out market.

Starting with the supposition that quality is defined by the customer, the customers who frequent a fine dining restaurant have different definitions of quality in relationship to time and value than do customers who frequent family style or fast food restaurants. A hamburger, no matter how well prepared, may never meet the quality standards of someone who frequents fine dining restaurants, but may meet very high quality standards set by people who frequent theme or family-style restaurants. In the following examples, notice that the less a person is able or willing to pay for food and service, the more quality is further defined by price and speed of service.

Quality in a fine dining restaurant may be defined by the following factors:

- Level of use of exotic or unusual ingredients
- Level of skill required to prepare a dish
- Use of wine, brandy or liqueur to finish sauces
- Style of service: leisure American service, French service, butler service
- Level of sophistication of the service personnel
- Size and depth of the wine and other alcoholic beverage services

Quality in a family-style restaurant may be defined by these factors:

- Size of the portions: large for adults and small for children
- Variety of common menu items
- Foods that are seasoned properly and served at the proper temperatures
- Simple preparations with somewhat sophisticated presentations and garnishes
- Appetizers large enough to share
- Entrées less than $20, including soup or salad, accompaniments and bread
- Entrées served in one hour or less

Quality for fast food restaurants may include these factors:

- Consistency of product
- Options in dressings and garnishes
- Speedy service; less than five minutes per order
- An entire meal for less than $10

VALUE IN FOOD SERVICE

Higher value is not to be confused with greater quality. Most of the TQM gurus like Deming, Crosby and Juran defined quality as the best possible. When discussing machines or machine parts perhaps this holds true, but in food service the best possible is further defined by a set of individual value factors:

- Speed of service required
- Customers' acceptance of pre-made items
- Customers' willingness to accept pre-wrapped and pre-garnished foods for the sake of speed
- Type of product used: ground filet or ground sirloin compared to ground chuck for a hamburger
- Type of service: counter service compared to drive-through and table service

These value factors and more make the definition of quality a multiple-level description in the hospitality industry.

Brillat-Savarin suggested in his treatise on food and dining that the reason for eating—pleasure versus hunger—also had an enormous impact on the choice of dining establishments and the perception of value in food service. In contrast to the primal instinct of eating versus dining, Brillat-Savarin had this to say:

> Such, in the nature of things, must have been the origin of the pleasures of the table, which must be carefully distinguished from their necessary antecedent, the pleasure of eating.
>
> The pleasure of eating is the actual and direct sensation of a need being satisfied.
>
> The pleasures of the table are considered sensations born of the various circumstances of fact, things, and persons accompanying the meal.
>
> The pleasure of eating is common to ourselves and the animals, and depends on nothing but hunger and the means to satisfy it.
>
> The pleasures of the table are peculiar to mankind, and depend on preliminary care over the preparation of the meal, the choice of the plate, and the selection of the guests.

In the twenty first century, both the pleasure of eating and the pleasures of the table are both commercial concerns.

VALUE IN BEING FIRST

According to Al Reis and Jack Trout, authors of *The 22 Immutable Laws of Marketing: Violate Them at Your Own Risk*, "It's better to be first than it is to be better." Another way to encroach on an already competitive business atmosphere, according to Reis and Trout, is to look for a different category to compete in.

Reis and Trout's example was Amelia Earhart. Everyone knows that Charles Lindberg was the first person to fly the Atlantic Ocean solo. Who was the second person? "If you didn't know that Bert Hinkler was the second person to fly the Atlantic," they say, "you might figure you had no chance at all to know the name of the third person. But you do. It's Amelia Earhart." Reis and Trout refer to this as the "law of the category." If you can't be the first, then create a new category to be first in; Earhart was the first woman to fly solo across the Atlantic.

In food service and hospitality operations, creating a category can be interpreted as being innovative and creative. Offering value and services not found elsewhere creates a customer perception of being different. That difference, when tied with quality, creates for itself a new category of services within a local competitive market.

BUILDING QUALITY COMMITMENT

Having a quality improvement program that works requires commitment from management and employees. The best way to develop commitment in people is through motivation and inspiration.

In an article from the *Harvard Business Review* (January–February 1968), Frederick Hertzberg summarized his approach to motivating employees. The article, "One More Time: How Do You Motivate Employees?" was reprinted in the *HBR Classic*. He writes:

> What is the simplest, surest, and most direct way of getting someone to do something? Ask? But if the person responds that he or she does not want to do it, then that calls for psychological consultation to determine the reason for such obstinacy. Tell the person? The response shows that he or she does not understand you, and now an expert in communication methods has to be brought in to show you how to get through. Give the person a monetary incentive? I do not need to remind the reader of the complexity and difficulty involved in setting up and administering an incentive system. Show the person? This means a costly training program. We need a simple way. . . . The surest and least circumlocuted way of getting someone to do something is to administer a kick in the pants.

Hertzberg's comedic summary of the complications of motivating employees leads him into a brief dissertation that delivers a synopsis of his motivational theories. Hertzberg, who clearly defines the difference between hygiene factors —that is, money, vacations, benefits, etc.—and motivational factors, says that job enrichment is the only permanent way to motivate employees. Hertzberg defines job enrichment as a vertical method of job loading giving these seven basic principles:

1. Removing some controls while retaining accountability.
2. Increasing the accountability of individuals for own work.
3. Giving a person a complete natural unit of work (module, division, area, and so on).
4. Granting additional authority to employees in their activity; job freedom.
5. Making periodic reports directly available to the workers themselves rather than supervisors.
6. Introducing new and more difficult tasks not previously handled.
7. Assigning individuals specific or specialized tasks, enabling them to become experts.

Hertzberg's theory of job enrichment is in direct conflict with Frederick Taylor's scientific management systems of the 1920s, but then the workers that

Hertzberg was trying to motivate were an altogether different demographic group. Taylor's was a mass of foreign immigrants and an expanding industrial workplace, while Hertzberg's was a more educated, more sophisticated worker whose psyche as well as physical security needed to be catered to.

In the hospitality industry, which has also seen a transformation of the demographics of people seeking jobs, and of the competitive demands of the hospitality business, which requires a more educated, skilled and motivated workforce, Hertzberg's approach needs to be considered a viable option to management practices.

Hertzberg, without saying it, supports the theories of TQM, but more directly he favors the theories of TQC (Total Quality Culture) as proposed by Joe Batten with the emphasis on the worker, and not on the system. However, Hertzberg and Batten are both assuming that the system of operation within the workplace has already been investigated and a good system of renewed evaluation is already in place. The next, and ultimately most important, step for Hertzberg and Batten is to plan to develop the personnel factor. Hertzberg says of job enrichment, "If only a small percentage of the time and money that is now devoted to hygiene, however, were given to job enrichment efforts, the return in human satisfaction and economic gain would be one of the largest dividends that industry and society have ever reaped through their efforts at better personnel management."

TRADITION VERSUS TQM

Hand in hand with efforts to improve personnel management goes the systematic review and evaluation that Shewhart started so successfully for Bell Labs, and Deming took over to Japan to turn its post-war devastation into world industrial domination. However, the argument is still present: How can a statistical measurement be used to evaluate a consumable commodity like food and lodging services? How do we even begin to collect the information needed through surveys or report cards? What happens to tradition and classical food preparations if the chef becomes too concerned with figures and profits and less concerned with the foods they are working with?

TQM does not dictate giving up on tradition with regard to products or services; rather, it focuses on the system of production. What Carême and Escoffier were faced with was total chaos of vocabulary and fundamental procedures. Their goal was simply to get chefs around the world to speak the same language regarding standard foods served, and to place some control over the introduction of invented food preparations that did not have foundation or science to back them up. One of the biggest mistakes modern chefs make is trying to be so original in their food preparation and service styles that the combinations do not make sense. The confusion comes from chefs who take

Escoffier's *Le Guide Culinaire* as gospel rather than as a guide. Escoffier himself said that his work was only intended to be the start of modern cuisine, and assumed that even his practices had to change as times and customs changed.

Many chefs already apply TQM techniques, perhaps without even being aware that they are doing it. Statistical analysis is not new to modern chefs; product usage, inventory control, labor control, food cost and menu sales are all fundamental food service management functions that are measured daily and charted against past performance. Neither is the concept that the worker is the best source of information new, because chefs too have worked up the ladder and have given their share of ideas to chefs before them. The adage "The customer is always right" seems to have been born with the whole concept of hospitality services. So what else is there to TQM?

TQM is the systematic evaluation of all processes, not just the isolated evaluation of sales quotas or food cost percents, but of all operational processes from ordering to sales. TQM is commitment to the customer and faith in the worker. It is a plan to succeed and a willingness to change that makes the difference between standard business operations and a business dedicated to quality.

A STRATEGIC ANALYSIS

Chefs who adopt TQMs basic tenets go beyond the numerical calculations of food cost percents to sales, labor cost percents to sales and menu item sales journals. They calculate and log this information in standard ways, but then they take it a step further. Where other chefs and business managers would simply collect this data as isolated information, the TQM chef would chart the information together with other pieces of information that affect it, and determine normal ratios and patterns of influence. For example, most chefs would determine food cost percents as a relationship to sales by following the basic formula food cost % = food cost ÷ sales, and labor cost percents using the formula labor cost % = labor cost ÷ sales, and leave it at that. Then they or their supervisors might say things like, "Your food cost is too high," or "Your labor cost is too high," but no one really knows what this means. These become simple judgment statements based on some predetermined quota or standard number. Deming warns against numerical quotas in number eleven of his fourteen points to management's success: "Eliminate management by objective. Eliminate management by numerical goals. Substitute leadership."

The real issues are the relationships between food costs, labor costs, overhead costs and sales. Take for example two menu items, stuffed lobster and the good old American hamburger. Stuffed lobster is relatively easy to produce (low labor) but has a high food cost; how do chefs determine the selling price? Do they base it purely on the food cost? If food cost is $10 per stuffed lobster, and the agreed upon food cost percent is 35 percent sales (a national average), then the selling price would be over $30. Who would buy it? An American hamburger has a very low food cost and takes relatively little time to produce; therefore, the selling price based on the same 35 percent goal might be around $3. Which one is more profitable to sell?

Obviously, cost is more complicated a question than first might be perceived. There might be a need in particular establishments to serve stuffed lobster tails, but few will buy them at $30. What is the operator supposed to do?

Various related data are collected and then charted together in order to see the relationships that develop. Such combined studies show how the selling price is affected by food cost, labor cost, availability and the intangible customer satisfaction. If stuffed lobster is something a restaurant wants to sell because their customers are asking for it, they decide on a price first that people will be able or willing to pay, then work backward. Because the labor cost in producing stuffed lobster tails is relatively low in relationship to other menu items, the operation can afford to have a higher food cost percentage than other items. Perhaps a 45 or 50 percent food cost to sales ratio then becomes acceptable. Look at the dollar return! A lobster tail with a $10 food cost that sells for $20, a 50 percent food cost percent, returns $10 to the operation in gross profit. Labor cost as a percent then goes way down, perhaps to 10 or 15 percent of sales, well below the national average of 25 percent. How many hamburgers at even a lower 25 percent food cost would it take to sell in order to clear an equivalent $10 in gross profit? Five or ten? Then what happens to the labor cost? It goes way up the chart. It is looking at numerical data in light of its proper relationships to all operational expenses, to customer appeal and to the restaurant's image itself that makes the decision-making process valid.

UNDER NEW MANAGEMENT

Chefs who follow TQM strategies go beyond the hierarchical organizational structure to lead and direct their workers to quality production. They understand that their job is to motivate their employees, and that by doing so the job will get done sufficiently well. Fear tactics do not work long term. They only appear to stimulate production. Fear destroys personal confidence and ultimately damages any ability to produce consistently, qualitatively or not.

TQM guided chefs know the value of their employees' knowledge and opinions. They seek their input and shape processes around their opinions. After all, employees are the ones doing the job hour after hour, day after day; are they not the experts?

Finally, TQM guided chefs go far beyond a passive relationship with the customer. They seek customer input by going into the dining room and talking directly to them. They insist on meetings with the dining room staff who come in contact with the customers every day to solicit their input into customer wants and satisfaction. Then they put aside their own personal tastes in order to meet the demands of the customer. Some chefs say, "Yes, the customer is always right, but why do we need to ask?" TQM chefs ask because asking is as much a part of their job as production and service. The customer is always right, and now we need to find out what customers want.

The business of quality food service is a complicated balance of art and profits, but it is exactly that complication and the energy and direction it takes a chef to manage it that produces quality kitchen leadership. Leadership is the true job of the chef; cooking and the service of food are merely tasks within the overall picture. Leadership produces a motivated staff, a consistent production organization and a high level of customer satisfaction. Leadership in the operation places the organization in a leading position among its competitors and makes long-term success possible.

CHAPTER 24

The Future
of Information Technologies

OBJECTIVES

When you complete this chapter, you should be able to:

- Describe some of the new information technologies that are affecting the way people communicate and do business.
- Explain the importance of obtaining training in information technologies and in keeping up to date with some of the progress in the field.
- Describe some of the management software programs available for the food service and hospitality industry.
- Discuss why food vendors are helping buyers hook up to their database systems via computers and specific software packages for easier ordering.
- Describe what is meant by POS and describe its use in food service operations.
- Explain the concept of exploring the Web in researching companies, organizations, and educational centers.

THE FUTURE IS HERE

Advances in information technologies like computers, fax machines, satellite conferencing, the Internet and cellular/digital phones are happening so quickly it is difficult to keep up with the progress. Technology that was revolutionary a few years ago is history today, while technology released today is outdated tomorrow.

Only a few decades ago, people were predicting that there would be a growing dependence on information technologies for businesses and home use alike. Today that dependence has become a reality. The future is here and food service managers cannot afford to fall behind.

Information technologies can affect all aspects of business and raise the level of expertise in recording and communicating information. Chefs and all managers need to embrace these new technologies and learn to use them in daily applications:

- The fax machine allows people to instantly send written messages, charts, drawings and pictures more quickly than hand-carried mail and verbal messages, more concisely and less obtrusively than phone calls.
- Computers have, for the most part, replaced the typewriter and calculator. They enable many specialized skills, like desktop publishing, typesetting, recipe development, and data analysis, to be done in house.
- Satellite conferencing has opened national and regional conferences, business meetings and even school classrooms to thousands of people who might not otherwise have been able to participate.
- The Internet allows people to send and receive electronic mail (e-mail) and places a world of research and information at a person's fingertips.
- Cellular/digital phones have revolutionized the way people communicate and do business, in some cases replacing traditional phones and many forms of wireless communication.
- Palm held organizers and planners have now gone beyond the capabilities of the cell phone and have begun to sweep across social and business enterprises. These devices connect students and business people alike to classrooms, libraries and offices through even more powerful wireless technology that continues to expand in scope and power.

These are only a few of the information technologies that can affect the management of food service and hospitality operations. Chefs and managers need to be trained in multiple facets of information technology to lead their staffs into the twenty-first century.

The Need to Learn

Some forms of information technologies are easy to learn and use, while others require special training and practice to master. The operation of fax machines and cellular phones, for example, can be learned quickly with the aid of written manuals and brief demonstrations. The knowledge and skills required to operate computers and manipulate the thousands of available software packages is not learned as easily.

Computer classes are offered at most community, state, private and other local colleges, ranging from basic to advanced studies. Many of these courses are open to the public and designed for non-traditional students (students not attending college on a full-time basis). Talk with a counselor at one of the colleges near you and create a study plan that will identify the courses you will need to advance your understanding of computers and their software applications. Once you've obtained this basic training, you are ready to learn some of the specialized software programs designed for the food service and hospitality industries.

MANAGEMENT SOFTWARE

There are dozens of computer software programs designed to help manage the production, sale and service of food and other hospitality services. Most are available in both Macintosh and PC (personal computer) formats for greater adaptability and flexibility. Software program developers often supply sample or demonstration discs for users to try before buying the whole program. Take advantage of these services to help you decide which programs are best suited to your operation.

Information about these specialized computer software programs is available in many restaurant industry magazines and newspapers and can be gathered at hospitality trade shows, association conferences and at local colleges that offer culinary and hospitality programs. The Internet can also be a source of information on software programs and can be used to solicit reviews from operators already using them.

Computer software programs are available in these areas:

- Employee management
- Inventory control and management
- Menu design and management
- Recipe development
- Nutritional analysis
- Costing

Many national food vendors now offer high volume customers a way to order supplies via computers and integrated software programs. This technology allows the independent operator to check vendor inventories and the price of goods before deciding which items to order. The host company supplies the customer with the software and some hardware needed to make the link possible. Hardware may include the loaning of a modem or entire computer system when necessary. The software allows the restaurant's computer to talk to the vendor's computer through phone lines. These integrated buying systems do not lock operators into any single vendor, but do encourage single vendor use with convenient access to their personal ordering systems.

POINT OF SALE (POS)

Point of sale computers are the new wave of food service cash register systems that integrate computer management software packages with touch screen technology ordering systems that allow wait staffs to communicate orders to the kitchen without leaving the dining room. These are revolutionizing the way wait staffs place food orders, guest checks are written, and managers gather and analyze critical sales and labor statistics.

Touch screen technology allows a person to send a command through a computer by touching the screen rather than typing on a keyboard. This makes it easier and quicker for wait persons to place orders, add to or correct orders and create guest checks to present to the customer. Information is presented on the main screen in a convenient and easy to read format.

The POS system is linked to remote printers in the kitchen and bar areas where orders for food and beverages are instantaneously transmitted. This allows orders to be processed as soon as the information is programmed into the computer terminal. The remote printers also eliminate the need for the wait person to hand deliver guest tickets to the kitchen crew. This keeps wait personnel in the dining room where they can give more service to the customer. The quick turnaround of orders and control of traffic in and out of the kitchen contributes to the efficiency of the entire operation.

Some POS systems can be linked to the chef's and/or dining room manager's PC in remote offices by integrated software. This technology allows the chef or other managers to access the information from the POS system at their own desks. This makes it easy to check sales, inventories, guest counts and other critical information as often as necessary to plan production or control costs.

PDAs

PDAs (personal digital assistants) are hand-held computers that serve as organizers for personal information. They generally include at least a name and address database, to-do list and note taker. PDAs may be combined with cellphones and other wireless technologies, providing a mobile office for people on the go.

PDAs are pen based and use a stylus to tap selections on menus and to enter printed characters. The units may also include a small on-screen keyboard which is tapped with the pen. Data are synchronized between the PDA and desktop computer via cable or wireless transmission.

THE BLACKBERRY

Blackberry represents a family of wireless e-mail appliances from Research In Motion, Ltd., Waterloo, Ontario (www.blackberry.net). Available in both pager and palm size, these popular devices are designed to synchronize with Microsoft Exchange and other e-mail systems. The units are on line and receive mail all the time. Internet content and other applications are available from third parties.

EXPLORING THE WEB

The Internet is a system of information technology first implemented by the U.S. Department of Defense in the 1960s as a means of sharing information across a wide range of networked computer systems. In the 1970s, American colleges and universities began using the Internet for academic research. Today the Internet is used by millions of people around the world in practically every country and by people from all walks of life.

The exponential expansion of the Internet has created a worldwide network of computers and services that allow the users to access information from millions of sources around the world, right in their own homes from their personal computers. The system of information networking is referred to as the World Wide Web (www).

Personal computers are connected to the Internet through a modem, which sends information along phone lines and uses an on line service that is usually purchased for a monthly fee. Once connected, the user can retrieve information from television networks, radio stations and individual companies that have created their own Web sites. A Web site is an information piece on a particular company, business or organization that is designed for access through the Internet.

Web sites can be accessed by using specific Web addresses. Web addresses are an identifiable series of letters, keyboard strokes and punctuation that identify the particular piece of information for easy retrieval. They are usually prefixed by the letters *www* and followed by an abbreviated name of the company or organization, and a designation of whether the item is coming from a company, an organization or an educational center. A typical Web site address might look like this:

www. (dot) name of the company. (dot) type of organization

Some common Web site extensions are:

.com–commercial	**.net**–network	**.nom**–individuals
.edu–educational	**.org**–organization	**.arts**–cultural sites

.gov–government	**.info**–info services	**.store**–business selling product
.mil–military	**.firm**–business	**.web**–site emphasizing the www

The most effective means of navigating the Web is through search engines. A search engine is basically an application that enables you to search efficiently through a database or listing of thousands, if not millions, of Web sites. By entering in a keyword, the database is queried and a search is launched which will scan the listing according to your criteria.

After the search engine has been queried, a list of links will be generated, with a brief synopsis describing each link. This list of links is ranked according to probabilities of matching search criteria, sequentially ordered from a high probability of matching the criteria searched for to a low probability.

The skill that everyone needs to acquire is how to generate effective search queries and how to sift rapidly through irrelevant links that search engines will often create despite efforts at creating a refined search.

WHY USE SEARCH ENGINES?

Search engines are the primary Internet resource that you must learn in order to harness the powers of the Internet and fully understand its intricacies.

Search engines are the on line resources that should be utilized when conducting any type of research, or when simply surfing the net. Search engines not only enable you to conduct research and find information quickly and efficiently, but they also expose you to new vistas or knowledge. As the Internet continues to grow, you can grow along with the Internet and track its dynamic progress and growth through search engines.

In order to master the Internet, you must begin to understand how to use search engines and become knowledgeable about which search engines generate the type of information you find most helpful.

The ability to create effective queries when using search engines is a critical Internet skill, as is the ability to screen and sift through irrelevant information. By becoming knowledgeable about search engines, you have the potential to become acquainted with and tap into almost all other Internet resources.

TYPES OF SEARCH ENGINES

There are many different types and kinds of search engines available on the Internet. Each search engine accesses information and generates lists of Web sites in slightly or radically different ways. Whether conducting in-depth research or just randomly surfing, you may want to utilize many of these search engines. Each search engine represents a unique way of accessing on line information.

By utilizing an array of search engines, information can be accessed in a multi-dimensional way.

Standard Search Engines

Listed below you will find some of the most popular and effective standard search engines and a brief synopsis of their strengths and weaknesses.

www.hotbot.com

If you are looking for a starting place, then Hotbot would be an ideal site to visit. This search engine has the uncanny ability to find what you are looking for rapidly. Hotbot has an array of options for screening information—most importantly, the exact phrase option.

www.yahoo.com

Yahoo is one of the Web's most popular search sites. It is also an excellent place from which to begin to learn how to search and navigate the Web. Yahoo is not actually a search engine; it is, in fact, a searchable directory. All items in Yahoo are cataloged and arranged into directories.

www.altavista.com

AltaVista is an excellent search engine and is a "must" stop when looking to do serious research.

www.lycos.com

Lycos has a fast, relatively comprehensive catalog but it simply does not have the ability to refine searches and screen information effectively.

www.google.com

Google is a fast and expanding searchable directory which in 2005 became a public company trading on the Nasdaq New Markets under the acronym GOOG. Google enables users to search the Web, Usenet, and images.

www.aol.com

AOL is a member portal and search engine combined. People can purchase a user license that gets them even more information and technology tools, including e-mail, instant messaging (IM) and chat rooms.

www.msn.com

MSN is another member portal created by the Microsoft Corporation which boasts to be one of the friendliest portals on the Web. Besides its search capabilities it allows the licensed user to customize a personal site to accommodate their particular interests and needs.

Multi or Meta-search Engines

A multiple or meta-search engine combines an array of single search engines into an all-encompassing search engine. If you want to search with broad sweeping strokes, then a meta-search engine is recommended. There are two different types of multiple search engines:

1. The first type of search engine combines several different search engines into one seamless search engine (such as Metacrawler).
2. The second type allows you to view all or some of its components simultaneously or sequentially.

www.webcrawler.com

Web Crawler is an automated "indexer" that "crawls" around the Web cataloging and indexing Web pages. Web Crawler is a very efficient search engine. However, it lacks the tools easily and effectively to screen information and refine searches that are available with other search engines. Web Crawler does have sub-categories to refine your search, but in a relatively crude fashion.

www.metacrawler.com

Metacrawler is arguably the best meta-search engine available because it is simple to use and it seamlessly integrates its array of single search engines into an easy to use interface. Metacrawler combines Lycos, Hot Bot, Yahoo, AltaVista, Excite and Infoseek to power all of its searches.

www.dogpile.com

Dogpile is a search cooperative that utilizes twelve search engines to power its searches. Dogpile is not as simple and elegant as Metacrawler, but its power to survey broad vistas of information is staggering. Dogpile queries each of its component search engines and lists the first ten to fifteen "hits" for each search engine. It lets you choose a particular search engine if it has created a list of Web sites that you find helpful. Dogpile is a search engine for search engines.

www.search.com

Search.com is a sequential multi-search engine, which means that it enables you to query seven different search engines, but only one at a time, via an easy to use interface. Search.com also offers editorial commentary about different search engines.

The Internet is beginning to have a great influence on the way people do research, promote products or ideas and communicate to others. In all likelihood, this influence will continue to grow and people will become more dependent on the Internet for exchanging information. If you do not have access to the Internet, you may not be as effective in management, business or your personal life as you could be.

Glossary

aboyeur: (Fr.) expeditor; acts as the liaison between the dining room staff and the cook's line to ensure that the foods ordered and recorded by the wait staff are prepared properly, plated and served according to acceptable quality standards.

Affirmative Action: U.S. federal legal term denoting an active approach to recruiting and hiring minority workers for the workplace.

Alexander I: Russian Czar who employed Antoine Carême in St. Petersburg, Russia.

allemande: one of the lead sauces standardized by Carême, thickened with egg yolks and cream.

American Culinary Federation (ACF): a national organization of professional culinarians promoting education, training and certification for the professional cook, chef and culinary educator.

Apicius, Caelii: fourth century A.D. writer who published *De Re Coquinaria* (*On Roman Cookery*) using recipes from Marcus Gavius; Caelli was probably not a relative.

Apicius, Marcus Gavius: Roman cook, first century A.D.; creator of the recipes and formulas used in *De Re Coquinaria*.

Appreciative listening: when the purpose is to show appreciation or gratitude for what someone has done and is then reporting to you.

au plumage: a cooked fowl garnished with the colorful feathers of the host bird.

authority: the ability to make decisions and correct problems without asking for the advice of supervisors or managers.

authority-driven leadership: a part of every organization that has a linear organizational structure.

Bailly: Paris pâtisserier who employed Antoine Carême and taught him the pastry arts.

Batten, Joseph: author of *Building a Total Quality Culture*, which places the entire emphasis of management on the human equation.

Bazaine: Marshal of French army given authority by Napoleon III to lead the troops during the Franco-Prussian War; commander under which Escoffier served as head chef.

Beauvilliers, Antoine: culinary writer and gastronomic authority who opened his restaurant La Grande Taverne de Londres in 1782.

béchamel: a milk and veal–based leading sauce first standardized by Antoine Carême.

Béchamel, Louis de: Marquis de Nointel (1603–1703), a financeer of Brittany for whom La Varenne named the famous white sauce béchamel.

Benedict, LeGrand: famous financier and Wall Street broker in eighteenth century America for whom Eggs Benedict was named.

Blackberry: a family of wireless e-mail appliances available in both pager and palm size designed to synchronize with Microsoft Exchange and other e-mail systems.

Blake, Robert: along with Jane Mouton, authored *The Managerial Grid III*, which describes different authority-based leadership styles and their effect on employee morale and production.

Blanchard, Kenneth: along with Paul Hersey, authored *Management of Organizational Behavior*, claiming that human resources are an organization's greatest resource.

boucher: (Fr.) butcher; responsible for all meat, poultry and seafood fabrication.

Boulanger, Monsieur A.: opened first restaurant in France in 1765, calling his shop *Restoratives*, which means to restore one's self.

brigade: a system of hierarchical leadership developed for kitchen organization by Auguste Escoffier.

Brillat-Savarin, Jean-Anthelme: eighteenth-century gourmet who authored *The Philosopher in the Kitchen*, the first serious treatise on the state of eating and the pleasures of the table.

Canterbury Tales: thirteenth-century poem written by Geoffrey Chaucer depicting the life of travelers and the use of roadside inns during a religious pilgrimage to Canterbury.

Careerbuilders.com: Internet Web site hosting jobs positions for culinary and hospitality workers and managers/chefs.

Carême, Antoine: the "king of chefs and the chef of kings," Carême was credited with standardizing four lead sauces and hundreds of recipes and procedures for fine cooking.

Carnegie, Dale: author of *How to Win Friends and Influence People*, a comprehensive study of human behavior and the things that influence and motivate people.

catering, off-premise: performing food service at any location other than your home kitchen.

Champy, James: co-author of *Reengineering the Corporation* and author of *Reengineering Management*, promoting the need to re-think how to manage others by starting with the re-engineering of yourself.

Chaucer, Geoffrey: (c. 1343–1400 A.D.) author of *The Canterbury Tales*, depicting the adventures of early travelers and the hospitality found in roadside inns.

Chefs de partie: ([Fr.] station chefs, or line chefs) are the working chefs on the production line.

commis: (Fr.) apprentice; often performing basic culinary/pastry tasks and working under the direct supervision of experienced cooks and chefs.

Comprehensive listening: When the purpose is to organize and make sense out of the message being delivered.

concept engineering: creating a company concept utilizing a variety of influential factors.

constancy of purpose: defines leaders who consistently demonstrate their commitment to high standards and inspire others to do the same.

Cost of Quality: a system of operational management developed by Dr. Armand Feigenbaum to examine all the costs related to developing a quality production and inspection system, as well as the cost incurred when the product fails to meet customer demand.

Crosby, Philip: TQM guru responsible for a Zero Defects strategy toward quality control.

D'Angelo, Dan, CEC, AAC: Catering Chef, D'Angelo's Summit Restaurant and Caterers, Philadelphia, Pennsylvania.

Delmonico, Giovanni: owner of first full class restaurant in America, Delmonico's in New York City (1827).

Delmonico's: first full service restaurant in America, opened in 1827 in New York City; Charles Ranhofer was chef from 1862 to 1899.

de Medici, Catherine: Italian matriarch who married Henry II of France in 1533; influenced the development of French cuisine with her chef Guillaume Verger.

Deming, W. Edwards: statistician who helped pioneer TQM and given credit for helping Japan rebuild her economy after World War II.

demographics: information on an identified group of people reflecting their cultural diversity and social and economic status.

dietary foodservice: foodservice provided in health and retirement institutions.

Discerning listening: when the purpose is to get complete information, determine the main message.

diversity: in personnel management it refers to the various makeup of people's cultural, religious and social backgrounds as well as race and gender differences.

Drucker, Peter: modern management theorist promoting Management by Objectives (MBO).

Dubrin, Andrew: author of *Effective Business Psychology*, which applies basic psychology theories and motivation techniques to the world of business.

Dugléré, Adolphe: chef of the nineteenth century restaurant Café Anglaise on the Boulevard des Italiens in Paris.

Earhart, Amelia: the first woman to fly solo across the Atlantic.

Empathetic listening: when the purpose is to support the sender, as he or she is telling you some of their concerns.

empowerment: giving authority to employees to make their own decisions and to try their own ideas without immediate acknowledgment from supervisors.

enabling: a concept of personnel management that ensures that employees have the tools and training to accomplish their goals.

entremetier: (Fr.) chef responsible for side dishes and accompaniments.

entrepreneur: a person who organizes, operates, and assumes the financial risk for a business enterprise.

Epicurean, The: first American treatise on cooking published by Charles Ranhofer in 1893.

Equal Opportunity Employer (EOE): U.S. legal term describing non-discriminatory practices in the hiring, promotion and pay given to minority workers.

Escoffier, Georges Auguste: known as the "father of haute cuisine." Reorganized the professional kitchen into the brigade system modeled after the French military; author of *Le Guide Culinaire*.

espagñole: (Fr.) a velvety brown sauce from the kitchens of Spain first popularized by Antoine Carême.

ethnicity: defines a person's cultural heritage.

Evaluative listening: when the purpose is to make a decision based on the information you are being given.

Feigenbaum, Armand: modern quality management theorist who developed the concept of Cost of Quality through an exploration of Poor Quality Cost (PQC); also promoted Total Quality Control (TQC).

Fishbone diagram: also called the Ishikawa diagram or Cause and Effect diagram. An analytical tool that provides a systematic way of looking at problems and the causes that create or contribute to them. Developed by Kaoru Ishikawa.

foodservice.com: an Internet Web site hosting job positions for culinary and hospitality workers and managers/chefs.

Food service director: similar in authority to the executive chef, or the person in charge of the food service operation.

garde manger: (Fr.) chef responsible for all cold food preparation.

gender: refers to a person's sex, male or female.

George IV: seventeenth century King of England who employed Antoine Carême for a short time; Carême did not like the English weather.

grillardin: (Fr.) chef in charge of grilling and broiling foods on the production line.

Hawthorne effect: term coined to represent the findings of Dr. George Elton Mayo at the conclusion of human relation experiments conducted for Bell Labs at the Western Electric Hawthorne plant in Cicero, Illinois; the theory states that worker productivity is directly related to social group dynamics, motivation, leadership and "human relations."

Hazard Analysis Critical Control Points (HACCP): a food safety protection system created for NASA utilizing quality control concepts, including Philip Crosby's Zero Defects strategies.

hcareers.com: an Internet Web site hosting job positions for culinary and hospitality workers and managers/chefs.

Heliopolis: ancient Egyptian city near present day Cairo; beginning of King's Highway.

Hersey, Paul: along with Kenneth Blanchard, authored *Management of Organizational Behavior*, which claims that human resources are an organization's greatest resource.

hospitality: the sharing of one's home and dinner table with friends, family and acquaintances.

impartial leadership: leaders who are constant in purpose and consistent in their delivery in order to turn a diverse work force into a cohesive team.

institutional foodservice: the business of supplying daily meals to generally captive audiences, e.g., in office buildings, school cafeterias, military bases and prisons.

International Association of Culinary Professionals (IACP): a national association of cooks, chefs and cookbook authors.

Internet: a system of information technology linking people at their computers to various types of information.

Ishikawa diagram: see Fishbone diagram.

Ishikawa, Kaoru: president of Union of Japanese Scientists and Engineers (JUSE) after World War II; responsible for bringing W. Edwards Deming's quality management practices to reconstruction Japan.

Juran, Joseph: a leader in quality management who proposed quality circles for the assessment of the processes.

Juran's Trilogy: a concept of TQM founded by Joseph Juran with an emphasis on Quality Planning, Quality Control, and Quality Improvement.

JUSE: see Union of Japanese Scientists and Engineers.

King's Highway: ancient trade route connecting Heliopolis in Egypt to Damascus, Syria.

Kitchen manager: the executive chef, or the person in charge of the food service operation.

lead cook: could be a shift manager, expeditor or main cook on the production line.

Le Guide Culinaire: written by Auguste Escoffier; became the world's bible on modern cookery.

legumier: (Fr.) chef responsible for all vegetable cookery.

Le Petit Moulin Rouge: famous restaurant in Paris which employed the young Auguste Escoffier.

Le Viandier: one of the earliest printed cookbooks, written by Tirel-Taillevent in the thirteenth century.

Lobster Newburg: famous seafood recipe created by Charles Ranhofer, who adapted a recipe brought to New York by a friend of Charles Delmonico.

Longo, Nancy: Chef Owner/Operator, Pierpoint Restaurant, Fells Point, Maryland.

Macrina, Thomas J., CEC, AAC: Hotel and Conference Center Chef, Desmond Hotel and Conference Center, Media, Pennsylvania.

Management by Objectives (MBO): a means of measuring the effectiveness of employees by analyzing their ability to meet certain objectives; promoted by management consultant Peter Drucker.

Mayo, Dr. George Elton: a Harvard researcher brought into the Hawthorne Plant to finish work begun by the National Academy of Sciences; responsible for developing the theories known as the Hawthorne effect.

McConnell, Penny: director of Food and Nutrition Services for Fairfax County Public Schools and past president of American School Food Service Association.

memorandum: a written communication designed to give specific information to a specific individual or group of people.

mise en place: (Fr.) a French cooking term meaning that everything is in its place and ready for production.

Modern Quality Control (MQC): the stimulating and building up of operator responsibilities and interests in quality, according to Armand Feigenbaum.

monster.com: an Internet Web site hosting jobs positions for multiple fields and positions, including culinary and hospitality workers and managers/chefs.

motivational leadership: the act of inspiring other people through example, equity, and constancy of purpose.

Mouton, Jane: along with Robert Blake, authored *The Managerial Grid III*, which describes different authority-based leadership styles and their effect on employee morale and production.

National Research Council (NRC): of the National Academy of Sciences, enlisted by General Electric in 1924 to conduct an impartial study to determine if there were any effect of lighting on employee productivity at the Western Electric Hawthorne plant located in Cicero, Illinois. This lead into what became known as the Hawthorne Effect.

National Restaurant Association (NRA): national association of restaurant owners, chefs and managers whose purpose is to keep themselves and the dining public educated on new trends and business management; promotes education and a public awareness of fine food.

Neff, Cary E.: Spa Chef, Woodloch Resort and Spa, Chicago, Illinois.

pantry cook: cook who is responsible for all cold food preparation, including cold sauces, dressings, appetizers, specialty condiments, salsas and other cold accompaniments.

pâtissier: (Fr.) pastry chef; responsible for all baking and pastry items used in the kitchen and served in the dining rooms.

Paul II, James W., MS, CCE, CSC, FMP: Chef Director, Culinary Arts, The Art Institute of Atlanta, Atlanta, Georgia.

PC: personal computer.

PDA: personal digital assistant; handheld computers that serve as an organizer for personal information.

PDCA cycle: see Shewhart's cycle; stands for Plan, Do, Check, Act.

Peters, Tom: modern management consultant and theorist insisting that the employee should be management's primary concern.

Philippe VI: fourteenth century King of France who employed Taillevent as his lead cook.

Philosopher in the Kitchen, The: published treatise of gastronomy by Anthelme Brillat-Savarin, c. 1825.

piece monteé: (Fr.) a decorated centerpiece for buffet platters intended to lend to a particular theme.

Pitz, Reimund CEC, CCE, AAC: Private Country Club Chef, Country Club, Orlando Florida.

Pliny: (c. 24–79 A.D.) ancient philosopher and archivist, author of *Natural Histories,* who credited Apicius with the practice of force feeding pigs with dried figs and then drowning them with honey wine.

poissonier: (Fr.) chef responsible for all seafood items on the menu.

Poor Quality Cost (PQC): a concept developed by Armand Feigenbaum to show management the true costs of poor quality, something business minded managers could understand.

POS: point of sale computers used in modern food service operations.

prep list: abbreviation for preparation list; a list of items needed for daily food production.

professional posturing: the act of seeking progressively more challenging positions.

proxemics: the study of the way we structure distance and space when approaching or communicating to one another.

qualifying: to evaluate based on pre-selected criteria.

race: a term used to group people with similar skin color, facial features, and other genetically influenced physical characteristics into distinct geographical groups.

Ranhofer, Charles: French/American chef who held the position of executive chef at Delmonico's in New York City from 1862 to 1894; author of *The Epicurean,* a collection of over 3,500 recipes and procedures for modern cooking.

Reis, Al: along with Jack Trout, authored *The 22 Immutable Laws of Marketing: Violate Them at Your Own Risk.*

Ritz, César: hotelier who teamed up with Escoffier to raise the level of sophistication in hotel staying and dining.

Rothschild, James de: wealthy banking magnate in Paris who employed Antoine Carême as head chef.

rôtisseur: (Fr.) chef in charge of roasted meat and fowl.

Rue du Bac: Paris, France. Birthplace of Antoine Carême.

saucier: (Fr.) chef in charge of sauces and sautéed items from the production menu.

Savoy Hotel: London, England. Where Escoffier was hired as Head of Restaurant Services and César Ritz as General Manager.

Scientific Management: theory of production management developed by pioneer Frederick Winslow Taylor utilizing time-and-motion studies to find the most effective way of completing each task in a project.

second cook: cook that is usually assigned to second most popular form of cooking for the particular establishment they are working in; could be the lead fry cook, sauté cook or broiler cook.

self-assessment: a process of self-evaluation to determine personal strengths and weaknesses.

Shaw's Guide for Cooking Schools: a guide to credit and non-credit cookery schools in the United States.

Shewhart, Walter A.: (1891–1967) inspector for Bell laboratories, who designed a system of continual assessment of processes known as Shewhart's cycle.

Shewhart's cycle: a system of continuous assessment of processes, developed by Walter Shewhart for Bell Laboratories; commonly referred to as the PDCA cycle.

sous chef: (Fr.) second chef in charge under Escoffier's brigade system.

specifications: an exact description of an item including brand name, type, size, shape, grading, and packaging.

Stacey, James E.: along with Frederick D. Sturdivant, authored *The Corporate Social Challenge*, a series of case stories on how modern businesses react to employee needs in the workplace.

standardization: creating a process or procedure that is so well designed that it can be reproduced by various individuals with similar results.

standard operating procedures (SOPs): specifically constructed procedures for doing things with exact steps and methods.

Statistical Quality Control (SQC): measuring the effect of certain production steps or procedures on the overall quality of the product, charting (quality charts) the results in such a way that the average worker could evaluate progress at various stages in production; first promoted by Walter Shewhart.

strategic management: an aggressive and deliberately systematic approach to management practices.

Sturdivant, Frederick D.: along with James Stacey, authored *The Corporate Social Challenge*, a series of case stories on how modern businesses react to employee needs in the workplace.

supervision: the act of supervising employees in the performance of their jobs.

Talleyrand, Duc de: famous Parisian statesman and early employer of Antoine Carême.

Taylor, Frederick Winslow: (1856–1915) industrial engineer who transformed the way American manufacturing businesses were designed and run.

third cook: often the lead preparatory cook responsible for the bulk of the higher level mise en place items.

time management: organizing yourself to be able to accomplish all the important tasks given to you, at the level of quality they have been prescribed with and in the amount of time given you to do so.

Tirel-Taillevent, Guillaume: (c. 1310–1395) cook to King Philippe VI of France (fourteenth century); standardized recipes using new innovations in cooking equipment.

toque blanche: (Fr.) tall, white stove-pipe hat worn by professional chefs; the size of the hat was used to depict the level of authority a person had in the kitchen.

Total Quality Control (TQC): a management concept developed by Armand Feigenbaum emphasizing that quality requires a "total" effort of management, not only the inspection department, to make sure inferior products do not make it to market.

Total Quality Culture (TQC): management concept defined by Joe Batten, author of *Building a Total Quality Culture*, addressing the need and the means for bringing about cultural changes in the work place that will have a positive effect on employee motivation, production and retention.

tournant: (Fr.) chef used in various positions depending on the need; rotating among the various positions.

TQC: Total Quality Culture; a concept of personnel management that goes hand in hand with TQM; promoted by Joe Batten.

TQM: Total Quality Management; a system of management based on quality planning and improvement. It involves procedures, policies and people.

Trial by fire: an interviewing technique which requires the administration of a skill test to potential employees as a demonstration of their culinary skills and knowledge.

Trout, Jack: along with Al Reis, authored *The 22 Immutable Laws of Marketing: Violate Them at Your Own Risk.*

truth in menus: legislation that demands that written menu descriptions depict accurate information regarding ingredients and procedures.

Union of Japanese Scientists and Engineers (JUSE): Japanese agency credited with convincing W. Edwards Deming to help them build a quality production culture for the reconstruction period after World War II. Kaoru Ishikawa was its president.

value-led visionary: term coined by human management specialist Joseph Batten that describes the total value of an organization as the sum of the values it promotes, teaches and practices, which begins and ends with management.

Varenne, François-Pierre, de la: chef under the Marquis d'Uxelles; author of three books on culinary art: *Le Cuisine Francaise* (1651), *Le Pâtissier Francais* (1653), and *Le Confiturier Francais* (1664).

velouté: (Fr.) roux thickened sauce standardized by Carême.

Verger, Guillaume: chef to the French court during the reign of Catherine de Medici.

Véry: eighteenth century Parisian restaurant frequented by the novelist Honoré de Balzac, the gourmet Grimond de la Reyniere and Brillat-Savarin.

Villeneuve-Loubet, Alpes: Maritimes, France; birthplace of Auguste Escoffier.

World Wide Web (www): a figurative description of the Internet and the access for information it allows its users.

www.acfchefs.org: Web site for American Culinary Federation, America's leading organization in the promotion and development of the American chef.

Zehnder, John, CEC, AAC: Large Scale Restaurant Foodservice Chef, Zehnder's Family Restaurant, Frankenmuth, Michigan.

Zero Defects: a concept of TQM fostered by pioneer Philip Crosby, whose notion of absolute quality is 100 percent adherence to standards and guidelines.

References

Batten, Joe, *Building a Total Quality Culture* (Menlo Park, California: Crisp Publishing, Inc., 1992).

Blake, Robert and Jane S. Mouton, *The Managerial Grid III* (Houston: Golf Publishing, 1987).

Brillat-Savarin, Jean-Anthelme, *The Philosopher in the Kitchen* (Middlesex, England: Penguin Books, 1984).

Carnegie, Dale, *How to Win Friends and Influence People*, revised ed. (Simon & Schuster: New York, 1981).

Carson, Ritchie I. A., *Food in Civilization* (New York: Beaufort Books, Inc., 1981).

Champy, James, *Reengineering Management, The Mandate for New Leadership* (New York: Harper Collins Publishers, 1995).

Coyle, Patrick L., Jr., *The World Encyclopedia of Food* (New York: Facts on File, Inc., 1982).

Crosby, Philip, *Quality Is Free* (New York: Times Mirror Publications, 1979).

Cummings, Long and Lewis, *Managing Communications in Organizations: An Introduction*, 2nd ed. (Scottsdale, Arizona: Gorsuch Scarisbrick, Publishers, 1988).

Deming, W. Edwards, *Out of Crisis* (Boston: Massachusetts Institute of Technology, Center for Advanced Engineering Study, 1982).

Drucker, Peter, *The Essential Drucker: The Best of Sixty Years of Peter Drucker's Essential Writings on Management* (Harper Collins, London, 2003).

Dubrin, Andrew, *Effective Business Psychology*, 3rd ed. (Englewood Cliffs, NJ: Prentice Hall, 1990).

Feigenbaum, Armand V., *Total Quality Control*, 3rd ed. (New York: McGraw Hill, 1991).

Hammer, Michael and Champy, James, *Reengineering the Corporation: A Manifesto for Business Revolution* (New York: Harper Business, 1993).

Herbodeau, Eugene, *Georges Auguste Escoffier* (London: Practical Press, 1955).

Hersey, Paul and Kenneth H. Blanchard, *Management of Organizational Behavior* (Englewood Cliffs, NJ: Prentice Hall, Inc., 1977).

Hertzberg, Frederick, HBR Classic, no. 87507, "One More Time: How Do You Motivate Employees?" (*Harvard Business Review*).

Juran, Joseph, *Juran on Leadership for Quality—An Executive Handbook* (New York: The Free Press, 1989).

Peters, Thomas J., and Robert H. Waterman, *In Search of Excellence: Lessons from America's Best-Run Companies* (Warner Books, UK, 2003).

Reis, Al and Jack Trout, *The 22 Immutable Laws of Marketing: Violate Them at Your Own Risk* (New York: Harper Collins, 1993).

Shewhart, Walter A., *Economic Control of Quality of Manufactured Products* (New York: Van Nostrand Reinhold, 1931).

Sturdivant, Frederick D., and James E. Stacey, *The Corporate Social Challenge*, 3rd ed. (Chicago: Irwin, 1990).

Taylor, Fredrick, *The Principles of Scientific Management, 1911* (New York: Harper Brothers).

Toussaint-Saint, Maguelonne, *A History of Food*, trans. Anthea Bell (Massachusetts: Blackwell Publishers, 1992).

Walton, Mary, *The Deming Management Method* (New York: Perigee Books, 1986).

Image Credits

Index